Inside the Virtual Product

NEW HORIZONS IN THE ECONOMICS OF INNOVATION

Series Editor: Christopher Freeman, *Emeritus Professor of Science Policy, SPRU – Science and Technology Policy Research, University of Sussex, UK*

Technological innovation is vital to the competitive performance of firms and of nations and for the sustained growth of the world economy. The economics of innovation is an area that has expanded dramatically in recent years and this major series, edited by one of the most distinguished scholars in the field, contributes to the debate and advances in research in this most important area.

The main emphasis is on the development and application of new ideas. The series provides a forum for original research in technology, innovation systems and management, industrial organization, technological collaboration, knowledge and innovation, research and development, evolutionary theory and industrial strategy. International in its approach, the series includes some of the best theoretical and empirical work from both well-established researchers and the new generation of scholars.

Titles in the series include:

The Economics of Power, Knowledge and Time
Michèle Javary

Innovation in Multinational Corporations in the Information Age
The Experience of the European ICT Industry
Grazia D. Santangelo

Environmental Policy and Technological Innovation
Why Do Firms Adopt or Reject New Technologies?
Carlos Montalvo Corral

Government, Innovation and Technology Policy
An International Comparative Analysis
Sunil Mani

Innovation Networks
Theory and Practice
Edited by Andreas Pyka and Günter Küppers

Systems of Innovation and Development
Evidence from Brazil
Edited by José E. Cassiolato, Helena M.M. Lastres and Maria Lucia Maciel

Innovation, Competence Building and Social Cohesion in Europe
Towards a Learning Society
Edited by Pedro Conceição, Manuel V. Heitor and Bengt-Åke Lundvall

The Dynamics of Innovation Clusters
A Study of the Food Industry
Magnus Lagnevik, Ingegerd Sjöholm, Anders Lareke and Jacob Östberg

Technological Systems and Intersectoral Innovation Flows
Riccardo Leoncini and Sandro Montresor

Inside the Virtual Product
How Organizations Create Knowledge through Software
Luciana D'Adderio

Inside the Virtual Product

How Organizations Create Knowledge through Software

Luciana D'Adderio

The University of Edinburgh, UK

NEW HORIZONS IN THE ECONOMICS OF INNOVATION

Edward Elgar
Cheltenham, UK • Northampton, MA, USA

Published by
Edward Elgar Publishing Limited
Glensanda House
Montpellier Parade
Cheltenham
Glos GL50 1UA
UK

Edward Elgar Publishing, Inc.
136 West Street
Suite 202
Northampton
Massachusetts 01060
USA

A catalogue record for this book
is available from the British Library

Library of Congress Cataloguing in Publication Data

D'Adderio, Luciana, 1967–
     Inside the virtual product: how organizations create knowledge
     through software/Luciana D'Adderio.
          p. cm. — (New horizons in the economics of innovation)
     Includes bibliographical references and index.
     1. New products—Data processing. 2. Knowledge management—
Data processing. 3. Information technology. I. Title. II. Series.
HF5415.153.D333   2004
658.4'038'0285—dc22
                                                      2003047224

ISBN 1 84376 210 2

Printed and bound in Great Britain by MPG Books Ltd, Bodmin, Cornwall

Contents

List of Figures and Tables   vii
Preface   ix
Acknowledgements   xi
List of Abbreviations   xiii

1. Introduction   1
2. Knowledge in Theory and in Practice   11
3. Distributed Knowledge, Situated Action: The Role of Qualitative
   Analysis and Participant-Observation in Organizational Knowledge
   Research   43
4. Integrated Software Systems: The Technology and its Embedded
   Assumptions   71
5. The Influence of Integrated Systems on Organizational Memory   105
6. Bridging Formal Tools with Informal Practices: How Organizations
   Balance Flexibility and Control   135
7. Crafting the Virtual Prototype: How Firms Integrate Knowledge
   and Capabilities within and across Organizational Boundaries   173
8. Conclusions   197

Appendix: Internal Company Documents   215
References   217
Index   225

Figures and Tables

FIGURES

5.1	Schema of the EPL in Lotus Notes	115
5.2	PDM and TMS EPL structures	116
5.3	PDM and TMS Engineering Parts Lists	118
5.4	Workflow process	125
6.1	Incidence of change along product design life cycle	145
6.2	Schema of the EPL in Lotus Notes	151
6.3	BoM and EPL reporting	152
6.4	'Request to Change' documents	153
6.5	The prototype BoM process	154

TABLES

6.1	Tensions: major issues	162

Preface

This book examines the introduction of Integrated Software Systems in Product Development (PD), focusing on their implications for the organization's innovative, learning and adaptive potential. Organizations worldwide are extensively adopting Integrated Software technologies in order to bridge the divisions and discrepancies created by an increasing functional and epistemological specialization. A major source of radical change, Integrated Systems are designed and adopted with the aim of reducing such fragmentation by helping to control and co-ordinate organizational activities, including those critical activities that are learning- or change-related. Notwithstanding the radical influence of Integrated Systems on organizational knowledge dynamics, the academic debate has been principally concerned with assessing the 'impact' of software on quantitative performance indicators, such as the speed of the PD process. This research demonstrates that the introduction of Integrated Software Systems and related 'virtual' technologies has much deeper implications, involving the fundamental reconfiguration of organizational knowledge and learning dynamics; these include: the organization's ability to create, acquire, store and transfer knowledge across discipline-specific boundaries; to co-ordinate and integrate activities and heterogeneous knowledge sources across functional domains; to use this knowledge to build and renew organizational capabilities. Specifically, this study shows that the introduction of software affects significantly the organization's ability to balance elements of change and stability, continuity and discontinuity, heterogeneity and standardization, flexibility and control, specialization and integration. While software tends to shift the emphasis towards standardized, automated and integrated processes, this research demonstrates that the final outcome is not given but emerges instead from the complex interactions between software-embedded and other organizational processes. Based primarily on a participant-observation at a leading automotive manufacturer, the case studies build on the Evolutionary, Innovation and Organization Studies' understanding of the influence of software on knowledge processes, as well as adding to their theoretical characterization of organizations as knowledge users and producers.

To Keith Pavitt

In memoriam

Acknowledgements

This book is dedicated to the memory of my mentor Keith Pavitt who died recently. Throughout the years during which I have had the honour to know him, Keith provided an endless source of intellectual inspiration and challenge as well as moral and practical support, without which this book would not have existed. The book also greatly benefited from the support, help and contribution, direct and indirect, explicit and tacit that I have received from all my colleagues at the Science and Technology Policy Research Unit (SPRU), University of Sussex. In particular, I would like to express my warmest gratitude to Ed Steinmueller, Michael Gibbons, Robin Mansell, Stefano Brusoni, Margaret Sharp, William Walker, Nick Von Tunzelmann and Martin Bell who, in many different ways throughout my time at SPRU, have provided invaluable scholarly input as well as practical advice and support. I would also like to thank all my colleagues at the University of Edinburgh, especially Robin Williams and Donald Mackenzie, for their enthusiastic and unrelenting encouragement throughout the painstaking final stages of this project. Many other colleagues have provided invaluable feedback throughout the years that it took to complete this work; among these I would particularly like to mention Patrick Cohendet of BETA (Strasbourg) who has provided precious feedback over the entire draft. All the remaining faults and shortcomings are entirely my own. I would also like to take this opportunity to acknowledge all those managers, engineers, designers and administrators, both at the software user and the software manufacturer's firms, who have dedicated so much of their precious time to sharing their knowledge and experience with me at such critical stages of software implementation and product development. Their names as well as the names of their organizations cannot be disclosed, to preserve confidentiality. On a final note, my most special thank you goes to Neil, whose strength, patience, unrelenting motivation and fresh intellectual inspiration have been among my most invaluable resources; to Luciano and Celeste, for their uncompromising love and guiding wisdom; and to Luca, whose arrival has provided my efforts with an entirely new meaning. Finally, this book would not have been possible without the financial contribution of several grants, specifically the ESRC Innovation Programme, the TSER

ESSY and TIPIK Programmes, and the EPSRC Systems Patterns Re-engineering and Dependability IRC Programmes.

Chapter 7 has been published in *Research Policy* 30(9), December 2001: 1409–24, Special Volume on Knowledge Codification. Reprinted with kind permission of Elsevier.

Chapter 5 has been published in *Industrial and Corporate Change*, Special Issue on the 'Theory of the Firm, Learning and Organization', 12(2), April 2003. Reprinted with kind permission of Oxford University Press.

Abbreviations

2D	Two-Dimensional
3D	Three-Dimensional
AI	Artificial Intelligence
BoM	Bill of Materials
BPR	Business Process Re-engineering
CAD	Computer-Aided Design
CAE	Computer Aided Engineering
CAID	Computer Aided Industrial Design
CAM	Computer Aided Manufacturing
CDM	CAD Data Manager
CHK	Check
CIP	Check in Progress
CNC	Computer Numerical Control
CORBA	Common Object Request Broker Architecture
COTS	Commercial Off-the-Shelf
cPDm	collaborative Product Definition management
CSCW	Computer-Supported Co-operative Work
DM	Digital Model
DMU	Digital Mock-Up
DPA	Digital Pre-Assembly
ECOs	Engineering Change Orders
EPL	Engineering Parts List
ERP	Enterprise Resource Planning
ERS	Engineering Release Systems
E/View	Engineering View
FEA	Finite Elements Analysis
ICTs	Information and Communication Technologies
ID	Industrial Design
IPD	Integrated Product Development
IPDMUG	Integrated Product Data Manager User Group
ISS	Integrated Software Systems
IT	Information Technology
LLP	learning as legitimate peripheral participation
M/View	Manufacturing View
OEMs	Original Equipment Manufacturers
OLE	Object Linking and Embedding
P/C	parent/child

PBS   Prototype Build Specification
PD   Product Development
PDM   Product Data Manager
PDS   Product Description Summary
PED   Product Engineer Designer
PLM   Product Lifecycle Management
PLT   Product Lifecycle Technology
PPS   Product Programme Submission
R&D   Research and Development
SED   Surface Engineering Designer
SOPs   standard operating procedures
SSTs   stable systemic traits
STEP   Standard for Exchange of Product Data
STS   Science and Technology Studies
TMS   Total Modular Statement
VP   Virtual Product
VPDM   Virtual Product Data Manager
VPM   Virtual Product Model
WIP   Work-in-Progress

1. Introduction

The pervasiveness of Information and Communication Technologies (ICTs) and the extent of their influence on many facets of our everyday life have produced in the past decade a phenomenal interest in software, information systems and virtual technologies. While such technologies have been studied from many different angles and for many different purposes, we have only begun to scratch the surface of this vast and fascinating realm. In particular, we still lack a deeper understanding of the complex workings of ICTs within organizations. For instance, how do we understand the deeper influence of Information Systems on organizations? How can we characterize their reciprocal interactions? This book argues that, while there are numerous contributions that, more or less directly, address the question of Information Technology (IT) and organizations, none of them has systematically attempted to characterize one of the most striking features of Information Systems: their profound influence on the way organizations are able to learn, adapt to change and innovate.

This book is concerned with the implementation and use of Integrated Software Systems (ISS) in Product Development (PD). Through an in-depth analysis of software adoption practices at leading manufacturers, it uncovers the ways in which ISS, and related digital technologies, influence the practice and outcome of the PD process. While the existing literature is primarily concerned with evaluating the 'impact' of software on quantitative performance indicators, this research reveals the deeper implications of software adoption for the organizational innovative, adaptive and learning potential. This entails exposing the radical influence of software on the organization's ability to acquire, use, create and transfer knowledge, and to turn knowledge into organizational capabilities.

The main hypothesis is that Integrated Systems, and other related software-based technologies such as rapid prototyping, fundamentally reconfigure existing organizational processes and routines as well as deeply affecting organizational cognitive and adaptive processes. These include the processes by which specialized knowledge is acquired, created, stored, shared and integrated across heterogeneous organizational functional boundaries; and the processes by which organizations are able to use such knowledge to create, expand and nurture their capabilities.

Specifically, the growth of the organization's innovative, adaptive and learning potential is understood in terms of its increased ability to: maintain flexible processes that allow for the exploration of a wide range of techno-organizational configurations; incorporate heterogeneous, local feedback and requirements into global product (and process) definition; modify its routines to respond to differential requirements for radical and incremental change at different stages of the product development process; flexibly control the (combined physical and virtual) evolution of product and process definition; integrate, synchronize and validate data, information and knowledge flows across the extended enterprise and along the total product life cycle. The initial hypothesis is that, while the conventional understanding of the main rationale behind the implementation of ISS is the search for increased efficiency, their influence is of much greater scope. This includes the radical reconfiguration of all those organizational knowledge and learning processes, which underlie an organization's ability to learn, adapt and innovate.

INTEGRATED SOFTWARE TECHNOLOGIES: THE CORE ISSUE

The nature of knowledge production within firms is becoming increasingly specialized and this is having important consequences for the nature and organization of firms. Innovation scholars, for instance, talk of an increasing 'cognitive' and 'functional' division of labour within firms (Pavitt, 1998). As a result, organizations are increasingly faced with the challenge of how to control and co-ordinate their activities, particularly those that are critical (such as activities that are learning- or change-related) (ibid.). Firms are often adopting integrated software technologies in order to respond to these difficulties.

Integrated 'Commercial Off-the-Shelf', or 'COTS', software application solutions represent an important sub-segment of the market for packaged software. They consist of generic systems made up of a number of complementary, system-compliant applications that are based on the same architecture and share the same development platform. Within the integrated systems category are 'enterprise-wide' application solutions. These are specifically designed to facilitate the integration among heterogeneous functions, activities and knowledge sources across the entire organization, including links to the extended enterprise. Among these are widely known application solutions, such as Enterprise Resource Planning (ERP) and Product Data Manager (PDM) software. The latter is the principal subject of this study, together with a number of integrated, systems compliant applications such as Computer-Aided Design (CAD) and CAD Data Manager (CDM) software.

Initially devised for the defence and aerospace sectors, integrated software systems have rapidly spread across the whole manufacturing spectrum influencing the design and production of a very extensive range of products and technologies. Examples include power tools, high-speed trains, automobiles, rocket engines and power stations. More recently, the range of adoption of these systems has spread across an ever-increasing number of firms and industries, including the public and private service sectors.

Integrated software technologies aim to provide organizations with the ability to simulate the properties and the behaviour of products and technologies digitally. This, in principle, includes: (1) the full 'dynamic' simulation of an artefact and its behaviour; (2) the simulation of the processes required to design, engineer, manufacture and maintain an artefact; and (3) the simulation of the 'physical' links between the organizational functions involved in designing, engineering, producing, manufacturing, selling and even maintaining the artefact. Being able to sustain such complex simulation capabilities, when we consider the increasing systemic complexity of products and technologies and the increasing fragmentation of design and manufacturing processes across the extended (and often geographically dispersed) enterprise, constitutes a rather ambitious aim. The need for firms to manage such an increasing technological and organizational fragmentation and complexity represents a major rationale behind the adoption of ISS.

Integrated software technologies are specifically designed to bridge the divisions and discrepancies created by the increasing functional and epistemological specialization within firms. They aim to achieve this goal by providing a centralized, global 'data and process core' that is intended to co-ordinate and integrate organizational activities and knowledge flows, both within and across organizational boundaries.

Notwithstanding the increasing rate of diffusion and the widening spectrum of adoption of ISS across industrial sectors, however, to date there has been no significant attempt to examine the consequences of their introduction for the innovating organization. This observation is striking, once we acknowledge that ISS constitute a source of radical technical change that, by reconfiguring the boundaries between the different process stages, and by changing the way products are conceived, designed, engineered, produced, manufactured and maintained, is transforming the very nature of product development.

The current academic debate has greatly underestimated the radical influence of software systems on organizational cognitive dynamics, being almost exclusively concerned with assessing the 'impact' of software introduction on quantitative performance variables (i.e. the speed of the concept-to-market cycle and the reduction of the number of physical prototypes). Authors, for instance, have discussed information systems mainly in terms of their potential effect on the efficiency and speed of the product development process (cf. Wheelwright and Clark, 1992).

While these are important issues, they fail to emphasize that the introduction of integrated software technologies is radically affecting not only organizational activities but also its cognitive and adaptive processes. Beyond reshaping the way firms process information, as argued in the Business Process Re-engineering (BPR) literature, in fact, such technologies are fundamentally reconfiguring all the processes by which knowledge is created, stored, reused and transferred. We shall demonstrate that they are also transforming the way organizations are able to integrate existing and new knowledge, skills, technologies, and capabilities; they therefore influence the organization's ability to react and adapt to change and to innovate.

Primarily, software systems attempt to harness specialization through controlling how organizational knowledge is typically transferred, co-ordinated and integrated, within and across functional boundaries and domains. An example is the 'Virtual' Product Model (VPM) technology and philosophy, which is designed with the aim of integrating digitally all the organizational activities and knowledge sources which underlie the creation of a new product (or process). The introduction of the Virtual Model technology affects radically the processes by which 'local', specialized knowledge sources from individual organizational functions or teams can be co-ordinated and subsequently integrated into a global product and process definition.

This leads us to the following observation: due to its potential for reconfiguring organizational cognitive and adaptive processes, the introduction of ISS can provide an ideal standpoint to analyse the processes by which organizations learn and unlearn, react and adapt to change, build and renew their capabilities. For instance, such a study could help to shed light over the continuously unresolved attempts of an organization to strike an appropriate balance between elements of continuity and discontinuity, flexibility and control, change and stability, heterogeneity and standardization. Moreover, it could uncover the processes by which complementary knowledge sources (i.e. tacit/articulable/codified, formal/informal, local/global, people-embodied/computer-embedded) can be co-ordinated and subsequently integrated into a single, consistent artefact definition. In doing so, it can help explain just how heterogeneous organizational functions and domains are able to co-operate while maintaining conflicting viewpoints, interests and goals, and while speaking idiosyncratic, discipline- and function-specific languages. Finally, and most importantly, it could provide a unique viewpoint to observe the evolution of organizational routines, including those mechanisms that can cause a routine to change or subside. It could in general provide us with a substantially new understanding of the sophisticated processes that allow organizations to create, maintain and renew their capabilities.

A study of the adoption of integrated software technologies by development organizations can, thus, significantly improve our understanding of organizations as knowledge users and producers, as well as filling some important gaps in the theory of organizational knowledge and learning.

INVESTIGATING SOFTWARE, KNOWLEDGE AND THE ORGANIZATION

Notwithstanding the increasing popularity of knowledge-related issues and the considerable amount of contributions that have attempted to capture the interrelationships between knowledge, (information) technology and the organization, there still remain fundamental gaps in both their theoretical conceptualization and empirical characterization.

First, while mainstream economists have recently acknowledged that the issues discussed under the heading of tacit knowledge are truly important, they still remain principally concerned with the questions of knowledge accessibility and diffusion (cf. Cowan, David and Foray 1998).[1] They therefore do not investigate the processes by which organizations manage to turn the knowledge they acquire into distinctive competences and capabilities (Iansiti and Clark, 1994; Malerba and Orsenigo, 1998; Teece, Pisano and Shuen, 1990). Exploring these pressing issues entails a conceptual move beyond Evolutionary Economics' essentially static view of organizational routines and capabilities to analyse how these evolve, change, and, at times, even disappear.

Second, the Economics, Organization and Innovation debates have often focused on abstract rather than actual decision-making processes, thus neglecting the study of how cognitive processes evolve in practice (cf. Newell and Simon, 1972). We suggest that, in order to overcome the unproductive dichotomy between cognition and the context in which knowledge is used and produced, we require to study knowledge as situated, that it is tightly coupled to a specific context (Bowker and Star, 1999; Suchman, 1987).

Third, much Organization Science and Innovation Economics literature has often adopted a simplified view of organizational learning as a summation of learning by individuals. More recent contributions, however, have emphasized that knowledge is not just embodied in individuals but distributed across many other forms of external memory, such as artefacts, routines and locally shared languages (cf. Hutchins, 1995; Nelson and Winter, 1982; Weick, 1979). We argue that the cognitive science-inspired analytical device of extending inferences from the level of the individual to the collective level is unproductive; moreover, it can prevent us from addressing the most relevant organizational issues, such as how collective and distributed knowledge-building activities operate.

Fourth, much Management, Organization and Innovation Theory has characterized 'organizational culture' as if this was internally homogeneous. This conception fails to account for the divisions created by 'communities-of-practice' and 'epistemic communities', which produce noticeable 'local' variations in the organization's landscape in terms of knowledge, language and culture (cf. Brown and Duguid, 2000).[2] We argue that it is only by acknowledging the heterogeneous nature of the organizational landscape that we can begin to shed light over fundamental issues, including the processes by which heterogeneous knowledge sources, activity levels, and conflictual interests are co-ordinated.

Finally, and most importantly, IT, Innovation, Evolutionary and Organization Theory have often narrowly described software as a tool 'impacting' upon people and organizations, a characterization that fails to take into account the two-way interactions between software and the organization. In order to avoid a narrow and partial account, we need to open the software 'black box' (cf. Rosenberg, 1982) to consider in detail how software-embedded processes co-evolve with other organizational processes (including search and learning processes).

RESEARCH QUESTIONS AND METHODOLOGY

How do we characterize the influence of information systems adoption on organizational learning and adaptive processes? This research attempts to shed light over this fundamental and, as yet, under-investigated issue. Our main hypothesis is that Integrated Software Systems, and related software-based technologies such as rapid prototyping tend to radically reconfigure organizational routines as well as deeply reshaping organizational cognitive dynamics. They therefore fundamentally influence the organization's ability to adapt, learn and innovate.

In order to characterize the influence of software on the organization's innovative, learning and adaptive potential, we have articulated the main hypothesis along three major themes. Each one of these themes principally addresses one of the evolutionary categories of knowledge retention, selection and variation (Ziman, 2000). Our analysis will later reveal the need to add a fourth category: knowledge integration. The main research questions are as follows:

1. *Knowledge retention*: what is the influence of software on the organizational mechanisms by which knowledge is structured, stored, and reused? For example, how does software affect the organization's ability to strike a balance between knowledge reuse and the creation of new knowledge? What are the organizational consequences of delegating product and process memory to software? In which circumstances does software-embedded knowledge facilitate or hinder co-operation and communication across heterogeneous organizational boundaries?
2. *Knowledge selection*: what is the role of integrated software technologies in selecting knowledge and actions/behaviour? For example, do they influence which knowledge types and sources can become an input into the design and development process (i.e. tacit, codified knowledge sources)? Does software influence the type of actions (i.e. formal, informal) that are allowed or disallowed? How does the software's selective behaviour influence the organization's ability to flexibly adapt and react to threats and to effectively exploit the opportunities brought about by change?
3. *Knowledge variation and integration*: how does software adoption affect the modalities by which heterogeneous knowledge sources (i.e. from various functions and domains) and knowledge types (i.e. tacit, articulable and codified) are co-ordinated and integrated across the organization? How are organizational functions able to collaborate while maintaining divergent (and often conflicting) knowledge, incentives and viewpoints? How does software influence the process by which new knowledge, skills and capabilities are integrated into existing ones (and, therefore, the balance between continuity and discontinuity)?

In order to answer these questions, we require a qualitative methodology that captures the influence of software on organizational processes in detail and in the specific context of software implementation and use. Such an approach entails moving beyond a 'purely cognitive' and abstract characterization of knowledge, present in much organizational theory (cf. March and Simon, 1993), to study organizational cognition as an ensemble of 'situated', collective, and 'distributed' processes (Hutchins, 1995; Suchman, 1987; Tyre and Von Hippel, 1997).

The fieldwork was principally conducted at a world-leading vehicle manufacturer, whereby the researcher participated in the phased implementation of the 'Virtual Product', an Integrated Product Development

Strategy. The results were later compared with those obtained by conducting interviews with two leading organizations in the consumer electronics and aerospace sectors that were implementing the same software strategy and technology. The collection of field data involved participant-observation, carried out during a one and a half years' period, complemented by in-depth, semi-structured interviews with engineers, managers and administrators at most levels and functions of the main case organization. A complementary set of interviews, conducted over a period of three years at various other organizations ranging from aero and car engine manufacturers to Formula One, was used to further validate this evidence. The results are presented in the form of several detailed case studies.

CONTENT AND STRUCTURE OF THE BOOK

This book shall argue that Integrated Software Systems radically influence: (1) the processes by which knowledge of product, process and organization is structured, memorized and reused, therefore affecting communication and the formation of shared meanings across heterogeneous organizational communities; (2) the selection mechanisms by which only certain types of knowledge and actions are allowed to become an input into the development process, thus affecting the organization's ability to react and adapt to change and to innovate; (3) the ways in which heterogeneous knowledge types (i.e. tacit/codified, formal/informal, software-embedded/people-embodied) and sources (i.e. from various organizational domains) are integrated across organizational boundaries. This also influences the patterns of collaboration and conflict absorption among heterogeneous organizational communities and reshapes the organization's ability to use knowledge to create and renew their capabilities. These results confirm the initial hypothesis that the introduction of integrated software (and related digital) technologies radically reconfigure all fundamental organizational cognitive and adaptive processes, thus exerting a crucial influence over the organization's ability to learn, adapt and remain innovative.

The book is divided into eight chapters. The Introduction (Chapter 1) is followed by Chapter 2 on 'Knowledge in Theory and in Practice', which principally focuses on the theoretical contributions by the Evolutionary Economics, Innovation Studies, Engineering Epistemology, and Organization Science debates. After emphasizing the limitations intrinsic in the current debates, the chapter proceeds to suggest complementary literature that promises to further our understanding of knowledge, organizations and (information) technology. The latter, which include the fields of Science and Technology Studies (STS) and Computer-Supported Co-operative Work

(CSCW), are ideally situated to provide complementary insights to the former debates, thus greatly enriching our theoretical analysis.

Chapter 3 on 'Distributed Knowledge, Situated Action' addresses the fundamental and, as yet, unresolved issue of how best to characterize the mutual influence between (information) technology and the organization. The chapter illustrates how, to capture such complex dynamics, we require a qualitative, hands on empirical approach that examines the co-evolution of software-embedded and organizational processes (including learning and adaptive processes) in the context of actual practice. Such an approach holds a much greater explanatory potential, when compared with more traditional technological- or socio-deterministic accounts of knowledge, (information) technology and organizations.

The fourth chapter, on 'Integrated Software Systems: the Technology and its Embedded Assumptions', lays out the main characteristics of the technology. These include the philosophy underlying software design and implementation strategies. The chapter analyses the ways in which the assumptions embedded in software by its producers are received and implemented by practitioners in our case organizations; it also raises the key issues, themes and questions that are subsequently developed in Chapters 5, 6 and 7.

Chapter 5, 'The Influence of Integrated Systems on Organizational Memory' addresses one of the major areas that existing literature has left largely unexplored, namely the issue of knowledge retention and reuse. The chapter shows the implications of enforcing a new software-embedded 'language' (database and product structure, plus a set of procedures) across heterogeneous organizational domains. Specifically, implications are drawn as to the organization's ability to balance elements of standardization and heterogeneity.

Chapter 6, 'Bridging Formal Tools with Informal Practices: How Organizations Balance Flexibility and Control' illustrates how software can act as a control mechanism by selecting (allowing or disallowing) certain knowledge and actions. Often the influence and benefits of ICTs are explained in terms of increased control: software acts as a stabilizing and standardizing element introduced to bring order and discipline into the chaotic development process. This chapter shows the differential benefits that can be achieved by introducing the software at downstream (i.e. production) or upstream (i.e. design) functions, where there are differing requirements for flexibility and control.

Chapter 7, 'Crafting the Virtual Prototype: How Firms Integrate Knowledge and Capabilities within and across Organizational Boundaries', examines the influence of software on the way organizational 'communities', collaborate and share knowledge in the process of creation and production of new artefacts. In doing so, it focuses on the role of virtual and physical prototypes as 'knowledge repositories' and 'intermediaries' among different communities and as the locus where organizational conflicts are absorbed, and temporary truces are reached. The chapter demonstrates that inter-functional co-ordination and knowledge-sharing depend upon the emergence of what are described in this book as 'translation routines'. In integrating various knowledge sources and levels, technologies and skills, these routines are shown to lie at the very basis of the formation and maintenance of organizational capabilities.

The Conclusions (Chapter 8) contain a summary of the main findings as well as indicating directions for future research and suggesting policy implications.

NOTES

1. The notion of tacit knowledge refers to 'that form of knowledge that cannot be easily expressed' (Cohendet and Meyer-Krahmer, 2001: 1564). For rich historical accounts of how engineers harness tacit knowledge see also Vincenti (1990), Ferguson (1993b) and Petroski (1996).
2. 'Epistemic communities' or 'epistemic cultures' can be defined as groups of agents working on a commonly acknowledged subset of knowledge issues and who at the very least accept a commonly understood procedural authority as essential to the success of their knowledge activities (Cohendet and Meyer-Krahmer, 2001; Knorr-Cetina, 1999). The notion of 'communities of practice' identifies groups of persons engaged in the same practice, communicating regularly with one another about their activities (Cohendet and Meyer-Krahmer, 2001; Lave and Wenger, 1991).

2. Knowledge in Theory and in Practice

INTRODUCTION

The relatively recent increase in popularity of the knowledge issue has been reflected in an upsurge of contributions that attempt to characterize how firms, industries and countries produce, use, augment and share their knowledge. Notwithstanding the vast amount of literature available, however, a number of issues remain as yet unexplored, or have been to date only partially addressed. These particularly concern our understanding of the fundamental role that knowledge plays in the economy and the role of organizations as knowledge users and producers.

This chapter begins by assessing the current state of the knowledge issue in the 'knowledge codification' debate and its failure to address the question of how both tacit and codified knowledge can be effectively exploited by organizations to generate their own source of competitive advantage. While making an important contribution, scholars in the codification debate have concentrated principally on the issue of knowledge diffusion, thus failing to acknowledge the fundamental difference that exists between 'having' and 'using' knowledge productively to generate organizational capabilities. While the innovation debate has acknowledged and, indeed, emphasized such a distinction, it still falls short of analysing in any detail the organizational processes of knowledge creation, acquisition, storage, transfer, integration, and of capability creation and maintenance.

It is argued that insights can be gained by combining the views of the codification and innovation debate with the organizational capabilities approach; this move, for example, can help augment our understanding of how the knowledge that is acquired or created by firms can be used to generate specific capabilities, which in turn lie at the basis of a firm's competitive advantage. Our approach entails therefore shifting our attention from knowledge-as-a-commodity to knowledge processes as the foundation of capabilities. In doing so it provides a framework to begin our analysis of the mechanisms that underlie organizational capabilities and the influence of IT upon these. But, first, we begin with the codification debate.

THE 'KNOWLEDGE CODIFICATION' DEBATE

The Boundaries between Codification and Tacitness

Neoclassical economists have traditionally paid little attention to information and knowledge. Those that have addressed the issue have often narrowly equated knowledge to (processed) information.[1] Such an epistemological flaw has frequently lead mainstream economists and other scholars to underestimate the importance of the semantic side of information (and therefore the process of interpretation and meaning formation) and to emphasize the value of the codified, explicit side of knowledge as compared to its tacit, or implicit side.[2] Innovation scholars, on the other hand, have traditionally emphasized the role of individual- or routines-embedded tacit knowledge as a source of organizational capabilities that underpins a firm's distinctive advantage (Nelson and Winter, 1982).

The knowledge debate has been recently moving away from the relatively simplistic juxtaposition of tacit vs. codified knowledge. Economists have recently admitted that 'tacit and codified knowledge are complements rather than substitutes' (Cowan and Foray, 1997: 600). In emphasizing that 'The now-classic contributions to the economics of R&D have been unwarrantedly simplistic in their handling of some subtle questions concerning "knowledge" and "information" and the relationship between the two', the codification side of the debate has admitted that 'the questions economists and others have been discussing under the general rubric of tacit knowledge are truly important' (Cowan, David and Foray, 1998: 5).

While, in innovation studies, the awareness of the complementary nature of tacit and codified knowledge has prompted greater attention towards their interaction and co-evolution,[3] the same realization has inspired some economists to develop a further theoretical distinction between the knowledge that is codified, codifiable and impossible to codify. After quickly dismissing the importance of the latter (as, by definition, it cannot be directly attributed economic value), these authors have proceeded to analyse that part of the knowledge spectrum which is seemingly (or temporarily) tacit but which could be codified if necessary incentives and investments were in place (Cowan and Foray, 1997; Cowan, David and Foray, 1998).

The authors have therefore proceeded to name as 'unarticulated' that knowledge which exists in a codified form but is not explicitly referred to in the typical course of knowledge activities. They quote as an example the case of a 'displaced code-book'.[4] 'Unarticulated' can also refer to that knowledge which is codifiable, but has not yet been codified. This happens, in their view, because codifiability does not necessitate codification; a paper, for example, may be thought out fully but not actually be written out (Cowan,

David and Foray, 1998). Their conclusion is, therefore, that the observed absence of codified knowledge in certain activities 'does not necessarily imply that only tacit knowledge is at play' (Cowan, David and Foray, 1998: 8). According to the authors, the introduction of the unarticulated knowledge category has considerably reduced the realm of tacit knowledge; in their opinion this justifies moving the theoretical 'boundary' between tacit and codified knowledge to also include those activities that involve the use of 'displaced' codified knowledge. The newly found 'location' of this theoretical boundary, however, is far from clear cut; rather, setting such a boundary entails significantly underestimating the problematic processes of knowledge reproduction and appropriation, as argued below.

The Increase in Knowledge Codification and Diffusion

The codification economists' argument rests on the assumption that significant recent advances in the tools available for innovation have implied an increased ability to formally represent or codify technological knowledge; this has in turn affected the costs of both generating and diffusing innovations (Ergas, 1994). While some have focused upon the role of 'Falling costs of information transmittal, deriving in large part from computer and telecommunication advances [in] encouraging a general social presumption favouring more circulation of timely information and a reduced degree of tacitness' (Dasgupta and David, 1994: 502), others have emphasized the role of information technology in supporting codification. According to Cowan and Foray (1995), 'The digital revolution has continued and intensified this move towards codification ... [by improving] ... our ability to codify and formalise knowledge and information ...'. The decreasing costs of knowledge codification have increased the ease with which codified knowledge can be transferred, which has in turn increased its value (Cowan and Foray, 1997; Cowan, David and Foray, 1998). Economists have mainly characterized this issue in terms of *diffusion*: an increase in codification is assumed to be implicitly good because it facilitates the diffusion of knowledge. However, an increase in knowledge diffusion does not necessarily imply an increased ease of knowledge reproduction and uptake (or appropriation) by organizations and individuals alike. Let us consider some major objections.

A first consideration is that *greater diffusion does not imply automatic use and reproduction of knowledge*. Knowledge reproduction is problematic, given that a substantial portion of knowledge is tacit and cannot be easily codified and therefore transmitted as information. In fact, 'The reconstruction of knowledge that has been codified, even where possible, may be a prolonged process that requires substantial extension of existing knowledge before it is effective' (Steinmueller, 1998: 10). This issue was initially raised by the innovation studies side of the debate,[5] where it was implied that, although codified knowledge may have lower marginal costs of transmission and it is thus slippery and hard to contain, it is also largely irrelevant unless its 'sticky' (Von Hippel, 1994), tacit counterpart is also available (Cowan and Foray, 1997: 3). Tacit knowledge, therefore, preserves its important function.

At its roots, the problem goes back to the issue of how we understand and characterize the knowledge codification and reproduction processes. Drawing from Levy (1997; 1999), we could argue that the knowledge codified in the code-book exists 'virtually', meaning that, before being used it must be reproduced, or 'actualized'. As we will argue in Chapter 7, the process of actualization does not simply entail *logic deduction* (i.e. the pure logic working of a software programme) but *creative invention* (i.e. the interaction between people and information systems) (ibid.). Creative invention in turn requires tacit and collective knowledge to be available. The process of writing a paper, as in Cowan, David and Foray's (1998) example, is often not just about automatic reproduction but creative invention. If codification is understood as a complex socio-technical process, then it cannot be resolved as a simple matter of language or code translation. If we accept that there are few cases of straightforward reproduction, then it follows that codification economists have not extended the realm of codified knowledge by a substantial amount.[6]

Similarly, the act of codifying organizational processes is not just a simple matter of making explicit something that is currently implicit. For example, the influence of Information Systems does not simply reside in their ability to support the straightforward codification of existing organizational processes;[7] processes are often being radically redesigned and rebuilt during codification. In this sense codification involves substantial self-learning by the organization. The knowledge involved in building and operating these processes is partly tacit. Every time newly codified processes require further modification and revision, that tacit knowledge will have to come again into play.[8] Only individuals and institutions that possess the tacit knowledge and the capabilities necessary to exploit it, can therefore utilize codified knowledge to their advantage.

The problem of knowledge stickiness is only partially resolved by the fact that codified knowledge is normally used by organizational communities that share tacit knowledge and the language required to interpret the 'messages' and thus provide them with meaning (cf. Cowan and Foray, 1997). This argument in fact does not capture the dynamic aspect of knowledge reproduction. An example is the issue of the evolution and maintenance of a firm's tacit knowledge base (e.g. how do organizations manage to preserve over time the tacit knowledge that is required to interpret new as well as stored information). This issue has so far been explained narrowly as the need for organizations to retain key individuals who embody that precious tacit knowledge. The argument's limitation is that, if we accept that there is more to organizational memory than the summation of individual memories (Cook and Yanow, 1993), then the task of acquiring and retaining tacit knowledge becomes more complex than simply acquiring or retaining key individuals. For example, how can tacit knowledge remain operational in renewed technological and organizational circumstances?[9]

A second objection concerns the issue of *knowledge appropriation or take up*. While IT-based tools can, in principle, simplify the diffusion and transfer of codified knowledge,[10] they do not necessarily facilitate the 'local' appropriation of codified knowledge by different epistemic or work communities. Given that different organizational communities (i.e. the various teams collaborating in Product Development) often differ in their language, objectives, and culture as well as usually only sharing a portion of their tacit knowledge, the problem of adoption is rather more complex than it might appear initially. For example, which are the complex organizational processes that lie behind an organization's ability to locally re-appropriate and re-adapt codified knowledge? If the codified knowledge available cannot be automatically deployed, then how are organizational communities able to exploit the (common) codified knowledge core?

Thirdly and finally, there is the issue of the importance of that portion of *knowledge*, which is *lost in the process of codification*. Given that codification entails a process of both simplification of knowledge and reduction of ambiguity, some fundamental issues arise. One important issue concerns the theoretical and empirical validity of regarding uncodifiable knowledge as unimportant. If 'non-articulable' knowledge was uninteresting, as some economists have argued, then we should do no further; but if it *were* interesting, then it would be legitimate to attempt to explore its economic significance (Steinmueller, 1998). For instance, what are organizations prepared to do (in both economic and cognitive terms) in order to preserve it? What kind of mechanisms need to be set up in order to facilitate its exploitation? A further important realization is that, as the codification of organizational routines involves a process of simplification and reduction of ambiguity, the resulting codified routines only reflect a small portion of the actual processes. The codified version of an actual routine is an idealized, 'normative' procedure, which tends to remain relatively stable. By focusing principally on codified processes, or the 'representation' side of routines, economists have often not considered their value as 'expressions'. A similar limitation is shared by those organizational theorists who have been heavily influenced by the cognitive psychology literature; they also have tended to focus on the rationalized, 'idealized' and abstract rather then the actual side of routines (cf. March and Simon, 1993).

The Process of Codification as Language Creation

According to Cowan and Foray (1997), the process of codification includes three aspects: model building, language creation and the writing of messages. The costs and benefits of these codification activities depend fundamentally on the knowledge environment in which they take place. They identify two cases: (1) a *stable environment* whereby the costs of codification are low and the benefits high, given that models and languages already exist (the fixed costs have been incurred) and therefore only variable costs must be incurred; and (2) an *unstable environment,* which is characterized by high codification costs and lower benefits, given that models and languages are yet to be built. According to the authors, the instability implies that codified knowledge might be difficult to use, due to the ambiguity of the language, and might only have a small number of users, due again to the fact that there are multiple interpretations, and presumably the potential audience will be divided among the interpretations (ibid.: 620). This argument presents a number of limitations.

First, the authors' optimism towards the benefits of codification seems to derive from *an excessive emphasis on stability.* As the advantages of codification are calculated in terms of costs/benefits, and the balance will bend towards benefits only in the presence of stable environments, we should not expect high benefits during all periods dominated by substantial technological change, such as, for example, the implementation of a new software system.[11] Periods of stability, however, are rare. This appears immediately clear when talking to industry experts and practitioners: the increasing pace with which technological change affects organizations implies that, at any point in time, there is some level of change affecting one or more parts of the organization. Justifying the benefits of codification according to periods of stability can therefore represent an elusive target.[12]

To assess the advantages of codification in terms of cost–benefit analysis, is, therefore, difficult and, to an extent, unsatisfactory.[13] If unstable environments were the rule rather than the exception, there would appear to be lower incentives towards codification. Once we acknowledge that a degree of instability in the organization's environment is the norm (cf. Iansiti, 1995), then the question that arises is exactly what happens (not in terms of costs–benefits, but organizationally) in situations of partial codification. Given that organizations can only bear a limited amount of change at any time (i.e. in order to support ongoing operations), the interesting question is just how are they able *to balance change and stability* at any point in time.

A second problematic inference from Cowan and Foray's argument is that the stability objective is to be achieved by *eliminating ambiguity and heterogeneity*; the underlying idea is that, once knowledge has been extensively codified, it can be made widely available and potentially used by anyone anywhere within a co-operating community. The elimination of ambiguity and heterogeneity, however, is an only partially realizable and desirable goal. It is difficult to achieve because institutions and organizations are often not homogeneous entities but made by different groups, departments and teams. Each one of these 'epistemic communities' (Knorr-Cetina, 1999; Steinmueller, 1998) or 'communities-of-practice' (Bowker and Star, 1999; Brown and Duguid, 1996; Lave and Wenger, 1991) is likely to speak different idiosyncratic, discipline-specific languages, as well as holding different tacit knowledge bases, culture and sub-goals. These differences are not eliminated by codification and indeed they should not be, as they represent important sources of local, tacit and specialized knowledge (as argued in Chapters 5 and 7).

A further problematic is that, due to organizational *heterogeneity*, codification alone is not likely to be sufficient to co-ordinate the work of practitioners across different communities. Once we acknowledge that knowledge creation and transfer are complex socio-technical processes, it follows that they cannot be reduced to simple code translation procedures. An interesting question, therefore, is how can the knowledge generated and acquired by *local communities-of-practice* be effectively captured and transferred across organizational boundaries. Also important is to establish how organizations are able to achieve at any point in time an appropriate balance between standardization and heterogeneity. This theme is developed further in Chapters 5 and 7.

A third, related, objection concerns the role of codification in supporting the creation of a *shared, common language*. While Cowan, David and Foray (1998) mention the difficulties of achieving a common language, they do not clarify what its role and characteristics should be. For example, should the common, standardized language substitute the local, idiosyncratic 'dialects'? Is the role of dialects essentially negative (i.e. they prevent us from reaping the benefits of codification) as codification economists suggest, or positive (i.e. can they convey tacit and context-specific knowledge)? In one example of bar code technology, the authors mention the obstacles encountered in codifying semantics. The question, however, is whether it is desirable (and indeed possible) to codify semantics. If it is true that some knowledge will always remain unarticulated (and therefore un-codified), then there are two possibilities: (a) that the knowledge that is not codified/able is not interesting (the codification economists' view), or (b) that this 'leftover' knowledge is indeed interesting. In the latter case the problem than becomes how organizations can learn to convey this knowledge into the process. This issue is addressed in Chapter 7.

The above considerations are particularly important when considering the introduction of Information Systems in organizations. The implementation of such technologies often requires the codification of existing product and process knowledge; such codification is often implemented by enforcing the software's own 'language' (i.e. structure) upon existing organizational languages. In these circumstances, the important issues are: how do heterogeneous epistemic communities learn to read and attribute meaning to the new (software-embedded language)? Is the introduction of a technical interface, which mediates the boundaries between community-specific and common language sufficient to generate shared meanings? Or are other elements also required in order to support the emergence of shared meanings among the various epistemic communities that make up an organization? These themes are developed in Chapter 5.

Here we encounter an apparent contradiction. On the one hand, radical change (i.e. the adoption of a new language) is required for the organization that intends to reap the benefits of IT. On the other hand, however, the adoption of the new language involves a painful process of codification and learning. Building on Chomsky's discussion of linear vs. structured languages and their acquisition, Steinmueller has emphasized that, while natural languages are structurally complicated but easy for humans to acquire, artificial ones are often not: 'Language acquisition is a major challenge and it should not be presumed that all that one needs to decode dialects specific to instrumental purposes, such as scientific and technological "instrumental dialects", is a phrase book' (Steinmueller, 1998: 8). While instrumental dialectics are clearly articulable, he argues that acquiring a facility in their expression may require reproducing the social dynamics and shared experience from which they arose (ibid.). The issues at stake are, in our case: how do functional communities manage to learn and adopt the new, software-embedded language? Does the new language exist in parallel or is it replacing existing idiosyncratic 'dialects' (i.e. supported by legacy applications)? What happens in the transition phase? If organizations resort to temporary meta-languages (Cowan, David and Foray, 1998), which characteristics are these going to display? Are communities likely to shed their idiosyncratic dialects to migrate towards a common standardized 'neutral' language?

The Influence of Information and Communication Technologies

The influence of ICTs (i.e. advanced simulation tools and Information Systems) is often associated with an increase in codification and division of labour. Economists have argued that the increased ability to codify technological knowledge 'tends to reduce the transaction costs advantages of in-house R&D, and ... is encouraging a shift to a more decentralised R&D system' (Ergas, 1994: 2). Arora and Gambardella (1994) have added that, while the experienced-based learning, tacit skills and capabilities embedded in organizational routines remain important, the ability to represent concrete information in abstract and universal categories allows for it to be used in a number of locations and organizations. This, in turn, encourages a division of innovative labour with different firms specializing in the stages of the innovation process where they have a comparative advantage.[14]

Contrasting evidence has been produced by innovation scholars who have argued that technical change supports the *integration* rather than the *division* of innovative labour (Rothwell, 1993). A well-documented body of technical and management literature has shown that the introduction of ICTs can support concurrency in design and development, and therefore the integration of work conducted by different organizational functions (Henderson, 1994). Thomke (1998: 71), for example, has shown how, after the (successful) introduction of software-based technologies, 'the data and personnel interfaces between [design] steps are seamless and integrated ... [and therefore] ... pose new challenges to the way R&D, its tasks and information are currently managed and organised'. Another example is the ways in which the introduction of computer-aided design at Boeing has supported inter-disciplinary and inter-functional collaboration: 'by having engineers and manufacturers share data and ideas ... and by having them work together in teams so that each knows what the other ... can do ... misfits and related problems were cut in the 777' (Petroski, 1996: 132).

To date, however, neither sides of the debate have fully explored the influence that codification and technical change exert on integration and functional specialization. This is especially true in relation to the role of ICTs: no contributions so far have analysed in detail the influence of information systems and technologies on organizational cognitive dynamics. In particular, this research shows how the study of organizational (distributed) knowledge dynamics is the key to understand the ways in which ICTs support the division or the integration of innovative labour.

This book builds on more recent contributions that have begun to address the issue of how functional groups are able to collaborate in the course of innovative work. Steinmueller (1998), for example, has identified important social elements in the process of knowledge codification. In particular, he identifies the creation of new epistemic communities and the preservation of existing ones as a key element in resolving the problems of incentive compatibility in the investment in the knowledge codification processes. According to this argument, ICTs work as individual, group, and social memory repositories; at all three levels, 'ICTs are playing a major role in augmenting the social processes supporting knowledge codification with effects that are likely to be very significant for both the *variety* and the *complexity* of available codified knowledge' (ibid.: 22, emphasis added).

While codification plays a fundamental role in facilitating co-ordination and cross-functional knowledge-sharing, however, it is not sufficient alone to explain how organizational communities are able to appropriate and share the knowledge required to 'get their work done'. The main issue here is that we need to understand the technological and organizational mechanisms that underlie the ability of heterogeneous communities to co-operate. The rationale behind co-operation in the knowledge creation process has too often been attributed to the works of authority (cf. Cowan, David and Foray, 1998). The concept of authority, adopted indeed by both sides of the knowledge debate, however, provides only a partial explanation: first, authority 'at work' is often difficult to identify and account for as it is often and increasingly distributed across humans, technologies (i.e. software) and organizational routines; secondly, the issue of authority cannot by itself explain how collective knowledge-building processes operate, as their rationale is complex and escapes straightforward social coercion explanations (cf. Zuboff, 1988). For instance, the notions of *'common intentionality'* and *'shared vision'*, often embraced by innovation scholars, are at the same time too vague and deterministic: individuals and organizational groups have often different intentions and goals, which can be sometimes contrasting and incompatible (Henderson, 1994; Katz and Allen, 1988). The *multiplicity* of languages, cultures, and tacit knowledge bases that characterizes communities-of-practice and epistemic communities has to be accounted for as it plays a fundamental role in organizational knowledge production and use. Indeed, we will demonstrate that they represent an important source of innovation and must therefore be preserved while being co-ordinated.[15]

Some fundamental questions are still left unanswered. For example, how can the barriers to codification and knowledge reproduction be (at least partially) overcome? Are there ways to bridge the tacit and codified knowledge 'pockets' to support collaboration across heterogeneous groups? Which are the fundamental barriers to reproducing knowledge away from the original context? How can the organizational processes of knowledge codification and reproduction be more adequately configured in order to exploit both the advantages of codification and of tacitness? Could organizations develop capabilities that would allow them to create knowledge more productively starting from their tacit background, and also to reproduce knowledge starting from codified knowledge sources? And, most importantly, can organizations learn to support the emergence of organizational mechanisms that facilitate the integration of knowledge sources and activities?

Beyond the Knowledge Codification Debate

While having provided a valuable contribution to our understanding of knowledge issues, the knowledge codification debate still presents some important limitations. First, there is a lack of both theoretical and empirical characterization of codification processes at the *organizational and at the collective level*. Existing literatures in fact focus principally on a simplified view of organizational learning as the summation of *individual learning*; we should instead be focusing on organizational memory as more than the summation of its constituent parts; this entails shifting the focus of our attention *from individual to organizational cognitive processes*.

Second, we need to improve our theoretical and empirical understanding of how information systems operate within organizations (Boland and Hirschheim, 1987) and the way their introduction reshapes organizational knowledge dynamics; for instance, there is no verification of *how IT tools really work*, and how their introduction reconfigures both organizational and individual, tacit and codified, knowledge processes as well as their interactions. Moreover, the influence of IT is too often read in terms of *one-way impact* and there is not much evidence of how information systems are shaped in turn by organizational variables.

Third, the emphasis is often set on stability and scarce attention is paid to analysing process/language *breaks* and *discontinuities* and how these could be remedied. Contributions often assume that language shifts are smooth and therefore fail to engage in the complex issue of organizational language creation and evolution. This issue is particularly interesting as it also concerns the co-evolution of common, artificial languages and local, idiosyncratic dialects.

Fourth, the focus is often placed on *individual* decision-making performed by an isolated engineer or inventor. This is hardly a realistic account of actual, collective and organization-embedded decision-making processes. Further, the attention is often centred on the normative, *'idealized'* side of product development and related business processes. This emphasizes the urgent need for analysing how tacit and codified, formal and informal processes co-evolve in theory and in practice.

Fifth, authors are only just beginning to acknowledge the existence of *communities-of-practice* and the *multiplicity* of organizational languages, cultures, and knowledge bases.[16] Literature also too often contains a narrow characterization of *authority* and *responsibility* that does not satisfactorily explain how collective knowledge-building activities operate. Instead, we need to unpack the notion of *common intentionality* to study the ways in which different individuals and organizational functions are able to collaborate, get work done and achieve temporary consensus.

All the above issues point to the need to extend our current understanding of knowledge to include the study of knowledge-building processes as organization embedded, concrete, collective and distributed. It is argued that important advances can be achieved by complementing the insights of the cognitive school of thought with those of the behavioural tradition. The proposed approach promises to remedy some of the existing gaps in our understanding of the evolution of organizational learning and adaptive processes, in the specific contexts of knowledge production and use.

TURNING KNOWLEDGE INTO CAPABILITIES

The codification debate has principally characterized knowledge in terms of its accessibility and diffusion. By implicitly assuming that *having access* to knowledge is all that is required, the debate has not adequately addressed issues such as how the knowledge which is acquired can be integrated into existing organizational capabilities to generate competitive advantage. This issue requires a shift of attention from knowledge per se, or knowledge-as-a-commodity, to knowledge processes as the foundation of organizational capabilities that are specific and not easy to replicate.

According to the dynamic capabilities approach, it is not sufficient for a firm to 'have' knowledge; important questions are: how is this knowledge integrated with existing organizational knowledge and capabilities? When we turn to observe cognitive processes as collective, organization embedded and distributed, we are faced with a number of new, fundamental and complex challenges. For example, how are new and existing knowledge and capabilities integrated? How are distributed and heterogeneous organizational knowledge bases and sources integrated? How does the structure and content of organizational cognitive dynamics influence the formation of capabilities? How do we prevent existing capabilities from turning into core rigidities? Finally, and most importantly, how does the adoption of IT influence knowledge dynamics and the formation and maintenance of organizational capabilities?

The capabilities' approach has begun to provide some answers to these fundamental questions. A substantial body of evidence, for example, has *linked capability and competition* (Chandler, 1977; 1990 and Lazonic, 1990, in Iansiti and Clark, 1994). The notion of capabilities, which draws from the resource based view of the firm, originated with the early concept of 'distinctive competence' (Snow and Hrebiniak, in Leonard-Barton, 1992) and has since expanded to embrace the notions of 'core competencies' (Grandstrand, Patel and Pavitt, 1997; Prahalad and Hamel, 1990), 'learning organization' (Argyris and Schon, 1978), 'organizational routines' (Nelson and Winter, 1982), 'absorptive capacity' (Cohen and Levinthal, 1990), 'core capabilities' (Leonard-Barton, 1992), 'combinative capabilities' (Kogut and Zander, 1992) and 'dynamic capabilities' (Teece, Pisano and Shuen, 1990).

According to this debate, the knowledge generated by learning activities is embedded in organizational 'routines' (Nelson and Winter, 1982). The concept of routines emerged from the criticism to the orthodox economic notion of *perfect rationality,* which assumes that the rational man makes 'optimal' choices in a highly specified and clearly defined environment (March and Simon, 1993; Simon, Egidi and Marris, 1992). According to this model, three major conditions are realized: all the alternatives of choice are given, all the consequences attached to each alternative are known (in terms of certainty, risk, or uncertainty), and the 'rational man' has a complete utility-ordering for all possible sets of consequences. In this world of perfect rationality in which markets perform the main role in co-ordinating information, organizations are seen as the result of the malfunctioning of markets.

The concept of objective rationality, however, is very far from what can be observed in reality (Simon, Egidi and Marris, 1992). Given the complexity of the environment and the limitations of the human brain (Arthur, 1994), behaviour can only be *satisficing* rather than optimizing; this involves setting an aspiration level, searching until an alternative is found that is satisfactory by the aspiration level criterion, and selecting that alternative (De Groot, 1965; March and Simon, 1993). The selectivity of the search, and its feasibility, is obtained by applying *rules of thumb,* or *heuristics,* to determine what paths should be traced and what ones can be ignored (Simon, Egidi and Marris, 1992). Heiner's concept of *rules* describes how, when our cognitive capacity is inadequate to cope with uncertainty and complexity, to the point that we cannot select appropriate actions in some contingencies, behaviour will be constrained by rules that neglect the corresponding options and contingencies (1983, in Nooteboom, 1992).

It is in this context that the concept of routines has to be understood: the choice menu of alternatives available to the organization is not broad, but narrow and idiosyncratic; it is built into the firm's routines which accomplish automatically most of the choosing. The *boundaries of a firm* reside in the collection of specific routines, capabilities and cognitive frames, rather than in the transaction costs; the limits to the expansion of firm boundaries are set by the type of knowledge they are able to understand and use in addition to the quantity of information they are able to process in any given time (Orsenigo, in Simon, Egidi and Marris, 1992).[17]

The routinization of activity represents the most important form of storage of the organization's specific operational knowledge: organizations 'remember by doing' (ibid.). Recalling Hayek's view on knowledge, Winter has argued that 'firms are organizations that *know how to do things*: a particular firm at a particular time is a repository of a specific range of productive knowledge, which involves idiosyncratic features that distinguish it even from superficially similar firms in the same line of business' (1988: 175). Firms can be therefore described as:

> Crucial (although not exclusive) repositories of knowledge, to a large extent embodied in their *operational routines*, and modified through time by their *'higher level' rules* of behaviour and strategies (such as their 'meta-rules' for innovative search, diversification, etc.). In this view, competences are the collective property of the routines of an organization. (Coriat and Dosi, 1994: 2, emphasis added).

Routines represent therefore the 'regular and predictable aspects of firm behaviour'.[18] They are *patterns of interactions* that represent successful solutions to particular problems. They are resident in group behaviour, though certain sub-routines may reside in individual behaviour. Because of the complexity of such behaviour, the knowledge embedded in routines cannot be completely captured in a codified form: it has a *tacit dimension* that often cannot be readily articulated. Hence, it is the routines themselves, and the ability of management to call upon the organization to perform them, that represents firm's business capability (Teece, Pisano and Shuen, 1990). Because routines involve a strong tacit dimension, they may not be easy to imitate: to the extent that this is so, routines contribute to a firm's *distinctive competences* and capabilities: 'By virtue of their evolution in particular environment and organizational contexts, capabilities are likely to differentiate firms from each other and provide the basis for differential performance vis-à-vis competitors' (ibid.: 20).

In shifting the attention from individual to organizational knowledge dynamics, the routines and capabilities' approaches can significantly improve our understanding of ICTs and organizations. Rather than a substitute, their predominantly behavioural perspective constitutes an important theoretical complement to the issues addressed by the knowledge codification debate. The following sections introduce some of the most relevant questions related to the notions of organizational routines and capabilities. We will argue that, although widely utilized, such approaches still retain several important problematic and unexplored issues that have so far prevented the full realization of the theory's explanatory potential. We will also suggest ways in which the current routines and capabilities debate can be lifted out of a relative impasse and effectively exploited to further our current understanding of knowledge and organizations.

Automatic Routine Behaviour vs. Deliberate Problem-Solving[19]

The routines debate can be roughly divided between those who argue that tacitness and automatic behaviour distinguish routines action from choice and problem-solving, and those who instead include deliberative choice under routines (Cohen et al. (1996). The first view, which stresses automatic behaviour, is based on a very clear distinction between what is and what is not a routine; in this case, *routines* are considered the '*fixed point*' of a learning process in a conceptualization which opposes non-routine behaviour (the dynamic path) to routine behaviour (the 'equilibrium'). Authors supporting the second view propose instead an *all-embracing definition of routine* that is equivalent to an executable procedure including both automatic and deliberative components: 'These authors would contend that at the beginning there were routines which get modified, selected, discarded in the learning process (itself driven by "learning routines") and give rise to other routines' (ibid.: 5).

The former view, favouring a distinction, seems to have had many followers among evolutionary economists and organization theorists. Along these lines, authors have distinguished between: *operational* (aimed at the execution of a known procedure) and *learning/search* routines (directed to identify changes to an existing set of routines) (Nelson and Winter, 1982); *static*[20] (embodying the capacity to replicate certain previously performed tasks) and *dynamic* routines (directed at learning and new product/process development) (Teece, Pisano and Shuen, 1990); others have contrasted '*routines*', elaborate procedures developed as a fixed response to a defined stimulus, with '*problem-solving*' activity, characterized by search, aimed at discovering alternatives of actions or consequences of action (March and Simon, 1993).[21]

Recent work in cognitive psychology has reinforced the distinction between automatic routine behaviour and deliberate problem-solving. Work on '*procedural*' memory in human individuals has shown that it has distinctive properties: it is centred on skills, or know-how, rather than on facts, theories, or episodes (know-that), which seems to be more the province of an alternative, '*declarative*' memory system. Procedural memory differs from declarative in its long decay times and greater difficulty of transfer and verbalization; therefore, the procedural/declarative distinction seems to support Nelson and Winter's characterization of routines as tacit and highly stable analogs of individual skills.

While the notion of procedural memory usefully aligns with many characteristics of highly routinized action patterns, others have argued that effective organizational performance involves a *mixture* of such 'automatic' or 'tacit' elements together with a certain amount of 'decision-making' or 'problem-solving' that is much more deliberative and self-aware in its character.[22] Warglien, for example, has emphasized that the problem whether to name 'routine' all 'recurring action patterns' in organizations or just those that imply non-deliberate, automatic action may be a question of terminological taste: 'Whether we want or not to call "routine" the working of a kanban system in an assembly line, what strikes me is that *we don't have yet a language* for going too far in analysing its working'.[23] He concludes that, whatever may be the terminological standard, the problem is finding a language for defining the *ingredients* of recurring action patterns and the *architecture* tying those ingredients together and giving them coherence (Cohen et al., 1996: 5).

While the distinction between automatic and deliberative elements of behaviour is relevant, a view seeking to understand how diverse action patterns come together could perhaps be theoretically more valid, as it overcomes an artificial dichotomy between the two sides, while being also empirically more interesting. An attempt to characterize the complex interaction of automatic action patterns is present in the evolutionary notion of '*stable systemic traits*' (SSTs*)*. According to Winter, SSTs are not themselves 'structural' but are *stabilized* over long periods by some combination of features of the organization. Stable systemic traits are *relatively invariant ensembles* of routines (narrow sense), and other quasi-evolutionary elements, such as rules of thumb and possibly heuristics; according to Dosi, they represent therefore the central level of observation required in order to identify corporate capabilities (in Cohen et al., 1996). While insightful, the concept of SSTs is limited to automatic patterns and does not help us to understand how routines (narrow sense, automatic) and problem-solving (deliberate, conscious) mutually evolve.

The evolutionary view of routines has, therefore, so far privileged the separation between essentially automatic and essentially deliberative behaviour; it has not explored in sufficient depth the way organizational routines (as 'programs') interact with more explicit and deliberate knowledge processes and activities. There is a danger that an artificial, theoretical dichotomy could be created between essentially 'repetitive' routinized behaviour and more proactive 'creative' problem-solving. Given that the two are not independent but tightly intertwined, research should aim to uncover how relatively static routines co-evolve with more dynamic (problem-solving) processes; and how the relative proportion in which these are present may influence the organization's adaptive and innovative potential. This book attempts to shed light over this issue by looking at how software embedded knowledge routines and rules interact with more informal knowledge processes and how these mutually co-evolve (Chapter 6).

Contextual Aspects of Routines: Physical and Motivational

Despite its importance, the context-dependent character of organizational routines has been largely overlooked in evolutionary literature as compared to their cognitive side. Such an oversight, however, can have important implications: given that 'The effectiveness of a routine is not measured by what is achieved *in principle* but by what is achieved *in practice* ... the routine might be declared effective in some specific contexts, but perhaps not in others' (Winter, in Cohen et al., 1996: 7). There are two sides to context: (1) the *physical aspect*, including both the *local/artefactual* complements to the routine (i.e. the requisite plant and equipment) and the *broader physical environment* that was not produced for the benefit of the routine (i.e. climate, air pollution); and (2) the *motivational/relational aspect*, which sees *routines as a truce* among organizational conflicts: 'once upon a time there was overt conflict, but in most cases it is largely over when the observer comes on the scene' (ibid.: 8).

The prevailing focus on the cognitive side of routines and relative absence of contextual factors from most discussions around routines is quite striking. A possible explanation for this shortcoming may be the over-reliance of evolutionary studies on cognitive psychology to explain the nature of organizational routines; moving beyond this 'cognitive trap' involves taking into explicit account the double nature of routines, both as *problem-solving* action patterns and as mechanisms of *governance and control*. The latter definition was present in Nelson and Winter's notion of routines as 'truces' which '... emerge and are implemented in organisations composed by a plurality of individuals who might have diverging interests' (1982, in Coriat and Dosi, 1994: 12, emphasis added). Similarly, other authors have pointed out that 'the painstaking establishment of a new set of routines ... involved both a different social distribution of knowledge but also a different distribution of power and control among individuals and social groups' (ibid.). Others have defined organizations as systems of co-ordinated actions among individuals and groups whose preferences, information sets, interests and knowledge differ. Organization theories have described the delicate *conversion of conflict into co-operation* (March and Simon, 1993: 2). These contributions have highlighted important research avenues left so far relatively unexplored. For example, the role of organizational routines as loci of *conflict absorption*, governance, and a way of codifying micro-economic incentives and constraints, has been widely underplayed: 'There is a need for an appreciation of the co-evolution of (highly imperfect) mechanisms of governance, on the one hand, and "what a firm is able to do and discover" on the other' (Coriat and Dosi, 1994: 3). This view holds important implications for characterizing the patterns of infra- and inter-organizational co-operation.

A twofold *cognitive and motivational* characterization of routines is required in order to understand how individuals and groups in different parts of the organization are able to collaborate. For instance, how are the conflicting interests among groups mediated within an organization and which is the role of routines in this? What would the consequences be of embedding governance (authority and control) rules in software? Due to complex mechanisms of interaction and co-production between routines and their 'context', failure to explore beyond the cognitive side of routines implies overlooking some fundamental issues; these include the study of the *relationship between routines and artefacts* and other loci of organizational distributed knowledge and the study of the role of routines in *absorbing emergent conflicts* among heterogeneous organizational actors and groups. As argued later in this book (i.e. Chapters 5 and 7), the contextual and cognitive sides of routines are tightly inter-linked and should not be studied as separate entities.

Being able to account for the motivational and physical aspects of routines is also important in order to improve our understanding of organizational *inertia*, which may have both cognitive and motivational origins:[24] both these factors in fact suggest that firms are likely to behave in the future according to the routines they have employed in the past (Nelson and Winter, 1982). In particular, *motivational inertia* is reinforced by the ability of routines to control locally solved *conflicts of interest*: in this context the truce represented by the prevailing routines is easily broken when an attempt to change is made (ibid.). Motivational inertia is therefore supported by the extent of reallocative efforts involved in the change of rules (March and Simon, 1993). The truces that emerge and are embedded in particular sets of routines tend therefore to foster conservatism by hindering the diffusion of technological and organizational innovation (Lorenz, 1994, in Coriat and Dosi, 1994). As a consequence, as new situations arise, the construction of an entirely new program is rarely contemplated: 'Whatever change takes place may be expected to follow the path of least resistance' (Nelson and Winter, 1982: 135). In other words, '*Path dependent* processes imply that "localized" learning and dynamic increasing returns amplify micro-fluctuations and may "*lock*" the system dynamics into attractors that may well be "inferior" from a normative point of view, but still be stable over time' (Arthur, 1977, in Coriat and Dosi, 1994: 6).

The mechanisms by which the continuity of routinized behaviour operates to channel organizational change are still not well understood, including preventing 'core capabilities' from turning into 'core rigidities' (Leonard-Barton, 1992; 1995). According to Egidi, the issue of how *local stability* is achieved remains a largely unexplored feature; therefore 'an important challenge for future research is to gain a better understanding of the *links between the cognitive and the conflictual forces* which give rise to the persistence of rules' (in Cohen et al., 1996: 33, 40). Accounting for the conflictual elements is especially important when analysing the *emergence* of organizational routines, as opposed to their steady, operational state characteristics. For this reason: 'we think that an item high on the agenda should be a better understanding of how the political relations among actors shape *cognitive and behavioural* patterns ... one would like to see also experiments that are set in ways which account for both dimensions' (Coriat and Dosi, 1994: 15). The double nature of routines as problem-solving skills and as mechanisms of governance appears with particular clarity when analysing the emergence of new principles of management and work practices (ibid.); in this sense, the introduction of information systems in organizations and the consequent radical process reconfiguration, provides an especially interesting platform from which to observe the co-evolution of such mechanisms. These issues are addressed throughout this book by examining how patterns of cognitive and motivational factors coexist and mutually evolve.

Routines as Representations and Expressions[25]

A further limitation in the evolutionary approach lies in the creation of a theoretical dualism between the notion of routine as '*representation*' and as '*expression*'. This is partly attributable to its reliance on the biological paradigm and its distinction between genotype and phenotype: a genome stores the pattern-guidance needed to reproduce its phenotypic expression, and the modifications of the genetic representation are the source of evolutionary variation. While some authors feel that this distinction deserves considerable stress, others find it of lesser priority, preferring to focus on the observable form of the actions as expressed. The second opinion is based on the observation that, where human patterns of action are concerned, the distinction between representations (such as learned, skilled responses of machinists) and action patterns (say, machine assembly steps) that occur when those representations are expressed is not at all as sharp.

The advocates of the dualism between representations of routines and their realization argue that this provides the basis for a theoretical characterization of the difference between *routines* and *standard operating procedures* (SOPs): while SOPs-as-representations consist of *formalized statements* of what actions *should* occur, the actions occurring as routines are expressed *in context.* A substantial body of literature has shown that real behaviour diverges substantially from formalized SOPs, and indeed, 'working to rule' has proven an effective labour tactic for bringing an organization to a halt.

While relevant, the distinction between representation and expression raises an important question: to which level do routines belong? If, as Nelson and Winter have argued, routines belong to the behavioural level, it follows that they can be reduced to expressions. The implication of this is profound: 'what is often reproduced is not the routine itself but some kind of "*coded knowledge*" which usually implies a mix of linguistic representation, rules, and artefacts'[26] (ibid.). Cohen et al. (1996) consider two examples.

The first concerns the reproduction of routines. According to diffusion theory, actual work experience generates successful routines to be reproduced and diffused as '*best practice*': it seems therefore to reinforce the automatic 'routine' view. However, when looking at the actual reproduction process of such successful routines, one invariably finds a large effort to set up a 'technology of replication' that usually implies: (1) *learning a language* within which to code successful routines; (2) *creating cognitive artefacts* that can be diffused (through flow charts and other replicable representations); (3) *translating* the high-level description contained in the cognitive artefact *in actual practice*, generating a new routine adapted to the new context (Hutchins and Hazelhurst, 1995). According to this view, *what finally generates value is therefore the routine* (the expression) rather than the code (representation). This relates closely to the problem highlighted in the first part of this chapter (the codification debate), indicating that there is a fundamental difference between diffusion and adoption (in this case of organizational practices).

The second example interprets the notion of business process re-engineering (BPR) in evolutionary terms as a form of 'organizational genetic engineering' and argues that existing routines are used as materials to be manipulated mainly through deletion and recombination of their elementary components. Also in this case, in order to make possible such manipulation, 'one has to *code the routine in cognitive artefacts* (i.e. work-flow graphs) amenable to engineering. Manipulation then happens at the representation level, and finally its outcomes are 'brought back to the field' generating new expressions (routines)' (ibid.: 18). As argued earlier, and investigated empirically in Chapter 7, the processes of 'codification' and 'de-codification' are highly problematic; the process of reproducing patterns of action, due to its inherent cultural nature, relies in fact on our ability to code experience, to communicate it, and to decode it in ways that may adapt it to new contexts.

What authors have not sufficiently emphasized, however, is that such 'translation' processes from expression to representation and vice versa, fundamentally reconfigure the shape as well as the content of existing routines, creating new routines while erasing others. New expression-type routines may contain parts of representation-type routines as *the boundaries separating them are far from clearly defined.* The relationships between the two levels of routines, in fact, is rather complex. Insightfully, Dosi has argued that: 'not the dichotomy between formally stated SOPs and actual behavioural patterns, but the *relation between the two levels,* however defined, is a promising area of investigation' (ibid.: 18–19).

This research attempts to characterize such interactions by highlighting the emergence of 'hybrid' level routines. This is particularly important with regard to the character and content of SOPs and other 'routines representations'. It confirms that it is not implausible to think of representations as sorts of imperfect and mostly *ex post rationalizations* of what has been done, should be done, one wished ought to be done. And, indeed, we provide evidence of this by illustrating how codified and software-embedded routines embodying 'frozen' meanings, intentions, points of view and strategic directions are translated into actual expressions (and vice versa).[27]

Individual vs. Collective Behaviour

The 'cognitive' approach essentially fails to emphasize that the characteristics of individual cognition can only be *imperfectly* mapped onto collective behaviour. In order to counteract this potential problem, some authors have introduced conceptual dimensions that are devised to *specifically characterize organizational cognition,* distinguishing it at the same time from individual cognition (Spender, 1995).

Organizational knowledge has therefore been characterized at different times as: (1) *implicit/explicit* (James, 1950), or, in Polanyi's (1968) terms, *tacit/codified;* (2) *knowledge intensive/search intensive,* highlighting the trade-off between undertaking new search or using existing knowledge as a basis for action (similar to Newell's preparation/deliberation trade-off);[28] (3) *distributed/local,* emphasizing that a given routine has no one place where it is represented and no one participant is able to entirely describe it, since *the routine arises from the interactions* among only partly overlapping, incomplete and inarticulate individual knowledge sources (Weick, 1979);[29] (4) *situated/context independent,* exploiting the idea that social knowledge is not only distributed among individuals but also *among individuals and their environment.* This brings us to the notion of *situatedness,* meaning that knowledge is tightly coupled to a specific context, which acts as external memory and information processor. Research in cognitive anthropology has suggested that many routinized competences can be of the situated kind (Hutchins, 1995; Lave, 1988; Suchman, 1987).

In a somewhat similar fashion Nelson and Winter (1982) have argued that knowledge stored in human memories is effective only when placed in an organizational context. This is because, (1) an organization typically includes a variety of forms of 'external' memory (i.e. files, message boards, manuals, computer memories, magnetic tapes); (2) the context includes the physical state of equipment and of the work environment; (3) generally, the context of information possessed by an individual member is established by the information possessed by all other members. The above assumptions, especially those concerning the role of artefacts as additional repositories of organizational knowledge/memory, have not been yet fully explored in evolutionary theories of the firm. This theme is addressed in Chapters 5 and 7.

Analogously, authors in the field of cognitive psychology have argued that the representation of an action pattern carried out by a group of actors in an organizational setting is maintained in the organization: (1) in the memories of *individual* actors; (2) by means of a *locally shared language*, e.g. Weick's (1979) conceptualization of shared meanings as a form of organizational memory; (3) via *physical artefacts*, such as tools, spatial arrangements, written codes of standard operating procedures, or computer systems; (4) via *organizational practice* such as archives, rotation of personnel, or by building key assumptions into organizational structure, e.g. Henderson's (1992) 'architectural knowledge';[30] (5) by means of *globally shared language forms*, such as formalized oral codes or stories (Orr, 1996 in Berg, 1998).[31]

By building on the notion of *distributed knowledge* this book illustrates how people-, software- and artefact-embedded knowledge processes interact. This work also draws from the notion of *situated action* and examines knowledge dynamics in context to uncover the interactions between formal/informal, global/local, tacit/codified, and computer-embedded/people-embodied knowledge. The latter point is further developed in the methodological chapter.

The Dynamic Aspects of Routines: Change, Stability and Adaptation

The question of how firms' action repertoires are assembled, maintained and modified has been to date essentially unexplored. While routines have been principally characterized as *stable* patterns, insufficient attention has been directed to uncovering how existing organizational *patterns of behaviour change* and how *new patterns are created*. The organizational mechanisms that support the emergence, maintenance and replacement of routines, however, are of utmost importance as they lie at the basis of an organization's ability to flexibly adapt to, anticipate and respond to change.

March and Simon have emphasized the distinction between *change* and *stability* and pointed to the fundamental difference between the *continuation* of an existing program of action and *change*. They have argued that, because of the approximating and fragmented character of action, only a few elements of the system are adaptive at one time, while the remainder are, at least in the short run, *'givens'* (March and Simon, 1993).[32] Others yet have argued that striking a balance between elements of *persistence* and elements of *change* is the key premise to adaptive behaviour: an organization must be *'dynamically stable'* (Crainer and Obeng, 1994). These contributions, however, do not address how organizations are able to achieve such dynamic balance (i.e. how they learn to exploit their accumulated knowledge while, at the same time, preventing existing knowledge and competences from obstructing the creation of new ones). While IT is assumed to be a critical factor in sustaining such dynamic balance, it is not yet known how its adoption can influence the organization's ability to manage the trade-off between stability and change.

Some of these critical issues were addressed in the 'dynamic capabilities' debate. By building upon the resource-based view of the firm, this approach has emphasized that the profitable growth of firms is both a process of *exploiting existing capabilities* and *developing new ones* (Penrose, 1959; Teece, Pisano and Shuen, 1990; Wernerfelt, 1984). Adopting a dynamic view of resource and capabilities accumulation implies acknowledging that 'it is not only the bundle of resources that matters, but the *mechanisms* by which firms accumulate and dissipate new skills and capabilities, and the *forces* that limit the rate and direction of this process' (Teece, Pisano and Shuen, 1990: 19).

The notion of dynamic capabilities emphasizes that *organizational capabilities are emergent* and thus cannot (and indeed should not) be taken for granted: once created and established, they have to be maintained; in fact, the *capability maintenance process* represents as great a challenge for the organization as much as their creation, because changing technologies and markets constantly make the existing firm's competence base obsolete (Chandler, 1990); it follows that we should focus on the process of *building and renewing capabilities over time* (Chandler, 1990; Dosi and Marengo, 1994; Iansiti and Clark, 1994; Penrose, 1959; Prahalad and Hamel, 1990; Rosenberg, 1982; Teece, Pisano and Shuen, 1990; Wernerfelt, 1984).

While valuable in emphasizing the dynamic aspects of organizational capabilities, however, this literature has not uncovered the processes underlying their formation and growth (Iansiti and Clark, 1994); for example, authors have often failed to identify precisely how the learning processes are carried out and which activities may be particularly critical in the building and renewal process; in order to begin to understand how capabilities become and remain a source of competitive advantage, it is therefore necessary to investigate the very processes that sustain the building and renewing of organizational capabilities. This book hopes to contribute to this effort by analysing how organizations are able to reconfigure their routines in response to external and internal change (Chapter 6).

A first important step in this direction involves acknowledging the relationship between a firm's knowledge base and its capabilities. Starting from recent work on the nature of organizational competencies (i.e. Dosi and Marengo, 1994; Leonard-Barton, 1992; Prahalad and Hamel, 1990; Teece, Pisano and Shuen, 1990), Iansiti and Clark (1994) place *knowledge and knowledge-creating activities at the foundation of capability*. It is argued that, in order to produce a capability, *knowledge must be implemented* in action-producing forms and specific assets, including: skills, the technical system (equipment, software, tools), the managerial system (routines, procedures, incentives), and the values and norms in the organization. These elements constitute an interrelated, interdependent knowledge system (Leonard-Barton, 1992). A *dynamic capability* can be thus defined as 'the capacity of an organisation to consistently nurture, adapt, and regenerate its knowledge base, and to develop and retain the organisational capabilities that *translate that knowledge base into useful actions*' (Iansiti and Clark, 1994: 563, emphasis added). In order to identify the important activities through which the firm adapts, nurtures and builds its capacity for action, we need therefore to capture *the processes inside the firm for managing and generating the knowledge base*.

In searching for new knowledge to execute desired actions, *problem-solving activities* drive the generation of new capabilities (Iansiti and Clark, 1994). Specific problem-solving competencies, for example, can deeply affect the ability of individual firms to generate and adopt new technologies (Coriat and Dosi, 1994).[33] Problem-solving is characterized as the basic unit of knowledge creation; this is consistent with Dosi and Marengo (1994), who argue that problem-solving routines are the essence of competence-building processes because they are an organization's basic increment of knowledge generation (Iansiti and Clark, 1994). They conclude that '*The capacity to integrate diverse knowledge bases through problem solving* is the basic foundation of knowledge building in an organization, and is therefore a *critical driver of dynamic performance*' (ibid.: 557, emphasis added).

The implications of placing an organization's knowledge system at the basis of the development of dynamic capabilities are fundamental. Since the organization's knowledge system and its associated capability base are complex and made up of many closely inter-linked elements, it means that *capabilities cannot function in isolation*, but they must fit with the broader context of the organization (Leonard-Barton, 1992). Capabilities, in fact, will not affect the realm of possible actions *unless they are integrated* into the existing organization; an effective capability-building process will act by framing the search for new possibilities in light of existing characteristics; existing capabilities will have to be adapted to achieve consistency with novel developments (Iansiti and Clark, 1994). This calls for the mutual adaptation of existing with new knowledge, assets and capabilities.[34]

According to Iansiti and Clark, a firm's *capacity for integration* is related to the organization's ability to build capability in response to 'external' (i.e. the evolution of customer tastes and/or technological possibilities) as well as 'internal' (i.e. the evolution of firm-specific resources, structures and approaches) contingencies (ibid.). Dynamic performance in Product Development, for example, lies in the organization's capacity for integration: *integration of knowledge*, both internal (i.e. the capacity for extensive co-ordination between different specialized sub-units within an organization) and external (i.e. the integration of knowledge of the market and the customer base as well as the integration of knowledge of emerging technologies) to the firm.[35]

In contrast with the information-processing argument, we argue that the capacity for integration is not simply a function of the communication of information between individuals or a consequence of the effective co-ordination of activities between organizational sub-units; *integration entails the generation, fusion and accumulation of knowledge*, or the capacity to merge new knowledge about the impact of possibilities with accumulated knowledge of the complex existing capability base of the organization (ibid.). Effective communication and co-ordination constitute, therefore, only part of the greater challenge of the integration capability.

Strikingly, we do not yet know just how such integration can be achieved. We know that the integration capability is founded on specific problem-solving routines that conceptualize new directions and evaluate their impact on existing organizational characteristics. However, all we have learnt about such routines so far is that 'they explicitly comprehend the inherent complexity of a firm's base of capability and that they involve processes that treat the evolution of that base as an integrated system, not as a sequence of isolated events' (ibid.: 602). While this represents an important finding, no attempts have been made to date to uncover the nature of such routines as well as of the mechanisms underpinning their emergence. This book attempts to provide a clear advancement precisely in this direction (see Chapter 7).

In Iansiti and Clark's example, NEC's integration engineers and Nissan's product management were functioning as an engine for the evolution of the firm's capability base. They achieved this by reacting to environmental changes, linking external trends with the internal competence base of their organization; initiating problem-solving activities to conceptualize options and evaluate possible responses when internal and external environments were perceived to be out of alignment: 'Their capacity for integration allowed them to adapt to uncertainties in the product's technical base or customer environment and continually to refocus the organization's competences in a timely and efficient fashion' (Iansiti and Clark, 1994: 600–601). While the role of individuals is relevant, this book demonstrates that it could not be effective in the longer term, unless it was supported by the emergence of specific, recurrent and relatively stable 'integrative' or 'translation' routines. These routines (introduced in Chapter 7) provide the 'glue' that co-ordinates automatic/tacit with more deliberative/conscious knowledge processes, integrates external as well as internal knowledge sources, and therefore facilitates the integration of new with existing knowledge and capabilities.

Malerba and Orsenigo (1998) have acknowledged the relevance of the issue and highlighted the need to analyse the knowledge processes that lie at the basis of competences formation; they have argued that, in order to constitute a capability, *different knowledge sources and types* must be integrated in a coherent whole which is finalized to accomplish specific purposes: 'if an agent's knowledge includes both codified and tacit knowledge, there must be something that links (even imperfectly) the two parts' (ibid.: 7). Specifically, the integration of different knowledge strands

> Must be the case if codified knowledge is itself composed of different parts, which are codified in different ways and through different codes ... thus, even if knowledge were completely codified, but *comprised knowledge about different domains and functions* (see for example the distinction between bodies of understanding and bodies of practice), mechanisms for integrating these pieces are necessary. (Ibid. emphasis added)

To support their argument, the authors introduce a distinction between two types of knowledge: knowledge as an *input* in the process of 'doing something' and knowledge as the *ability to use those inputs* in the transformation process finalized at the generation of new artefacts and knowledge. They therefore emphasize the difference between simply *having access* to some knowledge and being able to *use* that knowledge to produce products, services and/or new knowledge. It follows that what an agent can do cannot be simply described in terms of the knowledge that s/he possesses. If knowledge was only an input, we should be mainly interested in its diffusion. In this case the impact of knowledge codification (which reduces the cost of acquisition of that knowledge which is codified) would be of utmost importance. Instead knowledge codification has 'very few immediate implications on how such knowledge is then integrated with other fragments of knowledge in the process of production and the more so where processes of creation of new knowledge are concerned' and therefore its role is not quite as important as the diffusion debate assumes (ibid.). They conclude that, beyond knowledge diffusion, there is still another branch of the 'economics of knowledge', which needs to be developed, and this has to do with *the processes through which knowledge is used and created*.

The process of knowledge integration lies therefore at the core of capabilities' formation. Competencies are that part of knowledge that allows to *link* together the various bits of tacit and codified knowledge, and that *allows them to be mapped onto each other through codes, languages and practices*. They are therefore the equivalent of

> A *meta-structure* that allows to combine the necessarily different structures imposed on the codified and the tacit parts of the 'stock of knowledge', integrates its various sub-sets and enables the agent to 'use' the knowledge for specific purposes. This meta-structure is agent-specific and context-specific, precisely because it links agent-specific knowledge to context-specific domains. (Ibid. emphasis added)

There is still a lot to be uncovered in relation to the nature of such meta-structures, as well as the character of the problem-solving routines, which underlie capabilities. We can only begin to answer these questions by examining the processes that support capabilities in detail and in the context of actual practice. While existing approaches have been essentially assessing the presence of dynamic capabilities a posteriori (i.e. as a measurement of improved performance), this book hopes to uncover the very processes of capabilities' *formation and maintenance*. This should reveal some important aspects of the emergence of routines, i.e. their role in providing a strategic link (1) among knowledge types (i.e. tacit/codified, formal/informal, personal/social, computer-embedded/people-embodied), knowledge sources (i.e. heterogeneous specialized knowledge bases), and knowledge domains (i.e. knowledge residing across organizational groups or individuals); (2) between knowledge and action (i.e. bodies of knowledge and bodies of practice).

Uncovering the roots of the capabilities' formation process implies moving away from an *abstract model of problem-solving* to observe how processes evolve in concrete, actual circumstances. While Product Development represents an ideal standpoint from which to observe the evolution of the knowledge processes and activities that underlie capabilities, the adoption of Information Systems in Product Development offers an even more privileged point of observation. Software introduction is in fact often followed not only by the radical reconfiguration of activities or practices (as BPR would argue), but also the extensive re-engineering of organizational cognitive processes. The introduction of integrated software alters fundamentally both knowledge flows and activities, therefore forcing the organization to find new dynamic equilibria between accumulated knowledge and competences and new ones; it therefore puts to test the organization's ability to react flexibly to and exploit the potential brought about by change. Our analysis can therefore allow us to capture those instances in which the innovating organization is able to generate that glue that provides the balance between stability (accumulated knowledge, skills and capabilities) and change (new knowledge, skills and capabilities).

Uncovering the Roots of Routines and Capabilities

The routines and capabilities theories have addressed some of the issues left unresolved by the codification debate. Specifically, the notion of routines contributes to emphasize: the role of tacit, automatic and unconscious behaviour as opposed to more rational and deliberate factors; the importance of acquiring and creating capabilities as opposed to relying on more straightforward knowledge diffusion processes; the various forms in which capacities of action (including decision-making) can become embedded in relatively stable organizational mechanisms; the processes by which these become a source of stability by obstructing change. The contribution of the capabilities debate is valuable in emphasizing the need to analyse the dynamic factors that underlie the evolution of routines and capabilities. Theoretically, it has therefore helped counteract the over-reliance of the routines approach on the 'routines as genes' metaphor. This tends in fact to obscure important issues such as the need to investigate the nature of the processes by which behaviour producing routines emerge, evolve and decay along an organization's life span.

Nonetheless, several fundamental and problematic issues and challenges remain yet to be addressed. While the codification debate concentrates essentially on deliberate and conscious decision-making, the routines' approach moves perhaps too far in the opposite direction, at times underestimating the function performed by deliberate design and replication of structures to control and generate behaviour. An approach is therefore required which integrates the cognitive with the behavioural perspectives and which focuses on the interactions and integration between deliberate and tacit/automatic processes.

Even more importantly, we require to move beyond a predominantly cognitive view of routines (which characterizes both the routines and the dynamic capabilities approaches) in order to further our understanding of their contextual side; this includes both the physical context (i.e. the role of artefacts and distributed memory) and the motivational context (i.e. the emergence and absorption of conflicts and the co-ordination of actions among heterogeneous agents having divergent viewpoints). We also need to further analyse the patterns of learning and responsibility (distributed across an organization, together with explicit policies and procedures, physical artefacts and arrangements, social and political factors) that, in addition to cognitive inertia, can be responsible for lock-in.

Finally, we need to analyse, a priori and in the context of situated practice, the processes by which routines and capabilities emerge; approaches to date have essentially looked at routines 'a posteriori', or in a simplified simulation context. For example, we need to examine the co-evolution of routines-as-representation with routines-in-practice (expressions). The relationship between the two levels represents a promising area of investigation, and will be discussed further in Chapter 3.

NOTES

1. This is the case of 'information economists' (i.e. Arrow, 1974; 1979; Boulding, 1966; Coase, 1937; Hayek, 1945; Knight, 1921; Machlup, 1980; Marshak, 1974; Richardson, 1960; Simon, Egidi and Marris, 1992; Stigler, 1961; Stiglitz, 1977), who, in departing from the earlier neoclassical tradition's neglect of the knowledge issue, have recognized its centrality to the economic activity. In their framework, information is seen as a reduction in uncertainty and information acquisition as the process by which the dis-equilibrium generated by uncertainty is repaired. While acknowledging the presence in the economy of problems related to the nature of information, however, they treated changes in knowledge as exogenous and assimilate the nature of information to that of a (somewhat imperfect) commodity. Information is traded on the marketplace and there is no interest in the role of organizations in processing and creating knowledge. See D'Adderio (1996) for a review of the literature.
2. The different definitions of information and knowledge correspond to radically different characterizations of the role of the firm. These span from entirely disregarding the existence of organizations (perfect knowledge, as in 'orthodox' economics); to characterizing the firm as an information-processing machine (bounded rationality, cf. March and Simon, 1993); or as a knowledge repository and creator (emphasis on tacit knowledge and accumulated competences, cf. Nelson and Winter, 1982). For a review see D'Adderio (1996).
3. Although relatively new to the codification debate, the complementary nature of tacit and codified knowledge had already been emphasized by Polanyi (1968). Indeed, the observation of the need to overcome the Cartesian divide between tacit and codified, individual and social dimensions of knowledge, had inspired the recent organizational innovation literature's attempt to characterize the interactions between tacit and codified knowledge flows at the organizational level (Nonaka, 1994). While the operation of shifting the attention from the extremes to their interactions represents an important step forward, these contributions do not fully capture the sophisticated technological and organizational mechanisms that underlie these complex organizational dynamics.
4. This could be the case either because no 'codebook' exists which contains the knowledge that has been codified, or because a codebook exists but is displaced. In the latter case, a codified body of common knowledge is identified, which is present but somehow not manifest to the observer.
5. This view is also supported by the STS debate. Callon (1995), for example, argues that knowledge is embedded in the tacit understanding of individuals and working groups. See also Collins (1974).
6. This is not to deny the important role played by codification. To prove its relative importance, Steinmueller (1998) raises the hypothetical situation where all pharmaceutical research chemists were to die tomorrow; in this case it would take a much shorter time for

research to return to the frontier if scientists had access to the tools and databases that had been previously created.

7. Although IT implementation and codification are not the same thing, in fact, they often go together.

8. Are tacit and codified knowledge complements or substitutes? The codification debate has brought some seemingly contrasting evidence towards this issue. While earlier contributions seem to support the idea of substitutability (Cowan and Foray, 1995; Ergas, 1994), more recent ones argue for their complementarity. The key question is: '... whether additions to the stock of codified knowledge *always* involve growth in tacit knowledge' (Steinmueller, 1998: 9, emphasis in the original). The codification economists' answer would be: it depends which tacit knowledge. According to Cowan, David and Foray (1998), while some tacit knowledge is always complementary to codified knowledge (unarticulable), some other (articulable) is potentially substitutable with codified knowledge. If our answer to Steinmueller's question is yes, then it follows that the process of codification implies addition to tacit (uncodifiable) knowledge (tacit uncodifiable and codified knowledge are always complements), subtraction from tacit (codifiable) knowledge and addition to the codified knowledge stock (codifiable and codified are to an extent substitutes (cf. Dasgupta and David, 1994).

9. An example of this are situations where the language embedded in a technology has changed.

10. In practice, this is another matter for contention: the complex task of integrating technological interfaces constitutes by itself a major challenge.

11. The obsolescence of Information Systems is so rapid (Ullman, 1997), and it involves such extensive codification and reorganization efforts that often before one system's implementation is completed, another is likely to have begun. While often applied to IT, peripheral or support technologies, this argument can indeed be true also where changes in production systems, and other principal product and process technologies, are concerned, especially in turbulent markets (Iansiti, 1995).

12. Stability is often taken for granted by software producers, who market their products on the basis of the expected benefits that these can provide once they are *completely* and *successfully* implemented. In partial implementation circumstances, an 'intermediate' stage which can be very protracted, the costs (especially the organizational costs, such as communication break downs and knowledge sharing failures) can easily outweigh the benefits (cf. Chapter 5).

13. The reasons behind an organization decision to invest in substantial codification of their practices are often more complex than can be captured by a cost–benefit analysis; managers may feel compelled to codify to gain greater efficiency in the face of increasing competition; because of the need to integrate their practices with a higher tier organization's; or because they see codification as a means to acquire industry 'best practices', etc.

14. These conclusions derive from the problematic instance of equating knowledge to information (Fransman, 1994; Kay, 1994). According to information economists, knowledge displays properties of a public good and is therefore relatively easy to appropriate, e.g. the information disclosed in the scientific journals and various publications (Cowan, David and Foray, 1998). Innovation scholars have opposed this argument and emphasized that knowledge is unlike information; it cannot travel freely as it remains with the scientists and engineers engaged in its production. While codified knowledge may have low marginal costs of transmission and is thus slippery and hard to contain, that is largely irrelevant in absence of its 'sticky', tacit counterpart. According to innovation scholars, therefore, stickiness enables businesses (or other) entities to protect their ability fully to appropriate the benefits derivable from their research investments by controlling access to the repositories of uncodified knowledge. The economic benefits of tacit knowledge are consequently only available to be captured locally: the marginal costs of knowledge transmission rise very rapidly with 'distance' from the context in which such knowledge was generated (ibid.). A major implication of this argument is that, if technological knowledge is strongly tacit in nature, it is advantageous for commercial developers to situate themselves close to the locus of the discoveries (Pavitt, 1987; Nelson, 1992, in Cowan, David and Foray, 1998).

15. This issue is developed further in Chapters 5, 6 and 7.

16. 'Epistemic communities' or 'epistemic cultures' can be defined as groups of agents working on a commonly acknowledged subset of knowledge issues and who at the very least accept a commonly understood procedural authority as essential to the success of their

knowledge activities (Cohendet and Meyer-Krahmer, 2001; Knorr-Cetina, 1999). The notion of 'communities-of-practice' identifies instead groups of persons engaged in the same practice, communicating regularly with one another about their activities (Cohendet and Meyer-Krahmer, 2001; Lave and Wenger, 1991). While the theoretical distinction between the two notions of communities-of-practice and epistemic communities is useful and insightful (cf. Cohendet and Meyer-Krahmer, 2001), in practice their boundaries can be difficult to identify as each individual practitioner belongs at the same time to several epistemic communities and communities-of-practice.

17. See D'Adderio (1996) for a more comprehensive review of the literature.
18. The routine operation in a firm is initiated when a flow of messages is received from the external environment and time-keeping devices; the organization's members receive and interpret the incoming messages, evoking the appropriate performance of routines from their repertory; the performance of routines by one member of the organization generates in turn a stream of messages to other members of the same organization (Nelson and Winter, 1982).
19. The discussion in this section draws substantially from Cohen et al. (1996).
20. Routines are never entirely static, however, because with repetition they can be constantly improved (Teece et al. 1990).
21. In this framework, environmental stimuli evoke individual or organizational activity, which is a continuum having at one extreme 'routinized' responses, and, at the other, 'problem-solving' responses.
22. This is also known as the *problem of grain size*: 'Should a routine generally be taken to be a rather large block of action, implying that choices are part of one routine, or are routines instead small blocks interleaved with other small routines and other forms of non-routine action (in this case choices can be thought of as sutures joining several smaller routines)? (Cohen et al., 1996: 12).
23. 'To be sure, there is a lot of tacit knowledge and non-deliberate behaviour in the way workers can achieve co-ordination in a kanban system: there's more in it than workers or production engineers can say. But stability and replicability is assured to a large extent also by ... explicitly stated rules and instructions ... and by a carefully designed artefactual environment within which workers can learn co-ordinated behaviours' (Cohen et al., 1996: 5).
24. *Cognitive inertia* is generated by the fact that tacit knowledge (not consciously known and easily articulable) is stored in the routine functioning of the organization; this, however, also performs an important function of *co-ordination* with respect to the firm's activities, and is therefore at the basis of an organization's effective performance.
25. This section draws from Cohen et al., 1996).
26. Drawing from Lave and Wenger (1991), Cohen et al. (1996: 18) point out that '"apprenticeship" processes may directly replicate the routine itself through forms of learning by examples'.
27. See Chapter 6.
28. March and Simon (1993) have suggested that search can also be routinized to a greater or lesser degree, implying that the preparation/deliberation distinction applies also within the boundary of routines rather than defining routines themselves.
29. This concept also draws from behavioural work in Artificial Intelligence (AI), which has argued that artefacts and spatial arrangements form an essential part of the organizational memory from which routine performance is drawn.
30. See also Henderson and Clark, 1990; Ulrich, 1995.
31. It is important to note that this notion differs from the above notion of situatedness in stating that a *representation* of action patterns, and *not the actual action patterns* are distributed (see the discussion of routines as representation/expression).
32. Those aspects of pattern behaviour that are relatively stable and change only slowly (i.e. stable regulations and procedures that can be employed in carrying out the adaptive practices) constitute the organization structure or the 'boundaries of rationality' (March and Simon, 1993).
33. According to Coriat and Dosi (1994), this view is naturally overlapping with a much longer tradition of business studies pointing at the two-way causality between corporate strategies and structures, and their effects on performances (i.e. Chandler, 1962; 1990).
34. Theories of new technology adoption have shown that successful implementation involves innovation, so that, at the end of the implementation process, both technology and organizations are changed (Fleck, 1988; Leonard-Barton, 1995; Malerba and Orsenigo, 1998; Orlikowski and Gash, 1994).

35. Iansiti and Clark focus on product development as the locus where capabilities are directly
     generated as well as a window on the general capability-building process; they argue that
     the capacity for problem-solving that underlies effective PD is also the critical ingredient in
     dynamic capability more generally.

3. Distributed Knowledge, Situated Action: The Role of Qualitative Analysis and Participant-Observation in Organizational Knowledge Research

This chapter is divided into two sections outlining, respectively, the theoretical premises and the pragmatic implications of the chosen methodology. The first part addresses the theoretical foundations underpinning the choice of a qualitative, detailed, immersive, grounded and situated empirical approach; the second part illustrates how such assumptions unfolded in practice.

THE THEORETICAL FOUNDATIONS OF THE METHODOLOGY

From Abstract Cognition to Situated Action

Contributions in the fields of Economics, Organization and Innovation Studies have traditionally characterized knowledge as if this was separated from practice. Heavily influenced by earlier debates in cognitive psychology and artificial intelligence, such studies have often described cognition as a highly abstract process, detached from its context. Their underlying assumption is that such simplification and reduction represent a legitimate way of dealing with an overly complex and chaotic reality.

More recently, however, authors within the fields of Science and Technology Studies (STS) and Computer-Supported Co-operative Work (CSCW) have directed a strong attack to the rationalistic tradition's conceptualization of cognition. Drawing from anthropology, psychology and the sociology of science, these emerging fields have set out to ground activities previously seen as individual, mental and non-social as situated, collective and historically specific (Bowker and Star, 1999). Their argument states that, not only is an abstract and idealized representation of actual phenomena unsatisfactory, but it also draws our attention away from the most interesting issues and questions.

A fascinating critique of the rationalist tradition, for example, is Lucy Suchman's (1987) 'Plans and Situated Actions', a detailed study of human–machine interaction. Suchman points out that the design of traditional computer systems is based upon a simplified view that reduces human action to the execution of mental plans. Plans, she argues, are themselves located in the larger context of some ongoing practical activity; this means that they are always *situated*, notwithstanding traditional claims of disembodied, idealized formal notions of mind and thought (ibid.).

According to Suchman, therefore, planning must be understood as *locally contingent*, where 'local' means the complex interrelating of people, machines, documents, formal organizational arrangements and previous interactions (Star, 1992: 396). Given the contingent nature of planning and action, plans and goals themselves are fundamentally *non-deterministic*: they are 'resources for situated action' and therefore 'do not in any strong sense determine its course' (Suchman, 1987: 49, 52). This course itself unfolds only in the doing, in constant interaction with the actual, concrete and contingent circumstances that make up the situation (Berg, 1998: 460).

According to Robinson (1991, in Berg, 1998), Suchman has formulated an 'impossibility theorem': there can be no a priori or algorithmic connection between any particular plan and any specific action. Most computer systems designs, however, disregard this theorem in basing their assumption on isolated mental plans, 'as if users indeed followed clear-cut "plans" and were not in fact tinkering toward a practical solution by ad hoc tryouts and seeing where these lead to' (ibid.: 461). Computer systems built on simplified assumptions are therefore often destined to failure.

From this, it follows that cognitive processes should be understood and studied as concrete, organization-embedded activities. Conceptually, this entails a move beyond a purely cognitive characterization of both knowledge and practice, towards a situated approach, whereby knowledge and practice are studied as dependent upon, and indistinguishable from, their organizational context of application (Bowker and Star, 1999; Bucciarelli, 1988; Suchman, 1987; Tyre and von Hippel, 1997). A situated approach, it is argued, holds the highest potential to unveil the evolution of knowledge and learning processes in organizations.

Rational Characterization of the Design Process

A related limitation in the literature is the widespread characterization of the design process as a straightforward sequence of abstract stages that correspond to a series of perfectly ordered and logical decision-making steps. This, however, is a far cry from day-to-day 'muddling through' which decision-makers, or, in our case, managers and engineers experience (Lindblom, 1959).

Existing organization and innovation literatures, for example, are dominated by an essentially normative characterization of design as *a highly abstract* activity, made of distinct and idealized decision-making stages that are executed by engineers within the solitude of their own mind (cf. Newell and Simon, 1972; Wheelwright and Clark, 1992). According to Bucciarelli (1988), traditional models of engineering design 'are themselves designs: they are rationally constructed plans which are used by engineers to describe how the process *ought to* work. These images, which are the result of an abstraction from experience, express *an ideal* upon which designers pattern their efforts' (ibid.: 92, emphasis added).

Often invoked as an approximation of the actual design process, such models constitute unsatisfactory representations of practical design activity: not only do they provide the impression that design practice is an extra-orderly, rational process, but, most importantly, they can lead to underestimating the role of ambiguity and uncertainty in design. Rather than being orderly, the actual design process is in fact fraught with *ambiguity* and *uncertainty*, both of which are necessary elements of the design: ambiguity is essential to achieve some consensus among the differing participants' perspectives, while uncertainty is what makes the process challenging (ibid.).

Scholars who ascribe to the rationalistic representation of design have argued that, although simplified, the rational method is useful as it clarifies what normally is a very complex process. While we acknowledge that formal models can perform an important function, the sole reliance on these can obscure some of the most important issues and questions that relate to understanding design. For example, what is the function of an abstract model or chart? How do engineers use representations in everyday practice? What type of knowledge do formal models convey? And how does this knowledge interact with more informal knowledge during design activities?

In our quest to characterize how knowledge is used/produced during collective design activities, we must therefore consider the role of formal representations for what they are: *abstractions* that evolve together with informal practices and mutually influence one another (ibid.). These are unexplored issues that only become visible when looking at engineering design not as an abstract activity, but in the context of its actual, daily practice.

Recalling a point made in Chapter 2, we can argue that by setting an emphasis on the distinction between 'routines-as-representations' and 'routines-as-expressions' scholars in the rationalistic tradition have introduced an unproductive dualism between 'cognition' and 'practice' (Cohen et al. (1996: 15). The rationalistic tradition only captures the 'representation' side of routines, thus failing to capture and account for: (1) the actual content of routines; (2) the evolution of routines in the context of actual practice; and (3) the co-evolution of 'routines-as-expressions' with 'routines-as-representations'. According to Cohen et al., ethnographic research circumvents the hiatus between representations and expressions as authors focus on the observable form of the actions as expressed; it is therefore ideally placed to generate 'rich and suggestive results as well as providing the essential grist for theory development' (ibid.: 4).

Analogously, Brown and Duguid (1996) have criticized the chasm often present in literature between *precepts* and *practice*. In a society that attaches particular value to abstract knowledge, they claim, 'the details of practice have come to be seen as nonessential, unimportant, and easily developed once the relevant abstractions have been grasped ... we, by contrast, suggest that *practice is central to understanding work*' (ibid.: 59, emphasis added). In their view, conventional descriptions of jobs mask not only the ways people work, but also significant learning and innovation generated in the informal communities-of-practice in which they work (ibid.). Reliance on 'canonical practice' can blind an organization's core to the actual, and usually valuable practices of its members, including non-canonical practices, such as 'workarounds'. While canonical practices perform a useful normative role, '*It is the actual practices ... that determine the success or failure of organizations*' (ibid.: 59, emphasis added)

The divergence between 'espoused' practice and actual practice is also highlighted in Orr's (1987, 1990, in Brown and Duguid, 1996) ethnography of service technicians (or 'reps') in training and at work in a large corporation. Orr provides a '*thick*', detailed description of the ways work actually progresses, in contrast with the way the same work is '*thinly*' described in the corporation manuals, training courses and job descriptions (in Brown and Duguid, 1996: 60). Abstractions of repair work fall short of the complexity of the actual practices from which they were abstracted (ibid.: 61). A similar concept was advanced in Bourdieu's (1977, in Brown and Duguid, 1996) distinction between *modus operandi* and *opus operatum*: these illustrate the way a task, as it unfolds over time, looks to someone at work on it, while many of the options and dilemmas remain unresolved, as opposed to the way it looks with hindsight as a finished task.

Drawing from the work of symbolic interactionist researchers such as Anselm Strauss, Star also undermines the idea that work practices can be meaningfully modelled by means of predetermined, formal workflows and task descriptions. Complex social organizations, she argues, are characterized by 'ad hoc reactions to upcoming contingencies, by distributed decision-making, by multiple viewpoints, and inconsistent and evolving knowledge bases' (Gerson and Star, 1986 in Berg, 1998: 461). The connection between canonical and non-canonical practice is enabled by what Gerson and Star call the 'invisible work of articulation':

> [Since] no formal description of a system (or plan for its work) can ... be ... complete ... [a] very real world system ... requires articulation to deal with the unanticipated contingencies that arise. Articulation resolves these inconsistencies by packaging a compromise that 'gets the job done' that is, that closes the system locally and temporarily so that work can go on. (In Berg, 1998: 461–2).

Gerson and Star stress the importance of designing information systems which take into account the empirical knowledge of the context in which they are embedded: 'in order to accurately represent the open systems' properties of workplaces we should study them and incorporate *tacit knowledge* and *articulation*' (ibid.: 462, emphasis added).

As Brown and Duguid, Bourdieu, Suchman and Orr show, actual practice inevitably involves *tricky interpolations between abstract accounts and situated demands*. In Orr's example, the burden of making up the difference between what is provided and what is needed rests with the reps, which in bridging the gap actually protect the organization from its own shortsightedness. If the reps adhered to the canonical approach, their corporation's services would be in chaos.[1] The reps need therefore to understand the machine causally and to relate this causal map to the inevitable intricacies of practice. To discern such needs, however, will require that corporations develop a less formal and more practice-based approach to communities and their work (Brown and Duguid, 1996: 62, 66).

Individual vs. Collective Knowledge-Building Processes

Another important criticism has been directed against the prevailing characterization of design and experimentation as activities principally performed by individuals in isolation; the template for this is the lonely engineer or inventor, who iterates various solutions to problems within the solitude of his/her own mind. Within this literature, assumptions at the level of the *individual decision-maker*, engineer or agent are often artificially extrapolated to the level of the organization.

More recent work in cognitive science (Hutchins, 1995), however, has demonstrated that it is a mistake to assume that group cognitive action is the same as that of individuals. The implicit representation of design and experimental activities as individual processes is unsatisfactory and misleading as it obscures their highly interactive and collaborative nature. Recently, authors have therefore begun to emphasize the need to study cognition as a social phenomenon. Calling for a sociological and anthropological reappraisal of human–computer interaction, these contributions emphasize the need to study 'what actually happened with and around computers in modern workplaces' (Berg, 1998: 461). From these efforts derives the notion of '*distributed cognition*'.

Distributed cognition captures the notion that tasks that appear to be the product of individual minds are in fact distributed and collective (Star, 1992). The concept was first introduced by Hutchins in his study of navigation in which he described how 'The knowledge of the route was held in bits and pieces by many people and transmitted to each other as the occasion warranted in the course of a journey at the particular site where knowledge was needed' (ibid.: 396). Hutchins's work demonstrates that: (1) it is inappropriate to assume that all the individuals in a shared interaction have exactly the same schemata for a given situation; and (2) even if they did hold the same schemata, 'consensus on a schemata is not the same thing as consensus about the interpretation of events. Two individuals could have the same schema for the same phenomenon and still reach different interpretations of events' (ibid.: 457).

The notion of 'distributed cognition' was expanded further by the anthropologist Jean Lave (1988), who claimed that knowledge, far from being simply 'embodied' in individuals, is also *not divided between but stretched across* artefacts, procedures, capabilities (Suchman, 1987). Another way to phrase this is to say that knowledge is distributed across a number of external memory sources such as artefacts, routines and locally shared languages (Nelson and Winter, 1982; Weick, 1979).

Once we acknowledge the distributed character of organizational knowledge, a whole new set of exciting and important questions emerges: how are heterogeneous (function- or people-embedded) knowledge sources integrated and conveyed into artefacts? What are the implications of storing knowledge in software for our ability to retrieve and reuse such knowledge? Failure to focus on the distributed quality of organizational knowledge means that we also lose sight of such fundamental issues.

Beyond the Notion of 'Organizational Culture': Learning by 'Communities-of-Practice'

In rejecting transfer models that isolate knowledge from practice, learning theorists (i.e. Lave, 1988; Lave and Wenger, 1991) have developed a view of learning in which what is learned is profoundly connected to the conditions in which it is learned. According to Lave and Wenger's (1991) practice-based theory of *learning as 'legitimate peripheral participation (LLP)'* in 'communities-of-practice', the knowledge–practice separation is unsound, both in theory and in practice (Brown and Duguid, 1996: 59). Therefore, to understand working and learning, it is necessary to focus on the formation and change of the communities in which work takes place. Similarly, Daft and Weick (1984) have placed the community and not the individual 'inventor' as the central unit of analysis in understanding innovating practice (ibid.).

The notion of communities-of-practice is also present in Orr's ethnography. Here reps build a *shared understanding* out of a vast amount of conflicting and confusing data, therefore contributing to the construction and evolution of the community that they are joining - what Brown and Duguid (1996) call a 'community of interpretation'. It is through the continual development of these communities that the shared means for interpreting complex activity get formed, transformed, and transmitted (ibid.).

According to the above theories, learning essentially involves becoming an 'insider'. Learners do not receive abstract, 'objective', individual knowledge; rather,

> They learn to function in a community - be it a community of nuclear physicists, cabinet-makers, high school classmates, street-corner society, or, in Orr's case, service technicians. They acquire that particular community's *subjective viewpoint* and learn to *speak its language* ... Learners are acquiring not explicit, formal 'expert knowledge', but the embodied ability to behave as community members (ibid.: 69).

Such approaches draw attention away from abstract knowledge and cranial processes and situate it in the practices and communities in which knowledge takes on significance. Learning, understanding and interpretation involve a great deal that is not explicit or explicable, developed and framed in a crucial *communal context* (Lave and Wenger, 1991).

In order to understand how 'best practices' in knowledge management are adopted and shared, it is therefore necessary 'to look not simply at the transformation from knowledge to information (as in BPR), but *from knowledge to practice and groups of practitioners*' (Brown and Duguid, 2000: 6, emphasis added). This is because it is the practice shared in collaborative communities that allows agents to *share* their knowledge. Working, learning and knowledge sharing involves becoming a member of a *'community of practice'*, and thereby understanding its work and its talk from the inside. Learning, from this point of view, 'is not simply a matter of acquiring information; it requires developing the disposition, demeanour and outlook of a practitioner' (ibid.).

The above studies help to undermine the idea of learning by a 'lone thinker'. According to Brown and Duguid, practice both shapes and supports learning. In criticizing the limitations of Organization Theory and BPR, they argue that those frameworks based upon an information-processing model all share a misleading *homogenizing* vision. Organization Theory, for example, has often characterized '*organizational culture*' as *uniform*, thus failing to acknowledge that divisions created by practice produce significant variations within the organizational landscape. Analogously, BPR's very attempt to help organizations overcome the 'internal' divisions created by different practices has failed to understand the importance of the internally varied terrain of organizations and its *fractures* and *divisions*: 'Failure to read the topography may be at its most damaging as people try to predict the effects of new information technologies on organisations' (ibid.: 17).

Adopting the viewpoint of knowledge production and sharing by heterogeneous communities-of-practice, therefore, raises important questions: how are different groups speaking different idiosyncratic (i.e. discipline-specific) languages and holding different knowledge able to co-operate in product design and development? How are inter-organizational conflicts absorbed in the context of everyday practice? How do artefacts perform as loci of knowledge integration and conflicts absorption? These fundamental questions only emerge when we look at knowledge from the viewpoint of collective, group-based practice.

Beyond the Notion of 'Technology Impact'

Neoclassical economists have essentially treated technology as a 'black box' (Rosenberg, 1982). More recently, the fields of Innovation Studies, Evolutionary Economics and Organization Science have made important progress towards understanding the dynamics of technology within organizations. These works have shed light over macro- (country and industry level) and meso- (sector and firm level) knowledge issues and have been especially important in emphasizing phenomena of stability, continuity, lock-in, path-dependency in knowledge and learning processes.

While the contribution of these disciplines has been important, it has left a gap in our understanding of the micro- (firm and routine) level studies of technology and innovation, especially in relation to the actual working of technology within organizations and to the co-evolution of technology supported with organization-embedded routines. There have been indeed some very interesting and detailed technology case studies within the Engineering Epistemology tradition (cf. Ferguson, 1993a, b; Petroski, 1996; Vincenti, 1990), but these are principally historical accounts that consider the learning and capability formation processes only *ex post*, thus failing to situate knowledge in the context of its creation and evolution. Vincenti, for example, towards the end of his book acknowledges this shortcoming in proposing that the study of '*what engineers know*' should not be separate from our understanding of '*what engineers do*'.[2]

While valuable, these contributions have fallen short of answering some pressing questions. For example, how do we characterize the complex interrelationship between (software) technology and organization? How do technologies and human practices co-evolve? More specifically, how do software systems work within an organization? What are the implications of software adoption for knowledge and learning in the innovating organization?

In order to begin to answer these complex questions, we have to look into more recently emerging fields, such as STS and CSCW, which, in the last few decades, have attempted to cross the 'great divide' between social scientists and computer engineers. By concentrating on the actual processes of design and use of Information and Communication Technologies (ICTs), both these fields have challenged the 'technological determinism' intrinsic in much of the traditional computer Systems Design literature, as well as rejecting the idea that technology can develop autonomously from the realm of practice and human relations.

According to Berg, two opposite positions can be identified in the traditional view of technology: a *'utopian'* position, highlighting the efficient logic of technology and predicting a future of progress and rationality through its diffusion (i.e. increased democracy); and a *'dystopian'* position, arguing that the rationality of technology de-skills and controls, and, by being authoritarian and overly mechanistic, it empties human life of its meaning. The author argues that, 'In both versions, "technology" and "human work" are each characterized by *a specific ontology and logic*. The causal relation between them is *unilinear*: "technology" affects "human work" and either amplifies or erodes what was already there' (Berg, 1998: 464, emphasis added).

Computer-Supported Co-operative Work authors have agreed that these views remain too mechanistic, unilinear and stuck in a simplistic *'technology impact'* model. In reality, the influence of information technology on skills, work, managerial hierarchy, *can go both ways*. Kling (1991), for instance, argued that the technical and the social are so closely interrelated that it makes no sense to pry them apart; they do not occupy separate domains or operate according to separate logics, nor does their relationship develop in a unilinear way.

Technological artefacts, such as computer systems, should therefore not be studied in isolation but as interwoven with their organizational settings. We should study what Kling describes as the *'web of computing'*, that is the ensemble of artefacts, skills, applications and infrastructure that constitute the technical 'systems' whose functions are not predetermined but only evolve within specific socio-political contexts. A *focus on specific case studies* can help us to see a technical change as embedded in a larger system of activity (Kling and Scacchi, 1982).

Barley and Orlikowski similarly criticized deterministic accounts, emphasizing that new technologies do not determine organizational change – they trigger *unpredictable* 'social dynamics, which, in turn, modify or maintain an organization's contours' (Barley, 1986 in Berg, 1998: 466). As the materialized, objectified outcome of human design, development, appropriation and modification, technologies are highly consequential aspects of organizational structure: they shape the cognitions and actions of those who use them, embed specific distributions of power, choices made, and knowledge and norms valued (Orlikowski, 1992).

While valuable, the 'social constructivist' accounts have themselves been subject to some criticism. The problem, according to Button (1993), is that *technology seems to 'vanish'* from these accounts. In the attempt to leave behind the notion of technology as straightforwardly influencing human practices, technology is *reduced to its social origins*, thereby *losing its specific characteristics and nature*. The technological determinism is thus reversed into a form of *humanist determinism* as technology can only act out the meanings incorporated in it by humans through its appropriation by humans (ibid.).

The issue of how best to characterize the influence of technology on organizations remains unresolved. How to study the relationships between (information) technology and organization without falling into either the social or the technology impact modes? The work of Suchman and Gerson and Star attempts to overcome this theoretical impasse by arguing that working practice and technology *do not operate according to the same instrumental logic*, and do not inhabit the same domain, as maintained by the rationalistic tradition.

Human work cannot be described by the clear-cut logic of technology, as if it consisted of well-circumscribed tasks, executable in a predictable and pre-designed sequence (Berg, 1998). Traditional systems design does not see that work is performed accordingly to *a fundamentally different logic*, which is shaped by fluid interaction, situated action and local circumstances. They therefore demonstrate the richness and flexibility of social action vis-à-vis the mechanistic functioning of technologies; they also emphasize the *dangers of domination* of the latter over the former (ibid.). Gasser (1986), for instance, shows how the integration of computing tools in routine work requires the continuous, creative, and ad hoc work of employees. The computer's pre-programmed, formal representations of the work clash continuously with the actual, *contingent* and *complex logic* of this work. The employees must therefore constantly 'repair' the cracks and fissures in the flow of their activities. Similarly, Orr (1996, 1998, in Brown and Duguid,

2000) has argued that employees continually need to *articulate* the inflexible demands of technology to the practical requirements of the ongoing work.

This stream of thought emphasizes the *difference* between the logic of *technology* and that of *human work*: it uncovers the intricate actions that technology cannot accomplish and humans instead can and must. According to this argument, 'Overlooking the difference between the realms of technology and human work ... generates the failures of so many technology applications' (ibid.: 468–9). The implications are that 'proper technology' should be designed to intervene as little as possible in the informal interactions and ongoing workflows since they can only impede them (ibid.). A problem with this approach is that it links 'technology' with negative associations of being 'authoritarian', 'impoverished' and 'mechanistic'. It can therefore paradoxically lead to the assumption that '*the only proper technology is no technology*' (ibid., emphasis added).

Building upon the work of Suchman, Star and others, more recent contributions have begun to turn this negative analysis into a positive one. While the *analytical differentiation* between 'human work' and 'technology' remains, the analysis now focuses on what is or can be achieved through *creating connections* between the two realms. Through detailed studies of technologies-in-use authors have searched for ways in which (information) technology can start to support work, rather than limit it. Star and Griesemer (1989), for example, by paying attention to the precise and practical functioning of artefacts, examine how a rigid 'formalism of inscription' interrelates with an ensemble of local activities such as verbal reports, face-to-face meetings and other activities that never get inscribed on the artefact, and which remain invisible to other levels within the organization (Berg, 1998).

According to these authors, the interrelation between the realm of the technical and the realm of the human makes possible the *emergence of new worlds*, in which the complexity and consistency of tasks performed surpasses anything that could be achieved within either one of them. This is the theoretical and pragmatic position adopted in this book. The interrelationships between information technology, organizational routines, and search and learning processes generate *new design and search landscapes*, as well as creating new skills that are a result of the day-to-day interaction of engineers with technology. The book therefore contributes to illustrating the creation of new 'hybrid' knowledge and skills, which emerge from combining humans' and machines' knowledge and skills (Pickering, 1995).

A fundamental consequence of the complex interactions between technology and organization is, as already anticipated, the inability to draw *a priori inferences* in relation to the consequences or 'impact' of Information

Technologies. It is therefore more appropriate to talk in terms of '*influence*', as this suggests a reciprocal rather than a one-directional relationship. For example, while the introduction of CAD technology radically affects the equilibrium between flexibility and inflexibility at the process level, as argued in Chapter 6, this does not necessarily imply that it causes inflexibility or that it reduces or eliminates the importance of informal processes and tacit knowledge. Flexibility (or inflexibility) is instead the outcome of the complex interactions of software embedded with other relevant organizational knowledge processes. These interactions can be highlighted by analysing how software-embedded routines or 'scripts' interact with organizational routines. While this approach is theoretically and epistemologically consistent with acknowledging the distinct logics of technology and human work, at the same time it moves beyond this difference to analyse their interactions and reciprocal influence.

As argued in the flexibility and prototypes chapters (6 and 7 respectively), the important questions are not whether software tools are per se flexible or inflexible, but rather: how do IT tools affect the equilibrium between formal and informal, codified and tacit, people-embodied and technology-embedded processes, at any point in time? How does the knowledge embedded in software interact with other relevant organizational knowledge sources? These are more precise and relevant questions, and they can only be addressed by adopting a qualitative, non-reductive and in-depth research approach that analyses information systems in the wider context of the people, routines and organization. This issue is investigated further in the section below.

Beyond the Notion of Software as a Tool: Co-evolution of Technology and Practice[3]

The notion of 'software-as-a-tool' has proven popular among both academics and practitioners seeking to establish why computer-based systems succeed or fail. This notion, however, is only partially adequate as it draws our attention away from important interactions between tools and practices. The notion is strongly ingrained in the current academic debate, where two main schools of thought can be identified: the 'advocates' and the 'critics' (Berg, 1997b). On the one hand, there are the '*advocates*' who characterize technology as '*universal*', meaning that, in principle, it can be used anywhere, by anyone, on any problems that arise.[4] In the advocate's opinion, failure cannot be attributed to technology itself, but to the *setting* of which the technology has become part and in which it has to work. In other words, because a technology is universal, any blame for its failure is to be attributed to human practices (i.e. the inflexibility of users, lack of resources, etc.).

The '*critics*', on the other hand, reverse this argument and condemn the tools for fundamentally misunderstanding the world in which they are to function. In their view, the tools are being rejected because they are *basically misconceived*: human expertise, intuition, involved and skilled '*know-how*', in fact, could never be replaced by the detached, objective '*know that*' embedded in formal tools. Whereas the advocates argue for the universality of the technology, the critics emphasize that automating tools can only operate in *very specific*, confined areas: these include situations where know-how is not required, such as when the tools are to replace actions which are already *straightforwardly routinized*, or 'machine-like'. The process of embedding actual practices into formal tools is necessarily tied to the specific context in which it was generated: 'knowledge, according to the critics, is inextricably linked to specific practices, and therefore always *local*, its only truly universal feature being its impossibility' (ibid.: 157, emphasis added).

According to Berg, however, both the advocates and the critics share a wrong assumption: by comparing the actions of formal tools with those of human experts, they both inscribe 'tools' and 'practices' into two *fixed* categories. Highlighting the contrast between these categories has important implications: the measure of 'success' or 'failure' is reduced to analysing the extent to which formal tools can provide a *representation* of the structure of practice and of the decision-making process. In contrasting human practice with machine action, the critics emphasize the *ontological and epistemological chasm* that separates the two. For example, they compare the *poverty* of formal representations to the *richness* of the action represented and in doing so they 'expose the a priori failure of a map to capture the intricacies of the domain the map represents' (ibid.: 162). According to this view, formal tools cannot but fail, as they lack the *agency* and *tacit knowledge* that characterize humans. Advocates, instead, argue that human action and machine behaviour, while being two separate categories, share fundamental *similarities*; i.e. both 'tools' and 'practices' belong to the species of information-processing agents; both are structured according to a *scientific*, step-by step approach to problems.

Where both advocates and critics are mistaken is that *tools and practices cannot be so clearly separated*. On the one hand, *practices change* and become more amenable to formal tools; an example of this (as shown in Chapters 4, 5, 6 and 7) is the process by which organizations modify their routines to provide a more suitable setting for IT systems implementation. On the other, computer systems designers are increasingly *adjusting* their *tools* to function more in the background and to be better integrated into other larger IT products; in this case, by building upon an infrastructure which is already in place, they minimize the disruption to existing processes. An example of this is the implementation of integrated software systems mentioned in the Introduction and Chapter 4.

The *convergence* rather than the separation between tools and practices and their reciprocal transformation ought therefore to be brought to the centre of the attention of scholars. According to this view, 'success' or 'failure' cannot be characterized as *intrinsic properties* of either the tools or the settings: the tools' performance cannot be in fact separated from their *contingent history*:

> There is no meaningful way to talk about a tool without at the same time speaking of the practice with which it *co-evolved* ... 'The tool' or 'the practice' can no longer serve as an explanatory category: an understanding of the current situation requires an understanding of the way these categories *are intimately involved in each other's production* (Berg, 1997b: 164–5, emphasis added).

In agreement with these considerations is Bowker's (1994) notion of a 'working tool' as the outcome of the mutual convergence of tools and settings into a network in which *heterogeneous elements* are interconnected and transformed (in Berg, 1997a). These interconnections ensure that the tools are 'the right ones for the job' (Clarke and Fujimura, in Berg, 1997a). This view represents a move away from both the critics' and the advocates' characterization of IT tools as a 'product', to analyse the complex circumstances in which tools and practices co-evolve.

This book ascribes to this view as it sets out to analyse how software-embedded processes and assumptions co-evolve with operations and learning practices. It shows how, during the process of software design and implementation, practices are changed to fit the tools and how tools are reconfigured while being inscribed into local practices. As a consequence of focusing on the *interplay* rather than on the *dichotomy* between tools and practices, we are able to address new issues and questions that have been so far overlooked by both critics and advocates.

Analysing the interplay of tools and practices, for instance, draws attention to the work that makes tools feasible, that is how practices are transformed to fit with the formalism introduced by the tools. This work is described by Gerson and Star (1986) as 'invisible work of articulation': 'The technology seems to function on its own superb and universal power, while the work of meticulously creating and repairing the social and material infrastructure that makes this functioning possible (and in which the tool itself has taken shape) disappears from sight' (Berg, 1997b: 169). This highlights the need to investigate how formal and informal procedures co-evolve in practice and how information technologies may alter the balance between the two. One such example is Chapter 5's account of consequences of embedding the Work-in-Progress (WIP) functionality in software.

The convergence of tools and practices, however, should not be equated to *homogeneity*. Tools in fact retain and embed a *multiplicity* of notions of what rationality is, what the problems are and how these problems should be addressed. *Universality* therefore is not a static, pre-given property of technology but a *dynamic quality*, which is 'acquired through extending the tool's reach through disciplining a whole array of local practices, and achieving the pre-requisites demanded by formalism' (ibid.: 167). We should look, therefore, at *how local context and assumptions*, including not just one rationality but an array of embedded voices, *are built into the system*: 'every tool silences some voices and amplifies others; every tool helps to strengthen some knowledges and helps to forget others; every map has an author, a subject, and a theme' (Wood, 1992, in Berg, 1997b: 170). Chapter 7 (prototypes) analyses the relationship between '*universal*' and '*local*' knowledge; Chapter 6 (flexibility) captures instead the *unresolved tensions* between attempts to discipline and the persistence of fragmentation and loose ends.

Analysing the coexistence of informal practices and formal tools also points to the fact that while the 'map' is never able to perfectly capture the complexity of the domain, it is nevertheless useful: 'the map's crudeness (or, less disapproving, "selectivity") *allows it to work like a map*: to enable one to oversee large areas at a glance or to navigate one's way across long distances' (ibid., emphasis added). Critics fail to acknowledge this and thus try to substitute informality for formality to demonstrate how immersing a formalism in a practice's routine results in a complete subordination of the tool, and therefore its misuse or downright rejection. An example of this is Kathryn Henderson's (1991) story of CAD failure in replacing the richness of human skills and tacit knowledge. A straightforward 'rejection' story, however, is increasingly unrealistic given that: (1) Information Systems are increasingly widespread and integrated, their connections and ramifications making their outright rejection or disuse more difficult; and (2) software systems introduce formal routines which are either impossible to avoid as they are often invisible, or they are very difficult (or time-consuming) to bypass as they would require complex workarounds (as argued in Chapter 6).

The above argument suggests that a more constructive approach should be adopted which involves turning our attention away from straightforward 'substitution' issues, towards *the new design and work landscapes* that are created by 'the intertwining of procedures and tools, informality and formality, and the interlocking of representation and represented' (Berg, 1997b). The concept of new 'design landscapes' emphasizes that tools are not meant to replace humans but to allow them to perform *a task that did not exist prior to their introduction*. While, in fact, the vocabulary of '*representation*' leads one to compare a tool and a practice, it overlooks the *active* role of a tool. The production and use of the tool, or map, transforms the terrain opening up new avenues that were not visible before. An example of this is the digital scanning of physical prototypes (Chapter 7) whereby the tools support the articulation and codification of *the results* of tacit knowledge processes, which was so far infeasible.

Finally, by observing the co-evolution of tools and practices, we can also open up an interesting and important area of inquiry into the notions of *responsibility* and decision-making. These notions in fact shift when *control is distributed* between a tool and personnel, so that it is impossible to answer the question 'who or what is finally in control'. As argued earlier in this chapter, purified notions of 'human decision-making' are meaningless as *decision power is also distributed* among these heterogeneous practices. Given that different rationales are inscribed in both tools and practices, by narrowing down to the cognitive functioning of individuals, the decision-focused explanation overlooks the *interactive* and *heterogeneous* nature of Berg's medical practice or, in our case, of engineering design work. This is shown in Chapter 6 where we observe how 'authority to change' is distributed among engineers, software systems and design practices.

An important implication of this argument is the need to shift our attention from 'rational' design to what Suchman calls 'design as critique'. This concept points to the pragmatic activity, which attempts 'to transform a practice toward some pre-set goal in and through the production and implementation of an artefact in which this goal is inscribed' (in Berg, 1997b: 175). To do this, it is necessary to abandon any pre-given notion as to the potential benefit of a tool, or its proper (non-) use. The tool can no longer be perceived as the carrier of rationality, but neither can it be seen as essentially powerless – or essentially dehumanizing: 'Neither tools or practices can any longer be criticised from the comfortable position of the outside observer occupying some high ground' (ibid.).

A correct approach therefore entails *immersing oneself* in the networks described and searching for what is or can be achieved by a new interlocking of tools and practices (Suchman, 1987). It also involves adopting an analytical framework, which shifts the unit of analysis from either the tool or the practices to their *interrelation and historical co-evolution*: 'no longer denouncing tool or practice, ... [design as critique] ... means searching for ways in which such tools may become familiar yet never totally transparent, powerful yet fragile instruments of change' (Suchman in Berg, 1997b: 178). Focusing on the new landscapes generated by the mutual reconfiguration of tools and practices also importantly entails abandoning *the illusion of diffusion without transformation*, which is dear to much of the economics' literature. This exploration can only be conducted by means of a detailed, immersive investigation of these phenomena in the contexts in which they occur. These issues strongly indicate once again the need for detailed, in-depth qualitative analysis as the only method that can help to characterize the actual and complex unfolding of technology and practice.

Towards a Situated Approach

In the first part of this chapter we have demonstrated that adopting an abstract, normative and reductive approach to cognition is only partially adequate as it conduces to disregarding some of the most important and interesting issues concerning knowledge, (information) technology and organizations. Quantitative and 'purely cognitive' approaches inevitably fail to capture those very phenomena, which are at the basis of understanding how complex and unstable ensembles of technology and organization manage to work, learn and to innovate.

In order to begin to explore such issues we therefore need to study knowledge and cognition as situated and distributed organization-embedded activities. This is especially true in relation to the study of computer systems, whose increasingly widespread adoption and progressive integration into rapidly expanding networks demands that people, machines, work and other aspects of situations are considered ecologically. A comprehensive approach should also move beyond the simplistic characterization of software as a tool impacting on human practices to involve the study of the co-evolution and the (forever incomplete) convergence of technologies and practices. Only through a qualitative, situated, detailed and immersive study can we begin to make theoretical and empirical sense of the most important aspects of the technology adoption and evolution in organization and thus begin to characterize its influence on the organization's ability to create, accumulate, share and transfer knowledge, to adapt, learn and innovate. The second part of the chapter proceeds to describe how these assumptions translated in practice into a series of tools that allowed us to produce research output that was consistent with the above theoretical premises.

METHODOLOGY IN PRACTICE

The second part of this chapter contains the description of the process followed by the author to translate the above theoretical issues into practice. The objective of this section is to demonstrate that, while qualitative methodologies may be cumbersome for researchers in terms of time and learning investments, they represent an ideal approach to management policy research; this is because their deep connection with empirical reality often permits the development of theory that is at the same time novel, testable, relevant and valid.

Learning about Design, Software, Engineering and Engineers

The very early stages of this research project highlighted the importance of learning both about software and engineering design in sufficient depth and detail to be able to talk with ease to software producers and users at all levels and functions of the firm. As argued above, the nature of the theoretical questions addressed in this book and the level of detail required to address them demanded an insider's view of the ongoing changes. A fundamental aspect of this research, therefore, has been for the author to become familiar with the theory and practice of engineering design and, specifically, CAD design. This entailed undergoing a thorough learning process, which involved several steps.

The early stages of the research involved attending engineering and CAD design courses at the local Faculty of Engineering where the author actively participated in classes as well as taking examinations, which led to acquiring the theoretical and practical foundations of 'AutoCAD', a mainstream CAD application. This newly obtained engineering experience highlighted the importance of acquiring the fundamentals of the software application that was the object of the study. This enabled the author to formulate her own opinions, rather than exclusively relying upon the interviewees' judgement. To build on this knowledge and learn about a more advanced application (Product Data Manager) the author also attended a specialist course at the software manufacturer; this was populated by professional engineers and designers from a range of software-user organizations. As well as helping to gain an insider's view of the software, the course lead to important contacts by providing the background for the first informal conversations with practitioners.

The subsequent step was to learn about engineering practices and procedures, not as they appear in idealized diagrams, but as they are conducted in the real context of development organizations. This process soon revealed that the abstract and formal accounts existing in the literature were not sufficient to achieve this project's purpose. With the co-operation of the principal case firms, especially the automotive organization, the author therefore set out to spend a substantial amount of time discussing and learning from engineers and product/process administrators about all relevant processes. Those processes that, at that particular stage of implementation, were being affected by the introduction of a new software system became the main focus of the research. These included the Engineering Parts List (EPL) process, the Bill of Materials (BoM) process, the prototypes-making process, the Release process, and the Workflow process.

Interestingly, the managers, engineers and administrators were learning about the new processes as the implementation proceeded. In several instances, they were using the interviews as an opportunity to articulate their knowledge and as a means to distance themselves from day-to-day practice, and to clarify their thoughts. This experience emphasized the enormous difficulties introduced by the implementation of software, especially when this was conducted 'live', on ongoing programmes; software introduction at times implied such radical changes that the practitioners themselves struggled to keep up. Learning about engineering and business processes in detail at those selected firms was not only useful in itself but it also allowed to more easily identify and interpret changes as they occurred in other organizations where similar (or at least comparable) processes and procedures were in place.

All of these learning opportunities were an invaluable part of the research process and greatly contributed to strengthening both the nature and the extent of the findings. Unfortunately, this point of view is not widely shared in the economics literature, whereby scholars often prefer to attain to abstract models and detached, desk-based observations. Cohen et al. (1996: 24) are an exception in stating that 'ethnographic work which looks at documenting the actual contents of routines generates rich and suggestive results as well as providing the essential grist for theory development'. While they acknowledge that in-depth field observation is of major value, however, they also observe that the costs induced by an 'army of ethnographers' can be very high. While it is perhaps true that close observations require a substantial investment, in terms of time and most importantly, in learning terms, the benefits that this type of analysis provides in terms of improved understanding, empirical validity and frame-breaking theory building can be outstanding. This book hopes to demonstrate that the effort is often worthwhile.

Selecting the Software

Selecting the most appropriate software application to study was of utmost importance. The first stages of this research had focused on CAD, Finite Elements Analysis (FEA) and other 'stand-alone' software applications; however, it soon became evident that the most interesting changes were taking place not at the level of the individual application, but at the 'system' level, as more and more software producers were integrating isolated applications to provide integrated 'turn key', 'off-the-shelf' systems intended to support the management of the whole product life cycle across the extended enterprise. In their attempt to harness not simply information processing, but 'knowledge management', integrated systems represented the most interesting focus for the research.

Following this realization the research scope was refocused towards the study of one out of the many integrated software systems for design and manufacturing available. In addition to the thorough screening of the Internet and specialist publications, the choice was informed by conversations with software producer staff and practitioners at major software fairs and industry conferences. There are authors who have emphasized the frustration of academics in their (often failed) attempts to get attention and feedback at such events (Downey, 1998). The difficulty in this case was to find personnel at the software producers' 'stands' that had enough hands-on knowledge about the software to be able to answer in-depth questions. By then the author had trained as a software user (almost an 'insider'), while most of the stands personnel were Marketing employees, and therefore mere 'outsiders'.

The fact that personnel at the stand of the software later selected had proven on several occasions to be among the most competent obviously influenced the final choice. It also helped that the chosen software package is state of the art, holding a significant portion of the world market share (it claims 13 000 industrial customers around the world), as well as being a major player in the aerospace and automotive software markets. A systematic technical assessment of the software features and capabilities (achieved by comparing the information on the internet, in the specialist press and talking to producer and users) confirmed that this particular software product was outstanding enough to provide a solid basis for the study, at the same time being sufficiently similar to other leading competitors not to represent an 'exceptional case'.

Selecting the Software User Organizations

Once the software type and the specific 'application solution' was selected, the next step was to choose the case user firms. The decision was to study firms that had adopted the same (selected) software, so that the differences among applications would not bias the comparison. The specialist press was screened to gather the names of user firms, which would have made ideal case studies, but did not reveal the names of the appropriate people to approach. The Marketing personnel at the software producer firm helped to overcome this obstacle by agreeing to send a letter of request for collaboration out to the relevant individuals, while not disclosing their names and thus preserving their customers' confidentiality. Several firms replied, among which was a leading automotive organization, which demonstrated an excellent potential to represent the principal case firm. This was for the following reasons:

1. Automobiles (and vehicles, more in general) are increasingly interesting technologies to study, being characterized by a rather complex architecture which requires progressively more sophisticated design and development processes.
2. The organization selected is part of a large manufacturing enterprise with operations spread over many functions, departments and geographical regions, and was introducing an integrated software system with the aim to co-ordinate these dispersed units; such an organization would have provided interesting grounds to observe integration across functional, organizational and geographical boundaries.
3. The organization provided a leading, 'best in class' example of total implementation of the manufacturer's *integration* philosophy, and was committed to implement all the stages that were required to achieve the full simulation of product, process and organization (what will later be referred to as the 'virtual product', cf. Chapter 7).
4. Most importantly, the organization displayed a genuine interest in the research as well as willingness to grant open access and provide sufficient long-term resources (i.e. interviewees' time, desk space, secretarial help, access to internal seminars, conferences, and management meetings) to support the requirements of an in-depth empirical study. In return, the organization was expecting to gain from the research an insight into what they called the 'hearts and minds', or the human, 'messy' side of technology implementation and adoption.

Two more firms were selected to provide ground for comparison and validation of the results obtained with the former. The two leading organizations, operating in the consumer electronics and aerospace sectors, were chosen because, while having adopted exactly the same software technology, they substantially differed from the main case organization in that they: (1) represented, respectively, the case of a very simple, mature and a very complex product technology; (2) were at different stages of software implementation, the aerospace firm being the most advanced; (3) had adopted a different implementation philosophy combining integration with interfacing with existing proprietary software. The secondary case firms helped to provide the necessary grounds for generalizing and validating the insights acquired at our main case organization.

Selecting the Case Studies

The next step involved selecting the most appropriate case studies within the principal case firm. These were later compared to similar examples in the other two selected firms. The main selection criterion identified was the case studies' potential to support our attempt to build upon and expand the existing theoretical knowledge in the fields of Organization Science, Innovation Studies and Evolutionary Economics. In particular, the case studies had to fill those theoretical gaps and provide answers to the theoretical and empirical questions that were highlighted in Chapter 2 and in the first part of this chapter.

The focus chosen for the case studies was the ongoing implementation and use of Integrated Software Systems in the Product Design and Development Process; the assumption was that the radical changes that were taking place would at the same time highlight the pre-existing structures, issues and problems while also providing a window over the projected targets and aspirations. Three major case studies were chosen, each composed of two sub-cases. These were as follows:

1. To examine the mechanisms of knowledge codification, retention and sharing, and the influence of software over the structure of the knowledge retained, and therefore on its reuse, the decision was taken to study the process of unification and standardization of the Engineering Parts List (EPL) across the organization. The case of implementing a new product/database structure raised important questions in relation to the issue of codifying and embedding knowledge in software, especially in relation to the structure of embedded knowledge and how different functions are able to reuse this knowledge; in the final instance, it provided important insights about how to achieve an appropriate balance between standardization and heterogeneity. Two sub-cases addressed in Chapter 5 look respectively at the issue of delegating product/technology and process knowledge/memory to software.
2. With the aim to augment our understanding of the relationship between formal and informal knowledge and routines, between control and flexibility, and therefore to shed light over the ability of the organization to adapt and react to change, the second set of case studies examines the changes in two fundamental development processes (the BoM/EPL and the WIP process). These issues are in fact especially critical at the early stages of design were there is a trade-off between quickly freezing the configuration and communicating it downstream, on the one hand, and trying as many configurations as possible, interacting as informally as possible, on the other.

3. To shed light over the issues of experimentation, of knowledge, skills and capabilities integration and of inter-organizational conflict absorption, 'hybrid' (virtual and physical) prototyping activities were chosen; this is because they represented an ideal ground where to observe how heterogeneous knowledge sources and types from different parts of an organization could be drawn together and integrated into an artefact. Observing the process by which organizations built hybrid prototypes also allowed the exploration of how conflicts among different departments having different knowledge, objectives and incentives can be absorbed and co-ordinated. The two sub-cases here are concerned with the study of knowledge integration at the interfaces, respectively, between Design and Engineering, and between Engineering and Analysis.

Observant Participation and Participant Observation: Elements of Ethnography

Ethnographic research includes many variations depending on the extent of the researcher's involvement. These range between two extremes: at one end, the researcher can adopt the role of full participant in the lives and activities of the subjects and thus becomes a member of their group or community (Hammersley and Atkinson, 1995: 109); at the other, the researcher can adopt the role of a spectator, completely uninvolved with the surrounding environment. Participant observation is well documented in the literature. According to Mintzberg (1973, in Jill and Johnson, 1991) it can enable access to what people actually do (the informal organization) as opposed to what they might claim they do and which official sanctions impel them to do (the formal organization): it can be the only viable way to discover what is actually happening (ibid.: 109).

In this case a decision was taken to adopt a role that could be described as observer-as-participant (ibid.: 113). In this case the primary role of the researcher is that of an observer who, while not being a member of the organization, can at times take part in its activities as a member. This was the case, for example, when the author took part in company seminars, corporate games and 'change management' courses and lectures.

Not having a specific role to play within the firm, the access had to be negotiated. In return for their time and availability the author agreed to provide the firm with feedback about the major change project that they were undertaking: the migration towards the 'Virtual Product' technology and philosophy. The agreement reached involved signing a confidentiality document whereby, in the instance of publication, the identity of the organization and their employees would not be revealed.

Data was collected via both direct and indirect observation. The first case involved watching and listening to practitioners while working, across all levels and departments in the organization. A great amount of evidence was also produced by in-depth, semi-structured interviews. Access to indirect data was also obtained by reading IT and PD strategy documents[5] and by dropping into a live discussion database, which, unfortunately, was not used after the initial few months because it was too cumbersome and inflexible. These sources provided information about meetings and events, which the researcher could not, or was not allowed to, take part in. This data was complemented by library and Internet searches.

The attitude in field notes writing was initially 'to react rather than sift out' (Eisenhardt, 1989: 539) as it is often difficult to know what will, or will not, be useful in the future. Afterwards, such notes would be compared with previously collected evidence or assumptions highlighting differences and contrasts. Simple description would later be conducive to new theoretical insights. Afterwards, the methodology involved going back and checking if those inferences held in other cases. This method was important in triggering a change in research focus from the organization level, to the deeper level of routines and practices. As argued earlier in this chapter, this approach later proved fundamental in highlighting issues and questions which would have not manifested themselves otherwise. The effort therefore involved understanding each process individually and in as much depth as it was feasible.

Data Analysis

The above data collection methods generated an enormous amount of information. This is a recognized potential weakness of theory building from cases (Mintzberg, 1973) as it 'may lead to the researcher being swamped by data and being unable to distinguish the most significant variables from those peculiar to a case' (in Jill and Johnson, 1991: 119). On the other hand, there is substantial proof that simple, direct, inductive, semi-structured observations have produced wide benefits to management policy research. According to Mintzberg, small samples should be encouraged rather 'than less valid data that were statistically significant' (1979, in Jill and Johnson, 1991: 149). An important issue in this case was how to sift only that information which was relevant (Eisenhardt, 1989). The evidence was therefore organized according to the theoretical issues it contributed to; this methodology helped substantially to 'filter out the noise' from important evidence.

Another potential danger of immersive participant observation is that of producing research that is narrow and idiosyncratic. To counteract this potential problem the author conducted a series of semi-structured interviews in other development organizations (i.e. engine design, aircraft structures design, Formula One, etc.); these confirmed that all the issues that had been encountered in the three case firms were also a major concern in other industrial sectors. Evidence from user discussion lists on the Internet (Integrated Product Data Manager User Group [IPDMUG]) has also provided an important tool for cross-verification. For over three years the author constantly screened the debates ongoing in a user discussion list that was specifically dedicated to the class of software applications that are the object of this study. Beyond providing a wealth of insights from practitioners, the discussions were very valuable in confirming that the issues addressed in the research were also extremely relevant for a vast number of organizations across all manufacturing sectors and all over the world. JPL-Nasa, Boeing, Toyota, Lucent Technologies, BAe, Altair, Lockheed Martin, Ford, Siemens, Fujitsu, Chrysler, and many others, have all taken part in the online debate, having implemented the same or similar software technologies.

A third recognized problem with the ethnographic type of data collection is the difficulty for the researcher to distance her/himself from the fieldwork reality. This can be quite difficult when a strong relationship is built between the researcher and the practitioners, where there could be a loss of objectivity due to long term sharing of the managers' and engineers' concerns, troubles, stories. This issue is emphasized by Douglas (1976). In his opinion, depth probes are vital in getting at deeper aspects of social or organizational life; they involve 'de-focusing', that is immersion in and saturation by the setting through allowing oneself to experience them as much as possible as any organizational member. At the same time, however, he stresses that the researcher should retain a commitment to being a researcher and later moving to more systematic observations and analyses of that setting (1976, in Jill and Johnson, 1991: 110).

While participant observation retains important strengths, there is an imminent danger that, by becoming entangled in the everyday lives of subjects, the researcher can become unable to detach from and take a dispassionate view of events and unintentionally discard the researcher element of the field role. The opposite danger, however, is that the observer fails to gain access to and understand the elements underpinning the subjects' overt behaviours and actions. In this case the author experienced some difficulties at the stage where fieldwork exploration and the analysis stage overlapped. This was resolved by intentionally avoiding contact with the field organizations for a few months' period at the end of the data collection period. This was very effective in allowing her to regain perspective and consequently proceed with the analysis and writing up.

Developing Theory from Grounded Research

During the analysis and writing up stages, the concepts and theories emerging from the data collected were compared with existing theories and assumptions; consistent with Eisenhardt, special attention was dedicated to contrasting such findings with similar literature or evidence. At times the observation lead to insights that helped to fill in the gaps left by other literature. Probably the most important advantage of qualitative and grounded research consists precisely in this, in its ability to support the development of new theory (Eisenhardt, 1989; Glaser and Strauss, 1967). As Eisenhardt (1989) argued,

> The constant juxtaposition of conflicting realities [i.e. the investigator's preconceptions and the fieldwork evidence] tends to 'unfreeze' thinking, and so the process has the potential to generate theory with less researcher bias than theory built from incremental studies or armchair, axiomatic deduction. (Ibid.: 546–7)

Another fundamental strength of qualitative, grounded theorizing derives from the ability to immediately test the emergent theory with constructs that can be readily measured and hypotheses that can be proven false. A third strength is that the resultant theory is likely to be consistent with empirical observation. The intimate interaction with actual evidence often produces theory that closely mirrors reality (Eisenhardt, 1989: 547). According to Glaser and Strauss (1967), 'it is the intimate connection with empirical reality that permits the development of a testable, relevant and valid theory' (in Eisenhardt, 1989: 532).

The strong links with the empirical domain ensure potential usefulness of the findings for practitioners. A corollary is that, although the main aim of this research was to contribute to the theoretical debate, due to the level of depth achieved, many of its insights can be valuable to both software producers (i.e. contribution towards the design of less intrusive, more effective software applications) and software users (i.e. contribution towards a deeper understanding of the organizational implications of software adoption). This work, however, was not written with the false ambition to 'teach practitioners what they are doing wrong and tell them what instead they ought to be doing'. It instead provides them with a different, perhaps more detached and theoretically informed reading of their day-to-day reality. Rather then producing simplistic management or technology design recommendations, this book therefore largely leaves with the practitioners the task to find their own 'truths' by comparing these findings with their experience of their own and other organizations.

NOTES

1. Indeed 'working to rule' has been demonstrated to be an infallible means to grind an organization to a halt.
2. See also Chapter 7.
3. The discussion here draws substantially from Berg, 1997a; 1997b.
4. While admitting that the tools may not be yet perfect, they claim that their current limitations can be remedied by *advancing* on the current *path of development* (Berg, 1997b).
5. See the reference section at the end of this book.

4. Integrated Software Systems: The Technology and its Embedded Assumptions

The theoretical and methodological discussion in Chapters 2 and 3 provide the foundations for the 'theme' chapters that follow (5, 6 and 7). Before addressing the core of this book's evidence and findings, however, we first set out to explore the main characteristics of the software technologies that are the subjects of this study.

The aim of this chapter is to emphasize the assumptions that are embedded in software during its design and use; the theme chapters will then proceed to test how these assumptions perform in practice. The structure of the chapter is as follows: after a brief description of the technology, its relevance and diffusion, we examine some of the most widespread organizational practices for software adoption; the third section introduces the principal assumptions embedded in software; this is followed by a discussion that raises issues and questions that will be addressed by later chapters.

INTEGRATED SOFTWARE SYSTEMS: THE TECHNOLOGY, ITS RELEVANCE AND DIFFUSION

Integrated Commercial Off-the-Shelf Software Systems

This work is concerned with a segment of the software market that has experienced noticeable growth during the past decade: the market for integrated, Commercial Off-the-Shelf (COTS) application software. Commercial Off-the-Shelf systems are part of the 'middleware' market that is bounded from 'below' (closer to the computer) by the market for operating systems, programming tools, and utilities and from 'above' (closer to the user) by end-user applications such as desktop productivity solutions and multimedia software (D'Adderio, 2000).[1] In contrast with basic, independent software applications, these systems are often referred to as 'software application solutions' or simply 'software solutions'. Each solution consists of a generic system composed of a number of complementary, system-compliant applications; each application supports specific tasks and functions, at the same time also contributing to support the system's overall functionality. Within the integrated systems category are *enterprise-wide* application solutions that are specifically designed to facilitate the integration among heterogeneous functions, activities and knowledge sources across an organization, including links to the extended enterprise; among these are widely known application solutions, such as Enterprise Resource Planning (ERP) and Product Data Manager (PDM) software. The latter, together with a number of compliant applications, is the main subject of this study.[2]

The Integrated COTS software market segment has experienced an outstanding growth during the last decade; integrated software systems are in fact being adopted across an increasingly wide range of industrial sectors and industries. The PDM market, for instance, grew at a pace of 27 per cent during 1998 to reach $1.4 billion in sales; it was $0.6 billion in 1993 (Miller, 1999).[3] The worldwide growth of PDM is driven primarily by substantial investments by large manufacturing firms; among major adopters are the Automotive and Electronics industries (each accounting for 19 per cent of PDM sales in 1998), followed by Aerospace, Process and Utilities and manufacturers of heavy machinery. A similar pattern of growth has been experienced by other integrated application solutions such as ERP.

The reasons behind the increase in diffusion and adoption of integrated software solutions are numerous and complex; they include the strategies adopted by software producers to expand their system's range of capabilities, the resonance between the model embedded in integrated systems and the philosophy of Business Process Re-engineering, the perceived superiority of integrated systems over bespoke software, and of 'integration' strategies over 'interfacing'. These motivations are examined below.

The Increasing Generic Character of Integrated Systems

One factor behind the increase in diffusion of Integrated Software Systems is the migration of their characteristics towards those of generic systems. The increasingly generic character of Integrated Software Systems corresponds to a specific strategy by software producers who aim to encourage adoption by rendering the system applicable to a wide range of business and manufacturing sectors. The trend towards generic systems stems from the realization that no software developer organization alone can easily produce the entire set of applications required by different firms in different sectors. This is due not only to financial and/or operative but also to cognitive limitations: the producers' resources are limited and the professional expertise required for all sectors in which the system is used cannot be easily centralized within a single software producer organization (D'Adderio, 2000).

The division of labour between systems developers and specialized suppliers is technically supported by an increasing standardization and codification of software development tools, methods and procedures; this is also facilitated by the increasing standardization of the product architecture (i.e. platforms, interfaces) (Software Producer's Manual, 1998). In particular, the adoption by software producers of an open, object-oriented software architecture enables third-party firms to build specialized applications that are at the same time complementary and compliant with the main system's platform. By increasing the number and type of applications that are available to the user, the system's functionality range is also extended, thus potentially increasing the software's appeal to existing and potential customer organizations[4] (D'Adderio, 2000). An open, object-oriented strategy can also increase the system's market share as it can facilitate a progressive system implementation. Firms, for example, can phase software implementation by initially adopting only the core software modules and then adding the remaining modules over time; this strategy can make adoption easier to smaller firms by helping them to spread their investment over time (Miller, 1998).

The Resonance between Integrated Systems and BPR's Philosophy

A further reason for the sustained growth of the integrated software market segment is that such technologies are viewed by adopter organizations as principal enablers of a BPR strategy. Business Process Re-engineering is a management concept developed to describe enterprise strategies that are aimed at optimizing cross-cutting processes; the assumption is that information technologies with cross-cutting functionality, such as integrated systems, can potentially help an organization to realize the goals of BPR (Koch, 1998).

Integrated systems are designed to perform as the backbone for data communication and process control throughout the product life cycle and across the extended enterprise. According to Lozinsky (1998, in Hirt and Swanson, 1999), integrated systems are designed to allow information to enter at a single point in the process and update a database for all functions that directly or indirectly depend on this information. In principle, such integration should take place in real time, not through interfaces or programs that transfer information to one or more modules only after the information has already been processed and updated in the module through which it entered the system. Once input, the information should be available in all the necessary forms through which it may be accessed, throughout the system.

Product Data Manager software, for example, is designed to provide an information connection between many different applications, essentially serving as a bridge between various parts of engineering and manufacturing as well as areas such as marketing, purchasing, finance and customer services; it is also designed to manage product data throughout the enterprise, and to ensure that 'the right information is available for the right person at the right time and in the right form' (software producer's web page). In reconfiguring the patterns of communication and co-operation between functions PDM can provide the opportunity for an organization to restructure its Product Development and related business processes to support BPR.[5]

As a result, the implementation of integrated systems is generally followed by a substantial push towards 're-engineering' the organization; organizations often use software adoption as an expedient to trigger the process of codification and rationalization of their process know-how with the aim to achieve greater efficiency and integration. Integrated software adoption is in fact often perceived as essential by established organizations that view software as an opportunity to reorganize their wealth of (often sub-optimal) processes to gain superior efficiency; such reorganization aims to help organizations exploit their accumulated knowledge and capabilities while eliminating or reducing the sources of cognitive inertia and resistance to change embedded into their legacy systems. Software is perceived as useful also by firms that are new to a product/technology market and see the software as an opportunity to quickly update and improve their processes by acquiring knowledge about 'best practice' from established market leader organizations in the same industrial sector.

The improvements in the integration of activities and knowledge flows that these systems promise to deliver, both within the organizational and across enterprise-wide boundaries, represent a definite incentive towards adoption; so do the promise of increased collaboration and knowledge-sharing across project and functional boundaries, and the reduction of organizational inefficiencies and duplication of efforts. The issue of to what extent these aims are effectively achieved, and whether or not the goals of integration and BPR are desirable targets for the adopter organization will be addressed later in this book. At this stage it is important to emphasize that these are among the considerations upon which both software producers and users base their software design and adoption strategies.

The Perceived Benefits of 'Off-the-Shelf' over 'Bespoke' Software

Another principal motive behind the adoption of integrated COTS software packages is their perceived superiority over bespoke software systems. On the one hand, bespoke systems hold significant advantages: they are generally built around the contingent circumstances in which the adopter firm operates, and can be designed to accommodate its specific organizational routines and corporate knowledge flows. For this reason, the implementation of bespoke systems is often less traumatic than that of COTS systems, as it essentially entails the customization of software features and model around the organization, rather than the other way around.

On the other hand, bespoke systems are increasingly viewed as a missed opportunity for the organization in terms of re-engineering their critical processes and updating the organization's routines to their industry's best practice. Such systems may also put the organization at substantial risk that the large-scale effort and investment required to initially implement the system will have to be replicated, i.e. as the need for new functions arises or as a consequence of improvements in hardware performance. Moreover, the increasing technical complexity of many critical applications can make it difficult to develop client-specific solutions; users are therefore increasingly turning to adopt standard systems and customize them to construct their critical systems.

Standard COTS systems are being adopted across an increasingly wide range of sectors and organizations. As opposed to bespoke systems, which are specifically designed around the adopting organization, the implementation of COTS software involves an extensive customization effort which is required to adapt the generic, standardized software solution to the idiosyncrasies of individual industry sectors and segments, technologies and organizations. The design of any standardized software system, for instance, is based upon specific assumptions about the organization and its context, which can be more or less close to the characteristics of the adopter organization, and therefore will entail a greater or lesser customization effort.

The adoption of a standard, off-the-shelf system often provides an incentive for the organization to codify, adapt and rewrite its procedures until they fit more closely the 'ideal' model embedded in the generic system's design. The design of PDM, for instance, was inspired by and produced according to the idealized model of an aerospace organization (Interview/NG).[6] Manufacturing firms operating in sectors other than aerospace are likely to encounter a higher level of clashes and incompatibilities with the software, depending upon how closely their practices resemble the organizational model embedded in software. Those enterprises that are more unlike the model are expected to require a higher level of either software customization or organizational change (or both) in order to be in a position to achieve the benefits 'promised' by the software at the outset.

Our principal case firm, an automotive manufacturer, for example, is characterized by a much looser horizontal structure than usually found at an aerospace organization; it is also not as heavily regulated and strictly hierarchical as its aerospace counterpart. The chapters that follow demonstrate that, as a consequence, the software is often perceived as highly authoritarian, rigid and heavily structured; it tends to emphasize control while leaving a relatively diminished scope for upstream creative activities to take place and in general obstructing more informal knowledge-sharing practices.[7] In this specific implementation case, therefore, clashes are to be expected that are partly due to the mismatches between the generic software-embedded model and the specific structure and culture of the adopting organization. Similar mismatches are bound to occur whenever the adopter organization differs significantly from the software-embedded model.

In general, the mapping of the software-embedded model, routines and assumptions onto existing organizational processes can prove to be extremely difficult and resource consuming; this only excludes the extreme situations in which an organization decides to rewrite its procedures radically according to the software-embedded model (Brady, Tierney and Williams, 1992). It must be emphasized, however, that this represents an extreme and rather uncommon approach as most organizations could not and indeed would not attempt a total re-engineering effort; this is attributable to a number of reasons including their need to preserve the accumulated knowledge which is embedded in existing organizational routines, and the scarce availability of financial, business and/or human resources that would be required to sustain such a radical operation.

Alternative Paths towards Integration

When firms decide to pursue an integration strategy they generally face two major (but often non-exclusive) strategic options: (1) integrating by adopting a standard, generic (pre-)integrated system; or (2) integrating by interfacing individual software applications, often produced by different manufacturers. Organizations often opt for the former strategy as the level of integration supported by pre-integrated systems is perceived as superior to that obtained by joining together a set of independently conceived, non-compliant applications. The outstanding growth of the integrated software market segment testifies that firms are increasingly favouring integration (or a greater proportion of integration) over interfacing.

Integration basically consists of the adoption and customization of a (pre-) integrated, generic COTS system. Such a system is composed of one or more 'core' modules, plus a number of pre-integrated 'peripheral' applications that are often industry or task specific and are supported by the generic system producer's platform. A 'pre-integrated' system is designed to provide a firm with easier access to integration capabilities while also supporting the future expansion of capability; this is because all applications that are built according to the same platform and standards used by the main system producer can be more easily incorporated into the core system.[8]

Interfacing implies instead a continued long-term investment in discipline-specific tools, where immediate functionality, rather than systems compatibility and integration, is the deciding factor (Internal Document/PHI). Its major perceived advantage is to allow organizations to acquire tools, which are 'best-in-class', and/or high performance. The use of specialized FEA software applications discussed in Chapter 7 provides an example. In the case of interfacing, integration is obtained by combining isolated applications and can be supported by co-operation among the various software suppliers, by the definition and implementation of open standards that ensure interoperability, and by the long-term commercial involvement of third-party software integrators, such as consulting firms. In this case integration and customization efforts are focused towards achieving a smooth co-ordination of the various applications that compose the system, applications that are often based on different standards and interfaces. In the case of integration, efforts are instead essentially directed towards adapting the generic solution to specific and idiosyncratic organizational requirements.

It is important to emphasize that even when organizations opt for a fully (pre-)integrated strategy, they often end up using a mix of integrating and interfacing, for example by interfacing the standard generic integrated system (which constitutes a 'core') with several in-house or specialized non-compliant software applications. Indeed, even in cases where the user organization has opted for a 'totally integrated' strategy, as is the case for our automotive organization, it is common for some legacy applications (in-house or bespoke) to be retained instead of being replaced by compliant integrated COTS modules.[9] The integrated software modules, in these cases, retain permanent interfaces to several existing systems; these are regarded as 'best of breed' stand-alone applications which provide superior performance where it is needed and capabilities that the integrated system is not able to provide (Hirt and Swanson, 1999).

The decision whether to retain or shed legacy applications is related, among other factors, to the type of firm and technology. Firms that have a relatively higher portion of accumulated knowledge and experience in software development and that can rely on in-house software development skills, for example, are more likely to retain at least part of their legacy software and interface this with the new 'core' generic system. Also, organizations that produce leading-edge technologies are more likely to retain or acquire non-compliant high-end specialized software applications that are again interfaced with the generic integrated system.

While the strategies of integrating and interfacing are complementary, an emphasis on one or the other holds important implications. One major consequence is the difference in terms of the type and degree of integration that they are able to support. While interfacing is relatively easier and less costly to accomplish than integration, it does not create a persistent database. For example, interfacing translates data between applications that have different local data models and formats. As argued in Chapter 5, the data created this way is transient relative to the larger PD life cycle because it only produces changes in local databases; interfacing therefore allows for the sharing of data *but not of meaning*. This provides a further incentive towards the adoption of pre-integrated systems, as only these can provide a shared, persistent database between multiple applications containing the 'official' data; a persistent database can theoretically provide longer-term integration, therefore enabling advanced simulation concepts such as the Virtual Product, as discussed below.

THE ADOPTION OF INTEGRATED SOFTWARE SYSTEMS

Conceptually, the increase in adoption of integrated systems by business organizations can be characterized as the organization's attempt to face up to increasing competitive pressures by supporting a higher level of integration both within its own boundaries and across the boundaries with other 'external' partner and/or competitor organizations.[10] Achieving a higher level of integration is increasingly perceived as mandatory for a firm that aims to survive and prosper. As a manager at our automotive organization has argued 'there should be no question about whether we should or should not integrate our systems. The fact is, we will not be able to compete if we don't' (Interview/KT). According to an increasing number of adopter organizations, thus, the major issue is often not whether or not the enterprise should integrate, but, rather, which are the technological, management and strategic options that can help them achieve integration.

An Integrated Product Development Strategy

The implementation of an integrated PD environment is increasingly viewed by manufacturing firms as the most effective means to achieve greater co-ordination and integration of those elements that constitute their fragmented organizational landscape (i.e. heterogeneous technologies, functions, disciplines, processes, knowledge and activity flows) into a coherent, controlled and synchronized whole.

In order to achieve this goal, many organizations are opting for an Integrated Product Development (IPD) strategy. Adopting such a strategy entails 'an awareness that gaining and maintaining leading competitive edge involves establishing a proactive, focused company direction across all Product Development disciplines'; this presumption follows 'the recognition of the importance of utilising inputs from all disciplines to support early product characterisation and validation' (Internal Document/IPDS). Due to its ambitious goals and the extent of its scope, an integrated PD strategy entails efforts that reach well beyond the straightforward implementation of integrated software systems. According to Adler (1990a), integration entails a steep organizational learning curve which, depending upon its extent, can involve changes in up to five areas: the upgrading of skills (skills), the reconfiguration of processes (procedures), the co-ordination and integration of specialized and differentiated sub-units (structure), the harmonization of function-level long-term strategies (strategy), and the support of co-operative, inter-functional learning (culture).

Both IT and PD managers at our manufacturing organization share a similar view. One of their internal strategic documents argues that, in order to achieve integration, product, data and processes must form *a core* around which all other organizational variables revolve: organizational functions and groups, software tools, range of discipline-specific expertise, suppliers and partners (Internal Document/IPDS). The implementation of an Integrated Product Development environment must be based upon the integration of Product Development processes with those of the business as a whole, a model inspired by the software producer's own philosophy. Let us briefly examine these variables, as illustrated in our organization's 'Business Communication Model' (ibid.).

First, an integrated PD strategy requires the redefinition of existing *processes* and the synchronization of activities across organizational teams, disciplines and functions so to support simultaneous 'work in progress' development. Process redefinition often entails a steep learning curve by the organization involving the articulation, codification and reconfiguration of Product Development and related organizational processes (i.e. product definition, detailing, validation, and production).[11] The creation of a clear process infrastructure is aimed at supporting a higher level of integration between physical and digital product definition and validation (ibid.).

Second, an integrated PD strategy involves the integration of *organizational functions*; these include both 'internal' functions (i.e. Vehicle definition, Packaging, Design, Surface, Chassis, Power train, Body, Electrical, Analysis, Manufacturing, Testing, Production, Administration, Quality and Marketing) and 'external' functions (i.e. parts and materials suppliers). The integration of functions is aimed at ensuring that multidisciplinary data, information and knowledge inputs from the various parts of an extended enterprise are brought to bear into the PD process at an early stage, thus leading to a higher-quality product definition.

Third, according to the communication model, an integrated strategy requires the integration of *expertise and skill* in order to support the 'core' strategy. Identifying expertise requirements involves taking into consideration process, organizational and functional requirements, including: the definition of training requirements, the definition of core expertise and skills, the identification of internal and external skills requirement, the identification of gaps in internal staff number, expertise and skill levels, and the identification of outside capabilities and partnerships.

Fourth, an integrated PD strategy involves the integration of *development technologies*. Software technologies must be designed and implemented to support: (1) a single product definition model, which contains data, information and (codified) knowledge inputs from the various enterprise functions, teams and organizations; (2) a single product definition technology which uses open architecture to integrate with other complementary applications; (3) integrated activity and data management which facilitate the retrieval of the data stored and its utilization as input for New Product Development; (4) an integrated Information System which is able to support both Process and Functional requirements at three levels: Product, Work in Progress, and Company 'Data' and 'Activity' management.

Finally, an integrated PD strategy should facilitate the integration of *software tools suppliers,* selected with regard to required process, functional, and technical expertise, and *partnerships,* selected to complement the firm's and other partners' capabilities, and with consideration to the requirements of an integrated team.[12]

According to the company strategy document, a coherent PD strategy demands that all the above variables must be brought together. This must be achieved by setting up a 'common data and communication core', which is composed of two elements: a *data core* which collects the data contained in all distributed databases (i.e. local, function-specific databases) and a data *communication entity* (i.e. PDM software), which draws from, relates and structures all data contained in the data core.

According to their model, all business functions must draw from and input into the data core at various levels: at a *global* level, all organizations that form the extended Enterprise (i.e. R&D, Production, Maintenance Centres, often at different geographical locations); at the *organizational* level, all development programmes (i.e. vehicle programme 1, 2, ..., n); at the *project* level, all team participants that take part in a specific development programme (i.e. Programme Management, Production, Design of Vehicle 1); and at the *function's* level, all organizational departments involved in the development process (i.e. Body, Chassis, Vehicle Engineering, etc.).

All the above organizational layers must use PDM software (the communication entity) to access the relevant stored data, information and (codified) knowledge about product, processes and organization. Each function or level is expected to interact through this common core; the core therefore is understood as the reference centre whereby all PD-relevant data, information and formal knowledge is collected and stored; it is also intended to constitute a repository of collective, codified, up to date knowledge from which informal knowledge processes can draw. In synthesis, the integrated data and communication core is designed to ensure that all these different enterprise levels and knowledge inputs from different parts of the enterprise are integrated and contribute towards a *single* product and process definition.

While the software producer's notion of a central data and communication core has been widely and enthusiastically embraced by enterprises in most manufacturing sectors, the way the concept works in practice, and its implications for the adopting organization, are still unclear. For example, it is not explained how the adopter organization can achieve the alignment of the technological and organizational variables required to effectively implement an integrated PD environment. The extent and scope of an integrated strategy render its implementation a considerable effort for the adopter organization.

The Digital Mock-Up (DMU) or the Phased Implementation of an Integrated PD Environment

The scarce availability of organizational resources, together with the high organizational impact generated by the implementation of integrated systems, often dictates that software implementation is conducted over time as a phased effort. This is far removed from the one-off total re-engineering efforts often described in the Business Process Re-engineering (BPR) literature. Practitioners are rather more likely to describe software implementation as 'a continuous re-engineering effort' (Interview/KT). A phased implementation is also due to other reasons, including: (1) the need for continued refocusing, due to the changes in organizational requirements as the implementation proceeds and learning occurs; and (2) the shortening of the typical software life cycle, whereby the implementation of a new system or a new generation of an old system often begins before the previous implementation effort is concluded.[13] Unsurprisingly, the stage in the software implementation life cycle where an organization is using low resources and reaping high benefits (the 'factory' stage in Ward's matrix) is often theoretical and not achieved in practice.[14]

Organizations that decide to adopt integrated systems are therefore faced with the choice between a one-off, 'big bang' implementation and an incremental, staged one. On the one hand, the incremental approach is often slower and more expensive than its radical counterpart; this is because temporary interfaces have to be written that connect parts of the existing (soon-to-be-replaced) system with the newly implemented modules, in order to ensure uninterrupted data processing during the period of the DMU project. In addition, some of the configuration performed in earlier phases of the project may need to be adjusted in later phases to accommodate necessary changes when additional modules are linked to the system, or indeed when a new generation of the system is to be introduced (Hirt and Swanson, 1999). On the other hand, the 'big bang' approach is fairly risky as it requires going 'live' with all the newly implemented modules at the same time, while a staged implementation allows for sections of the system (or 'prototypes') to be implemented 'off-line' so as not to interfere with ongoing operations. Moreover, in dictating that all implementation activities must occur in parallel rather than sequentially, the radical approach requires that a significant amount of resources is employed at any one time.

Somewhat unsurprisingly, organizations are increasingly opting for the incremental approach, and choose to undertake the staged implementation of the integrated PD environment. As a consequence, most frequently organizations are positioned somewhere in the middle of a trajectory which leads from partial integration to (quasi) total integration.[15] Other reasons behind the prevalence of partial integration, beyond the adoption of a phased strategy, include: (1) the fact that the path to integration is riddled with difficulties ranging from the challenge of co-ordinating the various departments, groups, teams and disciplines that form an organization's landscape, each one of these holding different incentives, culture, requirements and capabilities; (2) the realization that the amount of resources (financial, skills, time) required to integrate are considerable, and the implementation process may have to be arrested or delayed until these become available; and (3) the threat that the succession of software solutions generations is so rapid that often a new solution is adopted before the past generations' implementation is completed, as mentioned above.

This is the case of our automotive organization. At the beginning of the fieldwork period, the management had just endorsed an integrated product development strategy, which entailed the implementation of a generic integrated software system as a major enabler (in addition to the re-engineering of their business processes). The principal aim was to use the software to achieve an integrated product development and organizational environment that would sustain the company's position in the world top ten vehicle manufacturers. The software implementation project was named Digital Mock-Up, or DMU. According to a senior PD manager:

> The scope of Digital Mock-up spans from the simulation of Product Concept (Digital Styling Models) to the simulation Product Engineering (from Digital Assembly to the Virtual Prototype), all the way through to the simulation of the

Production environment (including Virtual Manufacturing plant and assembly line simulation). (Internal Document/X100)

According to the software producers:

Digital Mock-up is the working environment for concurrent engineering teams. Disciplines co-operating with the design engineers (manufacturing and maintenance engineers, technical publishing specialists and so on) also consider the digital mock-up as the appropriate place to store their own data. (Software manufacturer's web page)

The assumption behind the DMU concept is that the rich multidisciplinary knowledge that constitutes a network of interconnections between parts, or even subparts like features, can only be optimized if

Engineers can access the myriad of 'technological links' that define a product – its mechanical contacts, the dependencies between the geometry and related NC program, electrical connections, links between geometry and knowledge stored in documents, etc. Technological links are key to allowing engineers to quickly propagate changes from part to part or feature to feature. By understanding completely the relationship between a product's components, engineers can run the necessary iterative simulations until the product's performance, manufacturability and cost have been optimized. (Software manufacturer's web page).

The Digital Mock-up or its most sophisticated version, the Virtual Product, in principle allows users to view three-dimensional (3D) data from many CAD sources regardless of vendor or file format (i.e. how parts and subassemblies fit into the context of an entire project). These models can reveal subtle relationships among components and operational details; as an integrated part of a PDM system, the model also provides a convenient entry point to access information associated with all parts of the product, including bills of materials, documents and specifications, engineering drawings and analysis results. Virtual product mock-ups are also useful to other functions beyond design: quality engineers could use the model to check specifications; manufacturing can create and verify process instructions; service groups can determine the best way to maintain products, etc.

Beyond being a synonym for the digital representation of an entire artefact plus its links to all organizational functions involved in its production, the Digital Mock-up also stands to exemplify the technology implementation path that an organization has to undertake in order to accomplish the migration towards a Virtual PD environment. At our organization, the implementation of Digital Mock-up technology was broken down into four different stages: Digital Pre-Assembly, Digital Model, Digital Product Model, and Virtual Product. Over a one and a half year period, the author assisted in the implementation of the first three stages, plus the preparation leading to the virtual product stage, that is to a fully integrated PD environment.[16] According to our interviewees, each stage of DMU represents a step forward in the organizational migration towards an Integrated PD environment. In order to achieve this, each of the steps requires the implementation of a specific set of software tools and organizational procedures.

The first stage, *Digital Pre-Assembly* (DPA), enables the assembly of 3D CAD models in the CAD environment; it is mainly used by engineers at the design stage to interrogate assemblies for clash and interference detection, tolerance stack, ability to assemble and serviceability. Digital Pre-Assembly is technically enabled by the functionality of advanced CAD software.[17]

The second stage, the Digital Model (DM), is intended to provide engineers with the ability to control 3D digital assemblies (DPA) through the CAD Data Management (CDM) environment; CDM is a local database designed to ensure that all data used is concurrent and correctly configured, and that it is accessible to all users within a model and design session environment. The CDM environment enables the control of mainstream engineering data (engineering geometrical data or CAD geometry models) plus Finite Elements-based and Computer Numerical Control (CNC) models. The implementation of a CDM environment entails the set up of specific design hierarchies, the mapping of the existing design working process, and the customization of design working practices.[18]

The third stage is the Digital Product; this has the properties of the Digital Model (above), with the added benefit of direct integration with the Product Data Management (PDM) environment. It supports full, direct configuration control allowing the user to access any available Bill of Materials (BoM)[19] in its correct configuration with fully concurrent data (full historical and configuration control). Product Data Manager also provides an environment for the linking of the Engineering Management Control systems or tools and the Parts procurement and control systems or tools, with the CAD Geometry data.

The fourth and final stage is the Virtual Product; this has the properties of the Digital Product, plus it provides the user with the ability to digitally test and evaluate the digital product. As described in the software producer's document, and reported by a senior manager at our case organization, 'Virtual Product is when you can fully describe all aspects of the final physical product in the virtual world. That does not just mean its configuration: it also means the capability to simulate its manufacture and its functional characteristics in a digital world' (Interview/KT). The Virtual Product contains connections not only to PD and manufacturing, but to the extended support functions, as well as the extended enterprise; its links stretch both 'functionally' to all functions of Product Development, and 'geographically' to all the organizations that form the global enterprise.

The DMU concept and strategy therefore exemplify the techno-organizational migration required to advance from a simple CAD representation of the product, to its full functional simulation. Interestingly, each more advanced DMU step requires a higher level of organizational restructuring and reconfiguration in order to render its potential capabilities effective. The implementation of the digital mock-up therefore holds important implications for the adopting organization.

While the DMU concept and strategy have been narrowly discussed in recent technical (Engineering and IT) literature (i.e. Miller, 1998), there have hardly been any attempts to explore how the concept is implemented in practice and what are the implications for the adopter organization. Integrated Product Development and BPR literature (Davenport and Short, 1990) have emphasized the 'impact' of a combined IT and Process Re-engineering strategy on quantitative performance variables (i.e. cost reduction, time reduction and output quality); however, the implications of integrated systems adoption on issues such as organizational knowledge, learning, adaptation and innovation have been so far largely neglected.

The Implementation of an Integrated Software Environment

While the scope of an integrated PD strategy reaches well beyond the scope of an IT implementation strategy, and indeed can theoretically exist without an integrated IT strategy, this is often 'technically' supported by the phased implementation of an integrated IT strategy. An important mechanism of co-evolution can be identified between the two strategies: while an integrated PD strategy is enabled by an integrated IT strategy, the latter would not be feasible or effective without taking into account the more complex organizational variables which make up this multi-layered equation.

The major stated aim of an Integrated PD environment is to help organizations to achieve 'an open and collaborative environment for them to graphically define, manage and share their product and process information, throughout the entire product life cycle and across the extended enterprise' (software manufacturer's web page). The integrated software environment is intended to accelerate the implementation of the digital enterprise, integrating consistent definitions of their products, processes and plant through a working environment that promotes advanced concurrent engineering (ibid.); this is achieved by providing access to an electronic representation of the product and the related processes, which should allow for early sharing of data and greater concurrency in the product development life cycle as well as supporting 'a manufacturer's requirements for innovation, evaluation and optimisation of their industrial products and processes across the extended enterprise' (ibid.).

The implementation of software applications in the form of an integrated product development environment is specifically intended to encourage involvement from all disciplines in the entire product development process. Such a strategy is supported by the large software producers, who are actively seeking open standards, development partnerships, as well as opportunities to widen the scope of their own development strategies. In particular, interdisciplinary integration is technically enabled by the software's open, object-oriented architecture and the use of common international standards.

An object-oriented architecture operates by treating the various data elements used by different systems as objects and by ensuring that related objects are associated together in logical relationships (i.e. the geometry data of a product part can be linked to the part's business and process information); the software is then designed to manage these objects so that they can be continuously shared among all relevant organizational systems; an open, object-oriented architecture also ensures that 'local', discipline-specific software applications can be integrated into the main information system environment. Interdisciplinary integration is also supported by the increasing adoption by software producers of common standards: 'So you end up with this ready-to-use, plug-in CAD/CAM/CAE/ERP/Publishing [system], obviously based on standards. You have got to have standards otherwise you cannot connect all these things together' (Interview/KT).

Prevalent standards include Standard for Exchange of Product Data (STEP),[20] an international standard which provides a means for networked companies to share data throughout the entire life cycle of a product by facilitating the linking with suppliers and other parties in the extended enterprise, and Common Object Request Broker Architecture (CORBA),[21] which supports the interoperability between past, present and future technologies. Another standard is Object Linking and Embedding (OLE) which aims to facilitate the integration of office and CAx[22] applications without the need for data translation from proprietary formats.

The principal assumption held by software producers is that the integration of software applications will support a higher degree of collaboration which 'includes simultaneously defining, configuring and optimising product definition, manufacturing process and product operations, and propagating changes consistently through the entire product definition' (ibid.). An integrated IT strategy therefore entails a migration from a model whereby the differing requirements of the various departments, teams and disciplines that compose an enterprise are supported by isolated 'islands' of discipline-oriented tools (legacy systems), to a model whereby such 'islands of automation' are integrated into a consistent whole (integrated system).

The adoption of a core, integrated business strategy is thus intended to replace independent discipline-oriented strategies (Internal Document/IPDS). At our automotive organization, for example, the Product Development process

> Is made up of many varied, independent but related disciplines, from Design through to Production ... with each respective discipline having their own specific requirement for product simulation and analysis, each with different levels of complexity and capability. Today, most of these requirements are being supported by isolated islands of discipline-oriented software tools. (Internal Document/IPDS)

According to our interviewee, this model creates a vicious circle, whereby the presence of many individual and unconnected software applications at the same time reflects and further reinforces function, process, and the organization's internal fragmentation.

In contrast, an integrated system is designed to encompass the capabilities and performance previously covered by the isolated software applications. Design-related data, for example, is often scattered among CAD, CAE, CAM and CAID systems. Product Data Manager aims to provide an integration framework for the fragmented CAx area by providing a single location from which functions can access all individual, 'local' sources of data (software manufacturer's web page). According to the software producer, the implementation of an integrated software environment, together with the creation of a data and communication core, should ensure that multidisciplinary inputs from different parts of the enterprise are integrated and embedded into product definition at an early stage.

The embedded assumption is that an early incorporation of downstream and multidisciplinary feedback into the digital product definition should facilitate the detection of conflicts and problems before a product reaches the physical validation and trial stage. This follows the software producer's and users' pragmatic consideration that it is cheaper and more time-effective to improve the digital product upstream in PD rather than having to find remedies downstream. This is because any problems that arise at the production or manufacturing stage would imply extensive and costly redesign. The early integration of knowledge inputs from both external and internal functions into product definition is also aimed at increasing the innovative potential of the PD process and its outcome.

By integrating all knowledge inputs and activities that contribute to the definition, engineering, production and manufacture of a product across group-, function- and discipline-based boundaries, an integrated software environment should encourage involvement from all disciplines in the entire PD process: 'as a consequence, the rich multi-disciplinary knowledge that determines what a product is, does and how it will be built to become available to all interested parties in the extended enterprise' (ibid.).

Integrated Software Applications

The resulting integrated PD Environment therefore principally consists of an integrated set of applications aimed at collecting, storing, organizing, managing and giving access to product, process and organizational data, information and knowledge. Among the technologies that make up an Integrated PD environment are Product Data Manager (PDM) and Virtual Product Development Manager (VPDM). While several other software applications are considered, including Computer-Aided Design (CAD) and CAD Data Manager (CDM), PDM constitutes the major focus of this book.[23]

Product Data Manager software is a leading category of integrated COTS software, extensively adopted across all manufacturing sectors. Product Data Manager aims to integrate product development data and activities along the whole product life cycle as well as across the entire enterprise (software manufacturer's web page). Specifically, PDM

> Manages heterogeneous product data and documents; it also manages data distribution and product release processes while providing wide access to this information on multiple geographical sites across the product life cycle. It enforces corporate processes throughout the product development cycle and across the extended enterprise. (ibid.).

Within the development context, the software serves as an information bridge connecting Original Equipment Manufacturers (OEMs), subcontractors, vendors, consultants, partners and customers. Specifically, PDM technology is designed to enable two major functions: (1) consistency of product definition, and increased access to this data; and (2) distribution of product information.

First, PDM controls the substantial quantities of information generated by engineers during the product development process. PDM acts as a *data 'vault'*, a *repository* of heterogeneous data, information and codified knowledge generated by the various organizational functions; this constitutes a *single source* of updated product information which, in principle, is made available to all functions directly or indirectly involved in PD. The range of technical information managed by the software includes data associated with design geometry, engineering drawings, project plans, part files, assembly diagrams, analysis results, correspondence, and BoM. Processes that create and use this data are also managed through the control of functions such as engineering change, project approval, parts classification and retrieval, configuration management, program management, authorizations, workflow and information exchange (www.CIMdata.com).

Second, controlling devices embedded in PDM regulate the *access* to such shared data, according to specific authority and hierarchy levels within the organization. Such *control* is intended to support concurrent processes by co-operating teams and departments; this includes managing critical enterprise functions such as engineering change co-ordination, location of control, multiple manufacturing effectivities, and advanced configuration. As product definition matures, PDM ensures that the correct design information is *distributed* to and accepted by enterprise organizations responsible for transforming the design into a finished product; this is supported by the software's 'workflow' capabilities. Finally, PDM also manages *configured product structures* that help to relate a product to its constituent components.

More recently, a second generation of PDM tools has been introduced (PDMII), with the intention to create a software infrastructure that would enable companies to 'digitally simulate new product development, along with necessary resources and even physical manufacturing facility in an integrated and much faster manner' (software manufacturer's web page). PDMII has been devised to provide: (1) common access to entire data sets which define physical and functional characteristics of a particular artefact; (2) support to multidisciplinary teams including design, engineering, manufacturing, procurement, customer support and others, in their efforts to develop new design in a concurrent environment. These technologies together provide the physical infrastructure that supports the emergence of an integrated PD environment.

PDMII encompasses two complementary software domains: Product Data Manager (PDM) and Virtual Product Data Manager (VPDM). Virtual Product Data Manager is designed to allow engineers to optimize a product by providing a shared model that captures both the geometry of the physical product under development and its technological behaviour. This is intended to facilitate innovation by 'helping define, configure and optimise product definitions and manufacturing processes' (ibid.). Product Data Manager and VPDM are designed to form a complete product modelling and management solution with common architecture and infrastructure:

> Combining VPDM and PDM, PDM II enables a smooth transition from design to manufacturing, despite differing data management requirements, by integrating data and activities within each domain. It enables customers to define, configure, manage and optimise product development, manufacturing resources definition, and plant definition (ibid.).

While the capabilities built into software systems have been widely discussed in the technical, management and innovation literature, existing contributions have often failed to highlight how software performs within the actual organizational context. As argued in the previous chapter (3), this constitutes both a theoretical and an empirical impasse. Often under-investigated or taken at face value, the assumptions embedded in integrated software tools hold important consequences for organizational cognitive, innovative and adaptive potential. In order to further our understanding of software behaviour within an organizational context, we require to access a deeper level of analysis. This entails examining the assumptions, rationale and routines embedded in software during its conception and design stage, to unveil how these features may influence the ways in which software-embedded assumptions perform in actual implementation circumstances.

INTEGRATED SOFTWARE SYSTEMS: EMBEDDED ASSUMPTIONS

The design of integrated, enterprise-wide software systems embodies a number of assumptions, or even an entire philosophy which reflects a specific characterization of what an organization is, how it works (and should work), how software is to be implemented and structured, and the benefits that it should bring to the adopting organization. This philosophy, together with its set of assumptions, rationalities and beliefs, is embedded in software in the form of 'scripts' (Akrich, 1992). In evolutionary economics language, software-embedded 'scripts' can be compared to 'routines',[24] once the software is implemented, these interact in complex ways with other organizational scripts or routines, which are embedded in other technologies and working practices. Analysing the software-embedded scripts and their interactions with other organizational routines, will provide us with a privileged standpoint from which to observe the organizational implications of software adoption; it will also provide us with the opportunity to move beyond much technical and management literature's narrow characterization of software and its influence by supporting a critical, in-depth analysis of these pressing issues.

By examining the assumptions, beliefs and frameworks encoded in software during its design, implementation and use, we can begin to characterize how these technologies are designed to behave, which can in turn shed light over the possible ways in which these technologies are likely to affect the organizations after implementation. In turn, we can also observe how organizational routines, scripts and assumptions may affect the design of software (i.e. in the form of feedback from industrial practitioners to software producers) and the process by which a specific software configuration may emerge out of the many potentially available. This issue is emphasized in Chapter 6, where different potential organizational outcomes of alternative software configurations are discussed.

The process of emergence of a specific software philosophy or rationality represents a complex and interesting issue in itself. It will not be addressed at length within this book, however, as our major objective is to find out how, once this rationality is formed and embedded in software, it can affect the adopting organization (and vice versa). At this stage we want to point out that such a philosophy at least partially emerges from the co-evolution of the software producers' business strategy and the user organizations' own strategic understanding of the directions the organization ought to take in order to prosper within their business environment. Our hypothesis is that the resulting philosophy and assumptions hold important implications at the user level (organization). The major implication of this thinking is that, when analysing the influence of integrated software systems on organizations (and vice versa), our main priority must be to uncover the sets of views, understandings, assumptions, philosophies and rationalities that are embedded in software.

Once we open the software's 'black box' to analyse the embedded rationality, we are thus faced with a number of fundamental questions. For example, what underlies the notion of integrated software systems? Which are the software-embedded beliefs, objectives and assumptions? Which model of the requirements and objectives of the adopter organization is embedded in software? And how does the software-embedded model of the organization differ from an actual organization? This section discusses some of these fundamental assumptions. The principal assumptions will then be addressed in depth in the three 'theme' chapters that follow.

The Integration of Software Systems and Organization

As software producers, practitioners and much of the technical literature have argued, the principal objective embedded into enterprise software is to support the integration of data, processes, organizational and enterprise functions and knowledge bases, both across the enterprise and along the product life cycle.

A first major assumption is that integrated software systems must support integration at several different levels: (1) at the *product/technology* level, software is designed to enable a single and validated product definition; this entails the integration of all component product parts, assemblies and systems into a coherent configuration (integration of product data); the single product definition is technically supported by the 'parent–child' structure of the software databases and by an object-oriented software architecture which enables product parts to be 'cut and pasted' from one section of the configuration to another; (2) at the *process* level, software's object-oriented architecture is designed to enable the integration of existing process parts (or entire legacy processes), into the revised, software-embedded and controlled process definition (integration of existing process knowledge); (3) at the *organizational* level, software is designed to support the co-ordination and synchronization of development functions and activities (integration of function-specific knowledge and activities); this is technically supported by the set up of a common data core from which all functions in principle can draw; (4) at the *knowledge* level, software aims to integrate all relevant heterogeneous data, information and (codified) knowledge sources originated in different organizational and enterprise functions, teams and departments (data, information and knowledge integration); this is again technically supported by the creation of a common data core and of a corporate knowledge base (obtained by integrating all distributed databases).

There is a significant gap in existing literature concerning precisely how these levels of integration interact, and how the theoretical software aims and assumptions can be effectively translated into actual organizational capabilities.

A Centralized Data Core and Single Product Definition

The notion of an 'integrated development environment' is based upon the capability of software to provide a single, centralized repository of product, process and organizational knowledge from which all functions involved can draw: 'This knowledge base will contain an entire product definition, including the processes required to build the product, as well as plant designs for the factories in which manufacturing will take place' (software manufacturer's web page). A second and fundamental aim of integrated software systems is, therefore, to assist the process of integration and validation of multidisciplinary and multifunctional knowledge inputs into *a single, consistent and reliable 'core'*. The integration of inputs from various organizational functions into a common core is intended to support the creation of a *single product data model*, which, in principle, can be accessed by everyone involved (at different PD stages, with different levels of access and authority) in order to update their own portion of work in relation to the most current, validated information. The single model is intended to help in co-ordinating different perceptions, synchronizing actions and increasing time saving by enabling concurrent work. The core is conceived to allow multiple disciplines to both access codified, software-embedded, knowledge of product, process and organization at any point in the development process, and to productively utilise that knowledge to progress their portion of the overall product development life cycle. According to the software producer,

> Allowing the design, analysis, manufacturing and maintenance discipline to define their respective deliverables *in concert* could have a substantial bearing on the overall cycle time by consolidating the influence each of these disciplines have on the product itself. (Software manufacturer's web page, emphasis added)

The multidisciplinary data inputs that are integrated into a digital product definition include: 'internal' inputs from the various organizational disciplines, functions and departments; and 'external' inputs both from those organizations that are part of the extended enterprise, and from the organization's external environment (i.e. information about customer preferences and regulatory constraints). These heterogeneous and fragmented inputs are integrated in the software's single digital product definition: 'When you take the digital side of product creation, you start pulling over all the pieces, and the interrelationships between all these pieces' (Interview/KT). A single product definition is therefore conceived to support data, information and knowledge integration and sharing along the product life cycle and across the extended enterprise.[25]

While the theoretical benefits of the software-embedded philosophy are more or less directly celebrated in much of the technical and management (and even some innovation and evolutionary) literature, there is scarce evidence of just how these notions work in practice, and what are the implications of its introduction for the innovative, learning and adaptive potential of the development process as well as the organization. These issues will be explored in the 'theme' chapters that follow, where we will be looking in depth at the actual role of the common data core, single product definition and digital model. The theme chapters will also discuss the organizational implications of the greater centralization of knowledge and activities supported by the introduction of an integrated software system.

From 'Serial' to 'Concurrent' Processes: The Synchronization of Data and Activities

A third embedded assumption is that the common data repository should enable the migration from serial to concurrent design processes. The process of evolution of an assembly drawing provides a good example.

An assembly drawing originates in Engineering and is subsequently circulated to other functions in order to obtain feedback. Such feedback is aimed at extending, improving, updating and validating the initial design. Paper-based engineering assembly drawings are traditionally sequentially updated by passing the drawing on to each department whose input is required. In a serial development process, thus, a drawing is subsequently handed over from function to function until the initial design is either approved or invalidated; any changes to a drawing which invalidate previously defined design data inevitably originate feedback loops as the design must return each time to the function where it was first originated in order to be revised in the light of the feedback received. Often, however, the feedback process is delayed to the extent that the feedback delivered to the original function is no longer current as, by that time, other changes to the design have been implemented which make that input obsolete. These intersecting feedback loops may therefore significantly hinder the exchange and sharing of knowledge across functional boundaries (software manufacturer's web page).

The assumption embedded in the software model is that, by copying the released drawing into a software repository or 'vault' accessible by all authorised functions, users can be made aware of changes to the design as these are taking place, and therefore feedback loops can be shortened and made more effective. For example, because downstream disciplines are able, in principle, to share information before designs are complete, design engineers can utilize this information to perform simulations, to understand performance, manufacturing processes, and maintainability constraints, all of which produce relevant feedback that can be incorporated in the initial product design. Some cost advantages can also be achieved, in principle, as early changes introduced at the upstream conceptual stage are significantly less expensive than changes introduced downstream.

Another expected advantage is that, as the data relative to a specific portion of design is 'released' by a function and recorded in the software vault, it can become visible and available to all (authorized) parties according to software-embedded authority rules.[26] The process of releasing and copying data in the common, central vault is intended to make the work of engineers much more visible to the rest of the organization, which in turn is meant to improve knowledge sharing and integration, as well as the synchronization of actions across functions. In order to achieve these benefits, however, a high level of data and process control must be introduced, in order to ensure stability. Greater process control can be achieved by codifying and embedding existing informal processes in software.

This holds fundamental implications for PD and the organization, which have not been so far addressed in the literature. Chapter 6, for example, discusses some instances in which the release processes supported by the software may prevent rather than enable inter-functional co-operation and the early exchange and acquisition of design feedback; there the greater transparency of design activities is linked to reduced scope of action. The above issues are related to the organization's ability to maintain flexibility and therefore to adapt to change and innovate, and are consequently of utmost importance.

Standardization and the Reduction of Data Re-interpretation and Ambiguity

A fourth assumption embedded in software is that this should *eliminate the need for data transfer, re-interpretation and conversion* which normally characterizes serial development processes, every time information is handed over from one function to another (software manufacturer's web page). This is supported by several software features: the existence of a centralized data core which gathers all data in one 'location'; the higher level of integration among the various software applications; and the push towards standardization of technologies, processes and epistemological languages introduced by integrated software.

Case study evidence in the chapters that follow illustrates the ways in which software restructures the patterns of information transfer between functions; specifically, it discusses cases in which software effectively eliminates the need for information re-interpretation and data conversion, as well as instances in which the expected benefits of the embedded assumptions do not materialize. Chapter 5, for example, examines some of the instances in which the push towards standardization introduced by software may eliminate or increase the need for data conversion and re-interpretation by different organizational functions. In doing this, it examines the role of technological and organizational heterogeneity (in the form of heterogeneous functions, technologies, dialects, etc.) and how this is reshaped as a consequence of software implementation.

A related software-embedded assumption is that the conversion of heterogeneous, multidisciplinary data into a digital, software-embedded format should help to *reduce the level of ambiguity* contained in that data, facilitating its interpretation by different functions and therefore the translation of dispersed data into useful information. This observation is a commonplace within much of the technical and innovation literature. Chapter 5 addresses the ways in which software helps reduce ambiguity and whether, or to which extent, this can be beneficial to the organization.

Co-ordination of Functions, Intent and Viewpoints

A further assumption is that, by creating a single digital product definition that everyone in the organization can simultaneously visualize, software can support the unification of the heterogeneous perspectives and viewpoints owned by the various organizational functions, teams and individuals.

According to software producers, software can help to co-ordinate efforts and viewpoints because its common data model ensures that people in various organizational functions are made more aware of the work of others. While this point is also rehearsed in much of the literature, its validity is far from proven. The following chapter (Chapter 5) discusses circumstances in which the heterogeneity of viewpoints and perspective tends to persist, and how this is attributable to variations in knowledge, culture and incentives within and across organizational functions.

Further, as discussed in Chapter 7, the process of co-ordinating actions and viewpoints among heterogeneous organizational groups having different knowledge (including different tacit knowledge bases), culture, objectives and incentives, and the task of reducing inter-organizational conflicts, is more complicated than it might initially appear. For example, it is not clear how the integration of knowledge and the co-ordination of heterogeneous viewpoints and interests among different functions and knowledge levels can be achieved, and how inter-organizational conflicts can be absorbed; it is also unknown which kind of knowledge processes and structures favour knowledge-sharing and integration.

Data Ordering, Sifting and Control

A further assumption is that integrated software technologies can help to store, retrieve, share and reuse product, process and organizational knowledge. Software is designed to eliminate data redundancy and duplication, for example by reducing the need for re-entering data, looking up information, researching a problem that is already resolved, etc. These issues are especially relevant during the early development stages, whereby a vast amount of data chaotically flows into product definition from the organization's internal (i.e. marketing, engineering, analysis, etc.) and external environment (i.e. manufacturing or legislative constraints, customer expectations, etc); they are especially relevant in the case of complex product development programmes, whereby an enormous amount of heterogeneous data is generated by various organizational functions, as discussed in Chapter 5.

In order to prevent data duplication and ensure the consistency of product and process definition, integrated software technologies are predisposed to sift, order, restructure and classify product, programme, process and organizational data. According to software producers, these software capabilities generate an increased ability to translate random data into useful information and eventually into corporate knowledge (software manufacturer's web page). If this assumption were right, then it would disprove Wildawsky's (1983) point that Management Information Systems tend to cause a data overload in the organizations where they are implemented. However, while software's data ordering and sifting capabilities may be effective in rationalizing and controlling development data, this bears fundamental consequences for the ability of certain organizational functions to interpret and therefore utilize such data. As discussed in Chapter 5, this can hold important consequences for the patterns of co-operation and communication between functions. Another related issue (Chapter 6) is how the software's data ordering and sifting properties may affect the balance between the reuse of existing (accumulated) knowledge and the creation of new knowledge; further, we need to investigate in which ways knowledge is reconfigured (i.e. articulated, structured, codified) as it is embedded in software. These issues bear important consequences for the learning, adaptive and innovation potential of the organization.

The Virtual and the Physical Product

Software gathers and structures product- and programme-relevant data in order to generate information which can support data management and control; this, in turn, is aimed at supporting the translation of heterogeneous, distributed information into a single consistent 'virtual product definition'. The Virtual (or Digital) Product[27] concept represents the complete *digital* description of the artefact together with the digital description of the links between its constituent parts and the organizational functions that are responsible for their design, engineering, production, testing, manufacturing and maintenance.

According to the software producer, the VP provides organizations with the ability to virtually design, test and evaluate an artefact before it is built. The main assumption behind the VP is that, once a clear (digital) a priori definition is in place, it can provide clearer guidance to the process of physically producing, manufacturing and maintaining the artefact along its entire life cycle. The links between the VP and the organizational functions involved are intended to ensure that heterogeneous data inputs (i.e. regulatory constraints, manufacturing and materials requirements, customer preferences and expectations) can be collected, ordered and subsequently incorporated into digital product definition. The assumption is that the higher the integration of such inputs into product/process definition, the more reliable and effective is the VP.[28]

While physical prototypes continue to play a fundamental co-ordination and conflict absorption role, as discussed in Chapter 7, the progressive migration towards a digital product modelling environment is shifting the emphasis from physical to virtual artefacts, as emphasized by a senior manager at our main case organization:

> The common objective of all disciplines within the PD process is to simulate the characteristics of the physical product within a virtual environment in order to validate the product design concept early and thus reduce reliance upon the use of physical models and prototypes. (Internal Document/DMU)

A solid definition of the virtual product, corresponding to a digital a priori definition of the physical product, is meant to ensure that the great majority of problems with a product/technology are resolved upstream; this renders physical integration activities more 'mechanistic' and less critical: 'This way, when you finish the design you've virtually built it. In the old way, you design it and seven years later you find if it will fit' (Fowler, 1998: 21).

A final fundamental related assumption is that, by, supporting the virtual explorations of techno-organizational configurations, software favours experimentation and therefore introduces greater scope for innovation. Chapter 6 discusses the instances in which the virtual product expands or reduces the scope of exploration of alternative configurations. The full implications for the innovating firm of adopting a digital prototype philosophy and technology are yet uncovered. This chapter has begun to explore the role of virtual prototypes and how their introduction can influence the ways in which multidisciplinary knowledge is integrated and embedded in artefacts. Chapter 7 provides a rich account of the processes by which combined physical and virtual prototypes co-evolve. This includes analysing the role of virtual and physical artefacts in facilitating inter-organizational conflict absorption and inter-functional co-operation. In doing so, the chapter opens up a window on the practices of prototyping and experimentation at the engineering end of R&D, an area often neglected by existing innovation studies.

ISSUES AND QUESTIONS

Having examined the assumptions embedded in integrated software systems, we will set out to investigate precisely how these assumptions work in practice, during software implementation, within an organizational context. In particular, we will begin to unveil how software configures the organization and how, in turn, the organization reconfigures software in order to adapt it to its specific logic and structures.

Strikingly, innovation studies, organization theory and evolutionary economics have largely neglected the issue of how to characterize the influence of information systems introduction on organizational cognitive and learning processes in the context of actual practice. Notwithstanding an upsurge in interest towards issues of organizational knowledge and Information Technology, there remain fundamental gaps in our theoretical understanding and empirical characterization of the implications of software on organizational cognitive dynamics.

Our main hypothesis, as mentioned in Chapters 1 and 2 is that the introduction of Integrated Software Systems (and related software-based technologies, such as rapid prototyping), reconfigure existing organizational processes and routines as well as organizational knowledge and learning processes. Because of their influence on cognition, adaptation and innovation, integrated information systems exert a much greater influence on the adopting organization that it has been so far acknowledged in existing literature.

The implications of software for organizations have so far been only narrowly addressed, and, even then, mainly at the firm level and not at the level of routines; we argue that the latter approach is much more promising, in that it allows a more in-depth and sophisticated analysis based on analysing how software-embedded assumptions and 'scripts' perform in the wider context of the organization. As argued in Chapter 3, this is intended as an alternative to the Management and IT literature's principal focus on the 'impact' of software on the organization. It also indicates the need to shift our attention from the impact of IT on quantitative performance indicators (typical of BPR and Product Development literature) to the fundamental issues of how software reconfigures and, in turn, is reconfigured by organizational knowledge, learning and adaptive processes. This includes observing the influence of software on cognitive processes (i.e. knowledge selection, variation, accumulation, knowledge and capabilities integration). It also entails analysing the influence of the standardizing, rationalizing and controlling rationale embedded in the software upon the organization. Further, it also helps to highlight in which circumstances software can effectively support or inhibit organizational flexibility, adaptability, innovation and learning processes.

The three chapters that follow attempt to shed light over these and other related fundamental and under-investigated issues; they are each dedicated to a specific 'theme' which is discussed and developed both theoretically and empirically. The themes selected emerge from the combination of the theoretical issues highlighted in the previous theoretical (2) and methodological (3) chapters, with the issues addressed in this chapter. The 'theoretical' themes draw from the gaps highlighted by our theoretical review and are concerned with advancing our understanding of the evolutionary categories of knowledge accumulation, selection and variation. A new category is also introduced, namely knowledge (and capabilities) integration, which has emerged from our discussion and findings. The 'empirical' issues mainly draw from the conceptual implications of software-embedded assumptions addressed above in this chapter.

The selected themes are: (1) knowledge retention and reuse (organizational memory); (2) knowledge selection (control and flexibility); and (3) knowledge variation, and the integration of knowledge and capabilities (cross-functional experimentation and prototyping). While each chapter focuses on one of the themes, all three themes are present in different measure in every chapter. While the evolutionary theory distinction between accumulation, selection and variation is valid theoretically, in fact, it proved far less so when confronted with the complex organizational empirical and conceptual reality. For each issue we have associated a specific set of research questions, as follows:

1. *Product, process and organizational memory (knowledge accumulation)*: integrated software often supports a trend towards the standardization of existing technologies and practices and towards the centralization of knowledge into a common corporate data repository. How does this affect the balance between the reuse of existing knowledge and the creation of new knowledge? What are the organizational consequences of delegating memory to software? What is the influence of software on reconfiguring the mechanisms by which knowledge is structured, stored and reused? Which are the circumstances in which software may facilitate or hinder inter-functional co-operation and communication? For instance, how does software influence the organization's ability to strike an appropriate balance between standardization and heterogeneity, between centralization and decentralization of functions, knowledge and activities within an organization, at any point in time?

2. *Control and flexibility (knowledge selection)*: software introduction often generates a push towards greater control of data and activities, towards greater codification, restructuring and control of processes, and towards the earlier codification of design knowledge. The latter may imply at the same time increased visibility and transparency of actions by other organizational functions, and reduced freedom and autonomy of action by the engineers and other practitioners. How does the introduction of software alter the balance between informal and formal, tacit and codified, computer-embedded and people-embodied knowledge? How do formal, standardizing tools and informal, flexible practices co-evolve? How can we characterize the influence of software systems on the organization's ability to react to the threats and to effectively exploit the opportunities brought about by change? What is the role that software performs in supporting or hindering control and flexibility of product, process and organization?

3. *Experimentation and prototypes (variation and knowledge integration)*: software introduction often provides an incentive towards stronger

centralization of knowledge and activities around a single (virtual) product model which becomes the common reference for the whole organization; it also often triggers an increase in the articulation and codification of engineering design knowledge, as well as reshaping the ways in which multidisciplinary knowledge is integrated and embedded into artefacts and the way inter-organizational conflicts are absorbed. How does software adoption affect the modalities by which heterogeneous knowledge sources (i.e. from various functions and domains) and knowledge types (i.e. tacit, articulable and codified) are integrated across the organization? How are new knowledge and capabilities integrated into existing ones? Does the use of integrated software systems facilitate or hinder the process of transfer and co-ordination of heterogeneous knowledge sources across various development, manufacturing and administrative functions? And how are organizational functions able to collaborate while maintaining divergent knowledge, interests and viewpoints?

While the above derive from the original research questions presented in the introductory chapter (1), these have been here revised and expanded to incorporate the knowledge acquired during the later stages of this book. In attempting to answer these questions, the following chapters will examine the influence of software on the organization in detail and in the specific context of software implementation and use. In particular, all of the theme chapters are concerned with one or more aspects of the wider integration issue: Chapter 5 addresses the issue of integrating different (software) technologies and organizational functions; Chapter 6 deals with the integration of formal and informal processes as well as tacit and codified knowledge; Chapter 7 discusses the issue of the integration of different knowledge sources and knowledge types across the organization as well as the integration of new and existing organizational knowledge and capabilities.

NOTES

1. Software below 'middleware' configures the platform upon which both middleware and end-user applications operate. The Integrated COTS software market segment has experienced outstanding growth during the past decade.
2. Related applications that belong to the same integrated platform include Computer-Aided Design (CAD), CAD Data Manager (CDM) and Virtual Product Data Manager (VPDM).
3. Forecasters have predicted that this trend will hold in the near future as larger enterprises broaden the scope of their adoption and migrate towards the second generation of integrated systems (Product Lifecycle Management technologies or PLM), and as the market for integration increasingly opens up to smaller sized firms (Miller, 1998). The consulting and research firm CIMdata, Inc. has recently reported that, despite the general economic downturn, the worldwide collaborative Product Definition management (cPDm)

portion of the Product Lifecycle Management (PLM) market grew 25 per cent to reach $3.6 billion during 2001 (Amann, 2002).

4.   This strategy can help to make a product the standard product of choice in one or more industry-specific markets, as our software's leadership in the aerospace and automotive sectors illustrates.

5.   In focusing on the software producers and users' *perception* of BPR and its merits, this chapter it is not concerned with either testing the validity of BPR's assumptions or its worthiness as a strategy or a management philosophy.

6.   This is not surprising when considering that, after the military, aerospace organizations were among the principal and earliest adopters of integrated systems.

7.   Chapter 6 discusses the circumstances in which software may affect flexibility.

8.   Integration can be rendered more effective, in this case, by setting up a partnership between the software developer and user organizations and by maintaining a consistent platform across tools and functions.

9.   This issue is discussed further in Chapter 5.

10. There are obviously a number of other reasons why firms decide whether or not to adopt integrated systems. These range from financial conditions and management style, to the imitation of the competitors' strategies, to an obligation for subsidiaries to follow the main company's strategy. This book intentionally leaves these reasons aside in order to focus upon cognitive motivations.

11. For example, processes can be characterized in terms of: product development functions involved, development support function, communications, data creation, data types, data use, data flow, etc.

12. The author's involvement in the IPD project was justified and indeed sought out as a form of strategic collaboration (university–industry).

13. This is often referred to in IT literature as the 'continuous building site' problem.

14. According to Ward (1987) the adoption cycle within an organization moves from a 'turnaround stage', whereby a high level of organizational resources are used to support the implementation and the benefits generated by the software are low, to a 'strategic stage', whereby the resources consumed are still high, but so are the benefits, to a 'factory stage' where resources are low but benefits high, to finally reach a 'support stage' where resources employed are low but so are benefits (in Brady, Tierney and Williams, 1992). Obviously the factory stage is the most desirable for the organization. The cycle of software development, however, is so fast that by the time an organization has moved to the strategic stage and begins to draw the benefits of the implementation, a new system comes in to bring the organization back to the turnaround stage.

15. It is important to emphasize the term 'quasi', as full integration reflects often an ideal situation rather than what firms experience in practice.

16. Originally the author had negotiated access to all stages of the DMU implementation. However, due to factors that arose in the firm's external environment, the project completion was substantially delayed so that the final implementation stage stretched beyond the period allocated to the fieldwork.

17. The CAD software that is the object of this study is the leading application in the worldwide automotive and aerospace CAD markets; it belongs to the market for integrated Commercial-Off-the-Shelf (COTS) software solutions, together with other software tools such as CAD Data Manager (CDM) and Product Data Manager (PDM). The integrated solution is also known as PLT or Product Lifecycle Technology.

18. CDM uses hierarchical tree structures, and enables 'zoned mock-ups', where parts are added as a consequence of their association with or proximity to another component. The elements addressed by the CDM environment implementation are: 1) *design hierarchy*, the control of model status and the authority of any user to either modify a given model, or change its status either vertically (WIP to Check to Release status), or horizontally (version or revision status); this is aimed at providing improved data access: the Product Structure Tree provides information on the structuring of data in an easily understood format, enabling the designer to find the data required for him/her to design his part with the correct and desired interfaces to associated parts; 2) *design working process*, whereby existing processes in various engineering functions (e.g. Vehicle Engineering, Body Engineering and Chassis) are mapped into the CDM environment, with a view to redesigning the process where possible with reference to best practice; 3) *design working practice*, is customized within the CDM environment to each engineering function, given that each function generates its design data using different methodologies within the boundaries of the common core tool.

19. A Bill of Materials is an ordered list of the parts, sub-assemblies, and assemblies and raw materials that define a product. Normally created and maintained within the Project Structure Management function (or Engineering Release function), it defines the type, number, quantity and relationship of parts and assemblies (software manufacturer's web page).
20. STEP AP 203 is the international standard for the representation of product model data for configuration-controlled 3D designs of mechanical parts and assemblies (software manufacturer's web page).
21. CORBA is based on the assumption that a component of a distributed system can be constructed independently from all other components, so long as the object interfaces it provides are well defined, the (external) object interfaces it uses are well defined and there is a standard means for performing the invocations over the network (www.omg.org).
22. CAx includes Computer Aided Design (CAD), Computer Aided Manufacturing (CAM), Computer Aided Engineering (CAE), Computer Aided Industrial Design (CAID), etc.
23. Other software applications were also considered; these comprise specialized high-end applications such as Finite Elements Analysis (FEA) software, company-wide communication software such as Lotus Notes, product administration databases such as Total Modular Statement (TMS), sketching and drawing applications such as Alias Studio, and several others. In an integrated environment, these individual applications are often integrated or interfaced with the main generic integrated system.
24. Here intended in the narrow sense of automatic procedures (see Chapter 2).
25. At Nissan, for example: 'A flexible communication system [PDM] ensures that information is shared among design engineering, prototype engineering and manufacturing throughout every stage of the vehicle development process' (www.nissan.na.com). This includes manufacturing input during the design phase, feedback from the design department, which is incorporated into the product and components, and design refinements as engineering and production trial begins.
26. According to a rigid authority system, some engineers/administrators are authorized to change a release set of data or product (part, assembly, system) configuration. Others in the organization can instead only view the part, but are not authorized to modify it.
27. There is no agreement around the definition of Virtual Product (VP). The VP is one of those concepts that, while being used in an extreme variety of contexts, is very often attributed different and diverging meanings. Within a user organization, the definition of VP provided by the software vendor acquires many different interpretations. Such divergence of meanings, however, is not always counterproductive as agreement is less important than the co-ordination of efforts and intents, as argued in Chapter 7.
28. For a deeper discussion of the notion of Virtual Product see Chapter 7.

5. The Influence of Integrated Systems on Organizational Memory[1]

Software systems exert a fundamental influence on the organization's ability to create, store, retrieve and reuse knowledge. Specifically, their introduction provides a substantial push towards the codification of organizational knowledge and practices at the adopter organization. This chapter argues that codification, and the subsequent delegation of organizational memory to software, entails fundamental structural transformations to organizational knowledge and routines as these are reconfigured and replicated in the form of new computer-embedded representations. It demonstrates that the process of embedding knowledge and routines in software holds fundamental implications for the ability of heterogeneous organizational groups, functions and communities to co-ordinate their efforts and share knowledge across function-, discipline- and task-specific boundaries.

INTRODUCTION

The recent diffusion of information and communication technologies (ICTs) has provided a strong push towards the articulation and codification of organizational knowledge and practices. Scholars, for example, talk of fundamental changes to the mechanisms of replication of organizational knowledge and routines being brought about by codification and the introduction of 'inscription technologies' (cf. Foray and Steinmueller, 2001).

As a result of such advances, increasing amounts of organizational knowledge or 'memory' are being embedded in software, or related computer-based media.[2] Integrated information systems, for example, contain centralized data repositories that are specifically designed to store and co-ordinate all knowledge and activities that contribute to the definition, engineering, production, manufacturing, and maintenance of an artefact across the extended organization and along its entire life cycle (cf. Chapter 1). Such repositories are aimed at supporting the organization's ability to store and integrate distributed knowledge sources and to co-ordinate and synchronize dispersed processes and actions across function-, discipline-, and task-specific boundaries.

This process of codification entails fundamental transformations to the knowledge and practices that are being codified. These transformations are of a structural nature as they involve the reconfiguration of both knowledge and routines often according to the assumptions and the rationale that are embedded in software during its design, implementation and use. We argue that such radical reframing holds important implications for the organization's ability to create, retain, retrieve and reuse knowledge.

Specifically, the act of delegating organizational (i.e. product- or process-related) memory to software raises two fundamental issues. The first concerns the process of embedding knowledge and routines in software. For example, what kinds of knowledge can be embedded in software? How is knowledge changed (i.e. reconfigured, restructured) in the process of embedding in software? What is the role of software-embedded representations? How are they created? What is the influence of software, and software-based representations, on the organization's ability to retain, retrieve and reuse knowledge and to construct 'shared meanings' across functions? The second issue concerns the reproduction of software-embedded knowledge and routines. For instance, once they are created, how are knowledge representations reproduced (i.e., circulated and adopted) across an organization? How are they enacted and incorporated in learning 'scripts'? In other words, how are such representations turned into actual expressions?[3] What is the influence of representations on the patterns of communication and knowledge sharing across heterogeneous organizational 'epistemic communities' and 'communities of practice'?[4]

This chapter argues that the process of embedding memory in software has radical implications for the organization. The case studies show that it is not so much knowledge codification per se, but the way in which knowledge is restructured in the process of being codified that holds important implications for the organization's ability to acquire, retrieve and reuse knowledge and therefore for its innovative potential. Specifically, the chapter shows that the ways in which representations are generated and reproduced across an organization can fundamentally affect that organization's cognitive dynamics.

The evidence, centred on the introduction of PDM at our main case organization, is based on two case studies. The first case study examines the influence of software on organizational *declarative* memory. The example shows that, while software aims to promote communication and the co-ordination of viewpoints and actions by imposing a single standardized product and process representation throughout the organization, it partially fails due to the persistence of local heterogeneities and idiosyncrasies, such as function-specific languages, cultures and knowledge bases. In contrast with much organizational literature, this example illustrates that organizational 'shared meanings' come not as a premise but as a result of learning activities aimed at establishing a sufficient level of coherence within the organization.

The second case study focuses on the influence of software on organizational *procedural* memory. It shows that the introduction of software restructures existing organizational processes and procedures thus radically affecting the way formal and informal knowledge flow into the product design process. Specifically, it illustrates how the assumptions and parameters used by software to manage the workflow process can obstruct experimentation and hinder informal communication and knowledge sharing in the early stages of the design process. In contrast with some Management literature's rather optimistic characterization of flexible software technologies, this example shows how their presumed benefits, such as the increased ability of functions and groups to communicate and collaborate, may only partially materialize in practice.

SOFTWARE AS A REPOSITORY OF DECLARATIVE AND PROCEDURAL MEMORY

Before we can proceed to analyse the influence of software on the processes of knowledge codification, storage, retention and reuse, however, we first need to identify exactly what types of knowledge and memory can be stored in software. A useful notion is Anderson's (1983) distinction between 'procedural' and 'declarative' memory. Procedural and declarative memory represent the *content*, or the 'what' of organizational memory (Walsh, 1995). They reside both in *social structures* and *practices*, such as shared information, group values or routines, and in *material structures* and *practices*, such as in blueprints, reports, procedures, etc. (Walsh and Ungson, 1991). Both social and material structures and practices evolve in relation to software structures and practices (and vice versa); however, because social structures and practices are more complex than the material counterpart, it is reasonable to expect that software cannot store or capture the former in their entirety (ibid.). We therefore need to identify how both procedural and declarative types of memory are reshaped while being embedded in software and during the process of memory retrieval and reuse.

PDM as a Repository of Declarative Memory

Declarative memory is 'memory for facts, events or propositions' (Anderson, 1983, in Cohen, 1991: 137); it can be stored in written documents, databases, group records, individual knowledge bases, and in intranet systems that make declarative memory widely available within an organization (Moorman and Miner, 1998). The databases or 'vaults' of enterprise-wide software systems, for example, are designed to store increasingly vast amounts of product, process and organizational declarative memory.

Product Data Manager (PDM) for example, is designed with the aim to store, control and distribute the whole of the enterprise-wide information and (codified) knowledge required for product development and beyond. Product Data Manager is designed to support the storage, organization, management and access control to heterogeneous product definition data; for instance, its vaults store systematic records of data about component and assembly drawings and their set of attributes (i.e. size, weight, where used, etc.) and options.[5] Documents relating to components and assemblies can be similarly classified, each document having its own set of attributes (i.e. part, number, author, date entered, etc.). Such software capability is intended to allow the organization's working stock of components to be organized in a clear, *hierarchical* network structure.

Product Data Manager is designed to store *structured* data, such as the relationships between parts, features, assemblies and systems that constitute a product or a technology. Within PDM, systems and parts are arranged into a multi-level hierarchy; by 'exploding' the structure of a Bill of Materials (BoM) for a specific product or item, for example, it is possible to visualize the hierarchy trees that identify the exact location of each part, feature, component, etc., within the overall product structure. This can allow an engineer to recall a complete BoM on screen, including documents and parts, either for the entire product or selected assemblies.[6] Structuring the product into a hierarchy of parts that can be easily modified and moved within a product structure is meant to facilitate the process of introducing changes at every stage of product development. Engineers, for example, can 'change an assembly by adding parts, taking away parts, or copying whole sections of an assembly tree from one part of the assembly to another' (Software Producer's Manual, 1998).

This capability is supported by the software's object-oriented architecture, which is designed to facilitate the process of the inscription of artefact structures and organizational procedures in software whilst allowing their modification as they evolve over time. Specifically, the object-oriented software architecture is designed to ensure that: (1) both product and software development can be optimized through the reuse of previously designed and tested components; in this case, the memory stored in the software is intended to prevent duplication of efforts; (2) that there is integration with other software applications that also support configuration control and manufacturing resources management; the software-embedded memory, in this case, is meant to enable higher level co-ordination among software applications and organizational functions.

Due to its data storage and control capabilities, PDM can be used to support the management of product/process changes along the entire product life cycle. For example, it helps the development team to keep track of the evolving product structure as well as of the evolution of the parts and models associated with it. The digital product configuration built into PDM is designed, managed and updated so to reveal at each query by designers, engineers, or managers, the configuration of the product and the development status of each associated part at that precise stage in time.[7]

This capability is meant to procure important benefits, including: facilitating product/process maintenance throughout the product life cycle; supporting the modification of configurations, from product definition to product release; helping to trace responsibility for failure in case of an accident; co-ordinating product development activities and stages; enabling product customization and the control and extension of product families. An example of this is the software's ability to store product configurations. Product Data Manager can store the configuration of every item that makes up a product or a technology, including all its configurational variations. In the case of a vehicle, for example, our software will store all possible configurational combinations (i.e. left-hand drive, three-door hatchback, air conditioning, ABS, etc.) for each vehicle model. All configurations are memorized in the software vault only once but can be retrieved many times, and used as input for many different Bills of Materials.

The software-embedded product configurations continuously evolve, during product development and beyond (i.e. during production, manufacturing, and maintenance). As the requirement for changes arises, the configurations are retrieved, changes are implemented and the revised configurations are again memorized in software. During product development, for example, PDM software can help to ensure that engineers are working with the most recent and correct configuration for each item (a part or a system); this facilitates the incorporation of feedback as well as preventing practitioners having to work on an outdated configuration. After product release, the software can help tracing faults in existing configurations as well as incorporating user feedback.[8]

Keeping track of past and evolving configurations can help *reconstructing* the '*whys*' and '*hows*' behind a part's design, testing or manufacturing, as well as providing a means to assign responsibilities for parts failures.[9] Identifying problems, faults and responsibilities implies a process of reconstruction, as, due to the complex socio-technical nature of decision-making and problem-solving, only a small part of the knowledge can be stored in software. Reconstructing the rationale behind a decision and understanding the process by which such a decision is implemented requires tacit knowledge and experience to re-apply meaning to the knowledge that has been codified and stored.[10]

A recent theory offers that, to the extent that software-stored information is *re-interpreted* and *re-contextualized*, it can lead to retrieving the original meaning of the embedded memory (Bannon and Kuutti, 1996). Such a view, however, is problematic for two reasons. First, in the process of embedding in software, the *meaning* of information *is 'standardized'*: only the syntax (the data) can be stored, not the semantics (its meaning). For this reason, the re-interpretation of stored information is always required. Because such interpretation occurs in the light of new knowledge, the content of the information retrieved is *changed* every time this is being re-interpreted and adapted to a new context. Second, the data stored is *'historical'* which implies that those (technological and organizational) conditions, which underpinned a choice of a configurational solution in the past, may not be any more retrievable or relevant.[11] *Learning retrospectively*, or the incorporation of new knowledge into past configurations, involves the re-interpretation of stored information/knowledge in relation to current knowledge/patterns/capabilities. While some recent software applications are designed to store also a *reduced* and *stylized* version of 'know-how' (i.e. a codified version of a routine, a formal description of the design workflow, etc.), the process of reconstituting the 'hows' and 'whys' remains essentially problematic.

In emphasizing the software's inability to translate raw data into information or even knowledge, Kogut and Zander (1992) have stated that the rationale behind a design choice is always complex so that (1) it is very difficult to rebuild the meaning of an action or decision just by looking at a 'configurational history' stored in software; and (2) it is largely infeasible to embed the tacit side of routines and actions in software. These considerations raise an important issue: if only part of the individual's or organization's knowledge can be 'captured' by software, what is it exactly that software can store, and what are the consequences of embedding knowledge in software? While the 'interpretive' literature stream has given these issues consideration (cf. Weick, 1979), it has not sufficiently investigated the organizational conditions that are required to enable the capability of interpreting stored memory and learning from the past. Our first case study shows that, unless an organization has achieved a high level of integration and coherence, the interpretation of software-stored memory can prove highly problematic.[12]

Software as a Repository of Procedural Memory

While 'declarative' memory is related to facts, theories or episodes or *'know-that'*, procedural memory is centred on *skills*, or *'know-how'* (Cohen et al. (1996). Its definition as 'memory for how things are done' or for 'things you can do', relates procedural memory to skills or routines; in its long decay times, and greater difficulty of transfer and of verbalization, procedural memory often represents tacit knowledge for individuals and organizations (Cohen, 1991; Winter, 1987).

While Computer Systems and Organizational Learning literatures have principally explained the role of software in terms of storing 'declarative' data into computer databases, we argue that there is another way in which software can play a role with respect to organizational memory that goes beyond providing a source of declarative memory to the decision-maker. As the capabilities of software systems progressively expand to include the storage, management and control of organizational processes, these are increasingly codified and embedded in software in the form of software-embedded 'routines'.[13] An important role is therefore created for software as a repository of organizational *procedural* memory.[14]

With the introduction of advanced software systems, an increasing number of organizational processes or 'routines' are embedded in software and managed through the enforcement of rules and constraints; these include the rules that ensure product/system integrity or reliability, or its coherence and compatibility with other products/systems; they also include constraints which can be of a legislative or regulatory nature or can be dictated by design requirements. Software-embedded rules regulate all changes in both the parts and model data, and their relationships in the hierarchy or product structure; acting as normative criteria they constrain changes and thus ensure their feasibility. For example, the software can help to ensure that any changes implemented are both valid and concurrent.

In embedding a set of rules and constraints, software behaves as 'dual enabler'.[15] it closes certain search spaces (i.e. technologically or organizationally infeasible spaces) while expanding others (i.e. feasible spaces). This function is intended to diminish the risk of 'reinventing the wheel', or preventing the discovery of faults or incompatibilities downstream in development, where the risk and costs of failure would be much higher. A large amount of stored memory is not in fact necessarily inconsistent with innovation as it does not by itself lead to core rigidities (cf. Leonard-Barton, 1995). In delimiting territories of exploration to those technologically or organizationally feasible, the software-embedded constraints mostly imply that creativity or experimentation can only be allowed within 'feasible' spaces. In constraining, therefore, software also enables.

There is another side, however, to embedding procedural memory in software. The process of embedding organizational routines in software is often preceded by substantial efforts to characterize and optimize all existing procedures. This operation often entails two steps: (1) the comparison of existing processes against a set of standardized procedures identified as industry 'best practice'; and (2) the modification of existing processes to migrate towards best practice and therefore realize the full potential 'promised' by the software.

The extent of 'process re-engineering' brought about by software qualifies not simply as the straightforward substitution of existing for new codified procedures, as is often suggested in the BPR literature, but as a form of 'genetic re-engineering' (cf. Cohen and Sproull, 1991) that affects the interplay between formal and informal, declarative and procedural, codified and tacit knowledge.[16] The main assumption here is that the way procedural knowledge is reshaped and reconfigured during the process of articulation, codification and inscription in software holds important implications for the organization's ability to retain, retrieve and reuse memory. How knowledge is embedded in software, for example, can influence the relative proportion of formal and informal, tacit and codified knowledge sources that become an input for the development process.

As mentioned earlier, only part of the designer knowledge can be effectively embedded in software. While the process of obtaining a solution can be codified, therefore, the process of codification is not able to fully capture *why* a particular design procedure or solution was chosen and *how* it was implemented (Bannon and Kuutti, 1996; Kogut and Zander, 1992; Wildawsky, 1983). According to the interpretive approach, since software tools are only able to capture part of the designer's knowledge (i.e. its codified, formal side), an engineer must every time reinterpret the software-embedded data or information in order to restore its meaning in relation to a new context. In this sense, memory retrieval is a type of learning in itself (Spender, 1995).

The active interpretation of software-embedded memory (especially procedural), however, is not always possible or feasible. A key characteristic of procedural memory is that it becomes *automatic* or accessible unconsciously (Moorman and Miner, 1998). As a result of its automatic character, procedural memory can have contrasting effects on innovation: on the one hand, by providing a rich vocabulary of action from which to choose, it can improve the likelihood that improvization will produce coherent action (co-ordination); on the other, a high level of procedural memory can constrain novelty, due to the habituated or uninspired use of a vocabulary pattern (Cohen et al., 1996). While this constraining effect, to some degree, may be true of all types of information stored in a memory (Leonard-Barton,

1992), its consequences are more problematic in the case of procedural memory, because this tends to be accessed automatically (Cohen, 1991).

A potential problem can arise as software tends to substantially increase the extent of automatic retrieval of procedural memory. Software can behave as an 'invisible agent' automatically triggering routines, influencing the process of beliefs formation, providing a 'path of least resistance' for action. Software-embedded memory can indeed both guide and constrain future behaviour. It can direct actions by embodying preferential rules and behaviours; and it can constrain action in a way that it is not always apparent to the decision-maker, as software-embedded rules and routines tend to sink in and trigger automatic rather than deliberate behaviour.

To some extent, and in some circumstances, therefore, the automatic behaviour generated by the unquestioning following of software-embedded rules and routines can substitute itself to active interpretation of software-embedded information.[17] Although automatic behaviour is always present in routines in some measure, this is emphasized when routines are embedded in software. During the process of inscription, for example, informal and tacit knowledge are abstracted and codified; it is the formalization of the tacit, 'interpretive' component of routines that reinforces a standardized and automatic behaviour.

Recalling Cohen et al.'s insightful characterization of routines 'as expressions' and 'as representations' we argue that only 'representations' can be embedded in software. The process of embedding in software in fact fundamentally alters the epistemic content of routines reducing them from expressions to representations.[18] In addition to this, as mentioned earlier, software embodies assumptions, and idealized, industry-standard processes that substantially reshape existing organizational processes as these are inscribed in software. The process of embedding routines in software has therefore important consequences over both the structure and content of organizational procedural knowledge.

Once we fully acknowledge the implications of delegating procedural memory to software, new issues arise that deserve further exploration. These include finding out to what extent and in which circumstances software-embedded routines, rules and constraints may induce conservative behaviour and lock-in into existing patterns of action. Our second case study will show that it is not the *level* of procedural memory stored in software that can hinder innovation, but the *formats* according to which memory is stored. The structure of software-embedded memory, for example, can influence the extent to which new knowledge and actions can become inputs for the development process.

SOFTWARE AS A REPOSITORY OF ORGANIZATIONAL MEMORY: THE EVIDENCE

PDM and the Integration of Heterogeneous Technology and Data Structures

The first case study provides an empirical account of the difficulties encountered in the process of structuring, storing and reusing *declarative* product memory, and of constructing shared meanings within a leading automotive organization implementing Product Data Manager (PDM) software. The introduction of PDM at the upstream (R&D) end of product development represents a fundamental step in the migration of technology and organization towards an integrated product development environment. The introduction of PDM at the Engineering end of development, however, appears to have created a mismatch between two generations of technologies and two Development (plus one Administrative/Control) functions that are the users of the technology.[19]

The coexistence of incompatible structures

Product Data Manager (PDM) and Total Modular Statement (TMS) are a new and an old technology used, respectively, in the Engineering and in the Production departments of our organization. Both technologies are used to manage a complex document named the Engineering Parts List (EPL), which is a structured list of all the parts that belong to the same development programme, including their relationships; the List is used to generate and maintain the evolving configuration of a product, plus all its variants, over time.

A vehicle's EPL is a hierarchically ordered list that contains all the items that compose a product's configuration (i.e. a passenger vehicle), including all of its component Systems (i.e. car body), Sub-systems (i.e. a door), Features (i.e. door trim), Assemblies (i.e. gear box), Sub-assemblies (i.e. gear stick), etc., down to the finest detail (Figure 5.1).

An EPL is compiled for each and every vehicle being designed and produced; it contains all the product variants planned for a specific vehicle programme, and it is modified over time so to reflect the most updated version for a part or system configuration. Besides managing the product's parts, the List also memorizes the relationships between vehicle systems and their components, as well as links between each of the parts and the files containing that part's description, analysis files, CAD files, etc.

The List is used by both Engineering and Production,[20] but with different objectives. Engineering compiles an EPL in order to facilitate the process of vehicle configuration extraction; this is done by extracting those parts that belong to an individual product configuration out of the total list of parts contained in an entire vehicle programme. Production uses the EPL for 'prototype verification' of fully built production vehicles. Engineering Release Systems (ERS) is the function responsible for releasing the approved, or 'frozen', Engineering List to Production (Interview/KT).

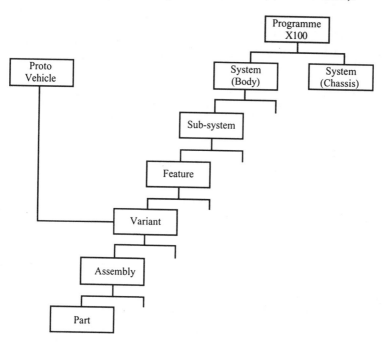

Source: Interview/KT

Figure 5.1 Schema of the EPL in Lotus Notes

While the Engineering and Production EPLs contain the *same data*, they vary substantially in the way they *structure* such data (i.e. the way they manage the relationships among the various parts composing a technology assembly). Product Data Manager and TMS technologies reflect this difference in the way they record data and their relationships (Figure 5.2). To generate an Engineering Parts List, PDM software orders product assembly data in a *hierarchical structure*, based on 'parent/child' type of relationships. Engineering Release Systems' (Production-released) EPL, instead, is characterized by a *flat file structure* where the relationships among different items and their exact position into product assemblies are captured by complicated, horizontal, Boolean statements. The more complicated is the product structure, and the higher is the number of configurational (vehicle) variants, the longer and more complicated are these algebraic statements (Figure 5.2).

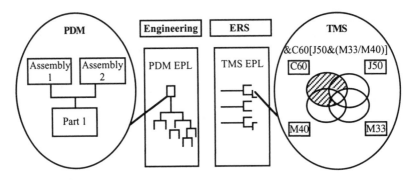

Figure 5.2 PDM and TMS EPL structures

In our organization, as a result of PDM introduction, PDM and TMS technologies are brought to coexist side by side. As a consequence, the basic incompatibility between the two different modalities in which PDM and TMS technologies organize information and compose product structures is emphasized. Product Data Manager implementation has in fact highlighted a mismatch between the way data is acquired and interpreted by two different ends of Product Development: Engineering and Production.

Before the introduction of PDM technology, both the Engineering and the Production EPLs were manually compiled with the assistance of a number of basic tools including Excel spreadsheets, paper drawings and CAD sketches. The manual process of extracting a vehicle configuration from the EPL is very complicated, given the overwhelming amount of data and configurational combinations existing for each vehicle and for each one of the vehicle variants; as a consequence, the information extracted and assembled in configurations through a manual process is liable to contain numerous mistakes. The risks involved are high, as these mistakes often go undetected until they get to the Production stage, where the configurations are tested on fully built prototype vehicles; at such a late stage, however, any major changes to parts or assemblies entail substantial disruption and significant time and profit losses, as modifying one part will have an impact on many other related parts and systems (Interview/MC). The recent increase in product/technology complexity in the automotive industry, related to a higher level of product–market diversification and customization, has greatly enhanced this problem. For each vehicle now there are many configurational variations, corresponding to the various vehicle variants and customer options. The introduction of PDM software is partly related to the intention to address this problem and to support the management and control of product variant complexity by automating the EPL extraction process (Interview/DA).

Another major motive behind the introduction of PDM and the implementation of a unique EPL across the whole organization, is the attempt to standardize and unify the actions and viewpoints of different groups and departments; this is aimed at achieving a higher level of inter-functional co-ordination and integration in design and development. The potential benefits of implementing a single, PDM-managed, EPL are, therefore, not simply related to the ability that the new technology provides to visualize and display assembly data; the act of embedding configurational data into PDM helps to ensure that the assembly data is at all times configured, controlled, synchronized and verified, and *can be shared* by different organizational functions throughout all stages of the development process, and beyond. In this sense it is intended to support the co-ordination and integration of knowledge and practices that is at the basis of the software implementation philosophy (Internal Company Document/IPDS).

According to a senior engineering administrator, the introduction of PDM at the Engineering end of PD has facilitated and possibly improved the management of the Engineering List, facilitating the process of EPL extraction upstream in product development (Interview/MC). At the same time as improving the process at the engineering end, however, the introduction of a PDM-managed List has created a fracture with the Production List; this fracture, as we have seen above, is due to the fact that TMS technology is structurally incompatible with PDM's parent/child database morphology. Because of their radical difference in structuring the data, it is not easy to shift between the two technologies. On the one hand, Production finds it difficult to understand PDM's EPL because they are not familiar with a parent/child structured List. On the other, only highly experienced practitioners are able to understand the complexities involved in structuring information according to TMS's logic. As an engineering administrator argued: 'Even with my experience I had to spend one week on this part of the configuration and found many mistakes' (Interview/MC).

Before PDM implementation, basic techniques were in place that enabled each department to independently interpret the data in order to adapt it to its own specific information needs. The two different ways of structuring data were allowed to coexist. In order to support the implementation of an integrated software strategy, however, practitioners in Production are now expected to adopt the PDM-structured EPL, which is unfamiliar to them. The PDM-EPL configuration is information for engineering because they have the knowledge required to interpret it. Production instead comes from a different sub-disciplinary background and is unable to make sense of the data contained in the engineering EPL.

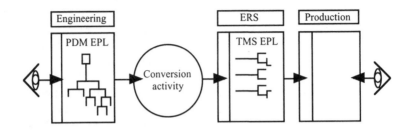

Figure 5.3 PDM and TMS Engineering Parts Lists

Engineering on one side, and Production, on the other, are looking at the same data from two different angles, and they see two different structures (Figure 5.3): 'Both Engineering and Production look at their own EPL and think it is the correct one, and that it is the other that is wrong' (Interview/KT). Clearly, neither of the two EPLs is wrong. Simply each EPL is structured in a fashion that is unfamiliar to the other function, and therefore it is perceived by that function as being incorrect. What is interesting is that the two EPLs contain exactly the same data, although this is structured differently. Engineering and Production basically speak two different configurational and database languages, corresponding to two different disciplinary and functional backgrounds.

Role of PDM in influencing meaning formation

Following the implementation of the integrated PD strategy, and the related introduction of PDM at the Engineering end of development, the parent/child typology of product configuration familiar to upstream functions is supported and becomes mainstream. This move follows the objective to introduce a single product definition that can (and indeed must) be shared by all functions. The common, standardized, product definition is implemented with the specific aim to co-ordinate and synchronize all actions and perceptions across the organization.

The PDM-embedded, parent/child-structured configuration, however, constitutes *information* only for the engineers who are able to interpret it and directly apply it to improve their processes; the same configuration is, in fact, simply *data* for Production, where practitioners are unfamiliar to the parent/child structure being instead accustomed to using Boolean logic statements to identify product combinations. The introduction of PDM upstream has therefore emphasized a pre-existing *gap* in shared meanings formation, a divide in understandings and practice between Engineering and Production. The two departments have different sub-disciplinary backgrounds (i.e. design vs. production engineering), different sub-goals (optimizing product design variants vs. verifying physical vehicles' prototypes), and different incentives.

The introduction of PDM has provided an opportunity and a strong push for the integration of upstream and downstream development functions via the elimination of existing technological and organizational incompatibilities and inconsistencies. According to the software producers, the elimination of such 'bottlenecks' can be achieved by creating a common infrastructure that supports smooth communication and the sharing of seamless information flows across the enterprise (cf. software producer's White Paper); in their view, this would support the formation of common meanings among various groups within an organization, and various organizations within an enterprise.[21] In order to achieve these potential benefits, the software-embedded rationality therefore dictates that the PDM-embedded configuration should be adopted across the entire organization; this includes downstream functions, whereby the new configuration should, in principle, replace any existing legacy technology such as TMS.[22]

This is not what took place at our case organization, and indeed other organizations interviewed were presented with similar issues. There, the decision taken was to maintain the two incompatible configurations and set up a complicated conversion procedure between PDM's parent/child configurations and TMS's Boolean algebra statements. Such a decision was due to a number of reasons including financial considerations (i.e. the costs involved in simultaneously implementing the new technology across the entire organization); business considerations (i.e. the requirement to keep the production running while the rest of the enterprise caught up with PDM technology); and technology and departmental idiosyncrasies (i.e. Production's familiarity with, and preference for, Boolean configurations, and the superior ability of TMS technology to convey Production engineers' knowledge into product definition).

According to the software producers, the seamless integration of data flows between PDM's and TMS's EPL is mandatory in order to achieve integration. Such integration in fact would allow to 'close the [communication] loop' between Engineering and Production (software producer's web page). In terms of integration, the choice to set up a conversion activity rather than enforcing the implementation of a single structure across the two functions, corresponds to the adoption of an 'interfacing' as opposed to the 'integrating' strategy supported by software producers.[23] While the implications of the decision to retain both technologies is practically irrelevant from the point of view of exchanging information flows, this has important consequences towards the formation of shared meanings.

Both integrating and interfacing in fact allow for information to be transferred from engineering to production and vice versa: configurational information from engineering gets translated into configurational information for production, via a process of conversion which is laborious, complicated and error prone, but fundamentally feasible. However, while the conversion process ensures that the syntax is exchanged, this represents a missed opportunity for the (at least partial) integration of semantics; in other words, while interfacing is an effective means to exchange data, it does not support the formation of shared meanings across functions. As a result, the two functions cannot make sense of the other's EPL and are therefore unable to detect any mistakes generated by the automated conversion between PDM and TMS structures. This resulted in greater inefficiencies and inconsistencies than existed before software introduction.

It is important to emphasize that the integrated PD strategy has created the need to restructure product data according to a standard preferential format (parent/child). Rather than promoting inter-functional co-ordination and collaboration, the new configuration has emphasized a clash in function-specific languages, cultures and knowledge bases that, until that point, had been only latent; the attempt to impose a standardized representation across heterogeneous domains has emphasized existing incompatibilities attributable to idiosyncrasies of the development functions involved:

> If you think about our organisation, but, more importantly, about our Information Management Systems, it's nothing more than taking a picture. The problem you have got is: firstly, can everybody see the same picture? *The answer is, no way, we've all got different views.* We might all say we are in the same landscape, but we all have a slightly different view of what that landscape is and what it should be. It might be the same subject, but it is a different picture; that's one problem ... the second problem is that that picture representing our engineering information infrastructure is like a jigsaw puzzle, where *each piece must fit with the next piece.* The problem is, that we don't have the co-ordination required to create or cut out the pieces of the jigsaw. (Interview/KT, emphasis added).

An important issue is, therefore, that organizational co-ordination and integration (to an extent) must already be in place in order to support the integration of Information Systems. We can say that the two strategies mutually sustain one another. This does not imply that achieving superior integration of information systems should necessarily lead to unproblematic organizational integration. While some of the existing inconsistencies are likely to be eliminated as the implementation of the integrated PD environment progresses and a common configuration technology is introduced, in fact, others are likely to remain; this is due both to the fact that organizations tend to retain at least some of their specialized legacy applications, and to the persistence of departmental idiosyncrasies even in the most advanced and successful integration circumstances (D'Adderio, 2000).[24]

The emergence of shared meanings and organizational coherence

The evidence above has illustrated how the introduction of PDM can radically reshape the process of organizational meaning formation; these results were obtained by emphasizing the difference between the integration of data flows and the integration of meaningful information. These findings unveil the limitations intrinsic in a substantial body of literature which chooses to deal with problems of inter-organizational co-ordination by focusing principally on the exchange of information flows across departmental boundaries, rather than concentrating on learning (cf. Aoki, 1986; Sanchez and Mahoney, 1996). The need for co-ordinating heterogeneous specialized function, which derives from the increasing division of labour within firms and is central to contemporary corporate innovative activities, however, 'cannot realistically be reduced to designing flows of codified information across functional boundaries. It also involves co-ordinated experimentation ... and the interpretation of ambiguous or incomplete data, where tacit knowledge is essential' (Pavitt, 1998: 14). In our case, Production engineers are not able to use their knowledge to interpret and attribute meaning to the newly structured List. It follows that supporting the formation of shared meanings across the organization is not simply about ensuring smooth information and communication flows across functions, but also, and most importantly, about integrating meaning structures.

Another important observation stemming from our analysis is that the integration of organizational meanings does not inevitably follow the implementation of integrated software technologies. In the case of our organization, the introduction of integrated systems and the implementation of a new product and database configuration has instead emphasized existing clashes and incompatibilities between upstream and downstream development functions. These inconsistencies were not previously apparent, as before there was no need for the two functions to co-ordinate and synchronize their actions and perceptions. After the introduction of software, however, 'we have to operate in concert, towards co-ordinating our EPLs. Now we have to work together' (Interview/KT). In enforcing collaboration and co-ordination between these functions, via the implementation of a common (standardized and standardizing) product structure representation, the integrated strategy has therefore highlighted existing incompatibilities, as 'people often cannot see what they take for granted until they encounter someone who does not take it for granted' (Bowker and Star, 1999: 44).

In our case, therefore, rather than resolving inconsistencies as some economists have argued (cf. Cowan and Foray, 1997), software implementation and the subsequent codification and inscription of the product structure in software has created *new* bottlenecks. These emerge as a consequence of rendering the existing manual procedures and informal languages obsolete, while forcing all functions to draw from the new, engineering-structured and management-enforced List. Codification, in our case, has involved the radical re-ordering of the knowledge relating to the product structure according to a specific format that is heavily biased towards the engineering language. Standardization, and the replication of such a format across the organization has proven more difficult than predicted.

Our example can be thus interpreted as a failed attempt to create a common (artificial) language by a means of standardization. The objective of integrated systems implementation was indeed to eliminate the inconsistencies among functions by introducing a common configuration that would allow different disciplines to communicate while maintaining their specific point of view. This strategy has encountered significant resistance, also due to the persistence of heterogeneous, local, discipline-specific languages, technologies and understandings across the various organizational functions. This has emphasized a trade-off between enforcing standardization and preserving heterogeneity which is particularly significant in relation to the implementation of integrated software technologies; as Bowker and Star put it: 'a core problem in information systems design is how to preserve the integrity of information without a priori standardization and its often-attendant violence' (1999: 50). The issue of the persistence of heterogeneity (i.e. local knowledge 'pockets') across organizational domains has been also referred to as 'stickiness' of departmental contextuality of internally generated knowledge (Von Hippel, 1994). This dictates that, even in ideal implementation circumstances, differences in interpretation of the same data are likely to persist as they correspond to the idiosyncrasies that characterize different groups within the same organization.

A successfully implemented unique configuration could act as a standardizing device by helping to synchronize perceptions across heterogeneous domains, therefore, differences in interpretations are likely to persist. These differences in tacit knowledge, perceptions, interpretations, goals and incentives within and across an organization have not been emphasized by organization scholars who have instead often taken the notion of shared meanings and organizational coherence as given. The ability to achieve shared meanings comes not as a premise but as a result of learning activities aimed at establishing a sufficient level of coherence within the organization. In other words, rather than given, shared meanings and organizational coherence are 'emergent' systemic phenomena that must be explained, rather than assumed (cf. Cohen and Sproull, 1991; Holland, 1992). This emphasizes the need to unpack the concept of 'organizational culture' to study this as an emergent property that requires to be continually reconstituted.

Observing the processes by which our organization dealt with the escalating conflicts has helped us to characterize the circumstances in which shared meanings and organizational coherence can be achieved. We have shown that coherence, in our case, depended on the organization's ability to achieve a balance between forces driving the organization towards greater heterogeneity or greater standardization. Such tensions were exasperated by the implementation of integrated software-based environments and the consequent push towards standardization. We have demonstrated that not so much the *increase* in codification but *the way* in which codified knowledge is stored and structured in the process of embedding in software, as well as the way in which knowledge was reproduced through standardization, constitutes a constraint that can influence significantly the ability of individual functions to interpret data and to draw meaningful information.

PDM and the Management of the Engineering Workflow Process

The second case study focuses on the implications of delegating *procedural* memory to software. It analyses the case of embedding the engineering 'workflow' process in software and explores the consequences of this for the organization. Specifically, it shows that while software-embedded procedural memory can introduce coherence, support economy of action and facilitate the synchronization of efforts, it can at the same time obstruct informal actions and knowledge exchanges across design teams and organizational functions.

Workflow process definition and control

The management of the design workflow process is a complex task. During product development, many thousands of parts need to be designed; for each part, files need to be created, modified, viewed, checked and approved by many different people, many times over; different product parts call for different development techniques and require different types of data (solid models, circuit diagrams, analysis models, etc). Because work on any of these files has a potential impact on thousands of other related files, there needs to be continuous cross-checking, modification, resubmission and rechecking. Due to the sheer amount of chain-induced changes, it is not uncommon for an engineer to be working on a design that has already been invalidated by the work someone else has done in another part of the programme (Interview/MC).

Our automotive organization has implemented PDM software with the aim of bringing order into their workflow process; the software acts by disciplining and controlling the progress of each project by breaking down the workflow process into several different 'states' and by using predetermined 'triggers' and 'routings' devices in order to enforce these states.[25] Complex rules about the levels of 'authority to change' are embedded in the software, in such a way that only one department (or few people) at one time are allowed to implement changes to a configuration, while everyone else is only able to view it, by calling it up on their computer screen (Interview/NG). This represents one way in which PDM can manage the design workflow process. Different PDM systems may differ in fact in how much flexibility they permit within the framework discipline.[26] The most rigid systems, such as the one adopted by our case organization, utilize strict procedures to control the project's progress. There, every individual or group is made to represent a state in the procedure: 'initiated', 'submitted', 'checked', 'approved', 'released' (Internal Document/WIP). According to this procedure, a file record cannot move from one individual (or group) to the next without changing states. Every time, for example, an engineer working on a design wants to confer with colleagues as to the best way to approach a design, the system imposes that a change of state is triggered. Another way to express this is to say that, in this case, the 'authority to change' moves around with the file. This can constrain substantially the engineer's ability to communicate with others in the development team, as illustrated below.

The product engineering workflow
This is the process that regulates the handing over of a released configuration from Design to Engineering, ERS, and Production through many controlled 'release' (or 'freeze') stages. As part of the implementation of an integrated PD environment, the management of the workflow process is being delegated to Product Data Manager (PDM) and CAD Data Manager (CDM) software.

Before being inscribed in software, the Product Engineering workflow is articulated and codified into a structured chart; the chart shows the workflow through the various changes of status of each part, from Work-in-Progress (WIP) parts through to full released (USE) status parts. The workflow chart, at our organization, reads as follows (Figure 5.4):

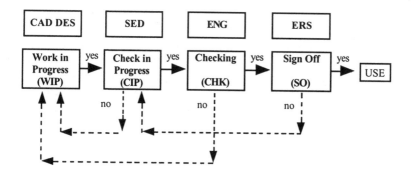

Figure 5.4 Workflow process

1. The CAD designer assigns the Work-in-Progress (WIP) status to a CAD model to generate a design solution. When design is complete, the CAD designer will change the status of the model from WIP to Check in Progress (CIP) and pass the model on to the Surface Engineer (SED) and Product Engineer (PED).
2. The SED and PED check the engineering content of the model; if this is not satisfactory they reset the status to WIP and pass it back on to the CAD designer for modification; if it is satisfactory they revise the status to CHK (Check) and forward the model to the Engineering Release System (ERS) group for release to Production.
3. The ERS group can either release the model by changing the status to USE or return it to the SED/PED for any required changes whilst resetting the Status to WIP.

This chart is then recorded into the CDM database, which is a relational database specifically designed to control the data and thus the workflow within the Product Engineering environment. CDM controls: (1) the evolution of a CAD model (status), which defines the position at which the part is considered to be at any given time, as it progresses to full released status; (2) who is the designer (or group) responsible for that model at any stage in time (ownership) (Software Producer's Manual, 1998).

The CDM database stores the specific attribute prerequisites that control the change of status of a CAD model from the beginning through to release; this will ensure that, before a change of model status and ownership can be instigated, the system will perform a number of checks to ascertain that these changes are feasible and compatible (Internal Document/DMU). In the CDM environment, CAD models are attached to the Product Structure Tree where the relationships between parts and systems follows the parent/child structure mentioned in our earlier example; models of any type can be attached to the

Tree, as long as they are model types recognizable within the CAD application adopted (e.g. Finite Elements Analysis, illustration, Kinematics, Assembly, Surface Data, Standard, Part, Package, etc.). Each CAD model is individually and temporarily 'owned' by a single user (engineer), who is the only person who has the privilege to update the model. Each user is able to relinquish ownership to a predetermined group of other users. A privileged user is also able to change the ownership of a model among a predetermined group (ibid.).

Co-ordinating such a complex workflow effectively requires the definition of the interdependence of the design tasks. PDM does this by creating a hierarchical relationship between files (i.e. the system can be instructed to prevent an engineer from signing off an assembly for release until all its individual parts have been released). A problem with this class of PDM systems is that the system can only handle data which has been *already released*, i.e. by an engineer or a group of engineers; the software cannot handle a *mix* of released and work-in-process data, which is typical of an evolving configuration. Within PDM, therefore, a model, file or record cannot move from an individual or group to the next without first changing status. The control exerted by the freeze/release procedure embedded in the software is such that the authority to change moves around with the file, does not remain with the design originator; the file, therefore, cannot be shown to other people who have a different level of authority (i.e. people outside the particular design group or in other organizational functions).

There are two major implications. First, a problem may arise when the type of control exerted by PDM systems is applied at the early stages of development. Introducing a strong emphasis on administrative product control so early in the development of the product could decrease the innovative potential of the overall development process. For example, only released configurations (i.e. finished work) can be passed on to others, meaning that the designer cannot easily obtain feedback from other colleagues. The level of interaction in the Product Engineering environment, instead of improving, is likely to be hindered. In these circumstances, PDM may restrict the potential for co-operation across functions/disciplines, as authority to change is attached to status, and a file cannot be shifted around unless its status is changed.

Second, PDM does not facilitate the *exploration* of many technological and configurational alternatives, because it cannot handle mixed 'development' (WIP) and 'released' (USE) part data. This means that a designer may not be able to adopt a part (or file) taken from previous development programmes and use it in a new configuration, because the old parts hold a released status, while the parts they are working on are still WIP. This may also cause the premature freeze of a design, because it does not allow the designers sufficient scope for trying out different alternative configurations. This process inflexibility can in principle restrict the innovation potential of the development process significantly.

If the rules embedded in the software would allow for authority to be detached from the CAD file (i.e. if the software was able to handle a mix of released and development data), than the designer could potentially more easily interact and gain feedback from his/her colleagues, as is the case of some PDM systems. Other PDM systems, in fact, make it possible to give the task an identity of its own, separate from the people working on it. These systems use 'packets', which allow the engineer to manage and modify several different master documents simultaneously, as well as providing various supporting documents for reference. In this latter case, not only each packet's route through the system must be controlled, but also the relationship between packets (Interview/MC).

By emulating paper-based processes, packets can facilitate the sharing of documents among team members. For example, although only one user can work on a 'master' design, colleagues working on the same project can be instantly notified that there is an updated master design and reference copies will be made available to them in their own packets. Packets also make it possible to move work around from department to department or from individual to individual, in logically organized 'bundles'. When an engineer requires the opinion of a colleague on a design, they can pass the entire job across to anyone else, as long as the master model and all the associated reference files are contained in and controlled by a packet. This operation will not trigger a change of state; besides, the formal workflow procedure is uncompromised by this informal re-routing because the authority to change the file's state does not move around with the packet, but remains with the designated individual (or 'owner').

This example demonstrates how software-embedded rules can potentially produce lock-in effects as well as obstructing flexible or innovative behaviour. While, on the one hand, the software-stored memory prevents 'reinventing the wheel' as well as co-ordinating and economizing efforts and producing coherent behaviour, on the other it can introduce rigidities by preventing the exploration of numerous alternative technology configurations and by obstructing informal interaction among engineers.

Observations about procedural memory and software
The previous example has illustrated how software can influence the organization's ability to maintain flexible processes that allow the reuse of stored knowledge, the input of new knowledge, and substantial exploration and search for alternative design solutions. Stored procedural memory, however, does not necessarily induce conservative behaviour; it is rather the

way in which such knowledge is structured (i.e. according to authority levels) that may be conducive to inertia. In the case illustrated it is the way in which procedures and rules are stored in software that can either help or hinder the possibility to 'capture' new knowledge as well as integrating informal knowledge in this formalized process.

By codifying procedures and specific sets of rules in software, certain actions are *constrained or impeded* (not necessarily implying that they cannot be bypassed, but that they can only be bypassed at great expenditure of resources, time or effort) while others are *supported, and encouraged*: software performs as 'dual enabler'. The control exerted by software ensures that the actions taken by the various functions during PD are coherent and synchronized. This can facilitate control and co-ordination as well as collaboration within and among development functions/groups. Thanks to such coherence, all departments can follow up the configuration as it evolves and deliver their input in the development process in a timely manner (concurrency, in other words). At the same time, however, the rules 'frozen' in software can hinder communication and informal exchange among designers and across functions.

Naturally, the interaction among engineers is rather more complex than exchanging files through wired connections. Designers can indeed share precious knowledge in very informal situations, and this remains a fundamental means for knowledge transfer, even after software implementation. The issue, however, lies in the fact that the behaviour 'embedded' in software often becomes invisible and/or unquestioned, and can therefore have greater influence over the final result than it may initially appear. The automatic behaviour embedded in software tends to become part of the status quo, 'the way we do things around here', and therefore its influence can be deep, pervasive and inconspicuous.[27]

An engineer can avoid the rules and procedures enforced by the software; he/she has some degree of freedom in establishing when and how to follow a rule supported by software, and when instead not to comply and to 'work around' it instead. Workarounds are in fact an integral part of the design process (Gasser, 1986); they represent a recognized way to introduce flexibility, variation and tacit knowledge in the process. While practitioners can in principle work around computer-embedded rules and assumptions, however, this is not always feasible. First, often actions and process steps are triggered automatically; as they often become 'invisible' to the eyes of the engineers, processes embedded into the software are often followed without questioning. Second, software embodies controls and switches that cannot be easily bypassed. Scholars have named those properties of software that inhibit customization as the 'power of default' (Koch, 1998).[28]

This case study has therefore shed some new light over the role of software in storing procedural memory, as well as over the process of embedding organizational routines and rules in software. The evidence presented has shown that the introduction of software restructures existing processes and procedures thus radically affecting the way formal and informal knowledge flow into the product design process. In contrast with the Management literature's often optimistic characterization of flexible software technologies, this example has shown how their presumed benefits, such as increased flexibility and ease in communication, may only partially materialize in practice. The case study has also illustrated how routines are changed in the process of software implementation; we have seen that this does not simply involve straightforward codification of routines but re-engineering of the way knowledge streams flow into the process. We have seen that delegating procedural memory to software can induce automatic behaviour that can in turn prevent the exchange of informal knowledge among designers working on the same development programme. We have shown the assumptions and rules to which software-embedded routines are subjected can induce conservative behaviour. This can hold important consequences for the extent of innovative potential of both the design workflow process and its outcomes.[29]

CONCLUSIONS

This chapter has shown that delegating memory to software bears important implications for the organization. Our evidence has demonstrated that software fundamentally reconfigures the very mechanisms by which organizational knowledge is structured, stored, retrieved and reused. We have argued that, in the attempt to impose a new, common, 'language', software generates a push towards greater standardization and reduction of technological and organizational heterogeneity (i.e., local, idiosyncratic 'dialects'). We have shown how, while the newly introduced (standardizing) 'language' and routines were aimed at reducing the duplication of efforts and at improving co-ordination by eliminating inconsistencies of data and actions across the organization, they clashed with existing organizational heterogeneities; these took the form of various 'epistemic communities' and 'communities of practice', each having their own knowledge base, culture, objectives, incentives and discipline- or activity-specific languages.

In our example of the two (incompatible) product structures, we have argued that the attempt to standardize across such heterogeneous organizational domains has paradoxically emphasized those existing inconsistencies and differences in knowledge bases and cognitive structures across functions. We have shown that, while standardization may eliminate some technological and organizational bottlenecks as some economists have argued (cf. Cowan and Foray, 1997), it also tends to create new ones. Our example can indeed be conceptualized as a failure to impose a common, artificial language, due to the persistence of local 'dialects' (i.e. existing database structures, technologies and routines). In other words, it can be argued that the software-embedded product and database structure have failed to perform as a 'boundary object' (Bowker and Star, 1999): the new structure does not in fact possess the interpretive flexibility required to support collaboration among heterogeneous functions; rather, its behaviour is more similar to that of an inflexible 'standardizing device'.

Achieving shared meanings in a heterogeneous organizational setting therefore requires more than the mere co-ordination of information flows advocated by some economists: it requires the integration of (often) incompatible meaning structures. The heterogeneous groups and functions that compose an organization significantly differ in their ability to learn, interpret, know and memorize. These inconsistencies are often heightened by the introduction of software, which tends to disintegrate existing organizational patterns while challenging the stability of existing routines.

This case study has shown therefore that it is necessary to 'unpack' the concept of *'organizational culture'* that characterizes much Organization and Innovation Theory; organizational knowledge bases, language, culture, objectives and incentives, rather than being static and homogeneous, are instead the result of a *continuously emergent* equilibrium among conflicting and incompatible elements.[30] A similar point was raised by Brown and Duguid who advocated the need for studies that account for the divisions created by 'communities of practice' and 'epistemic communities', which produce noticeable 'local' variations in the organization's landscape in terms of knowledge, language and culture (cf. Brown and Duguid, 2000).[31] Similarly, organizational 'shared meanings' are not given but require instead to be *continually reconstituted*: they are not the premise but the result of (and a measure of) techno-organizational integration and coherence. Rather than fixed, they are emergent properties. This leads us to a fundamental paradox for the organization: the need to exploit heterogeneity (of knowledge and practices), therefore fully exploiting the advantages of specialization, while at the same time reaping the advantages of software-induced standardization. Heterogeneity must (and indeed does) remain, but needs to be co-ordinated.

In the second case study we have examined the implications of delegating procedural memory to software. We have argued that software performs as a 'dual enabler', providing guidance and constraints that allow and support some actions while constraining or obstructing others. Further, due to the tendency of software-embedded rules and routines to sink in and become invisible to the eyes of the decision-maker, circumstances are created where active interpretation is replaced by passive, automatic behaviour. We have concluded that, while software introduction can support the synchronization of efforts and economy of actions, therefore, it can at the same time entail a risk of lock-in and reduced flexibility.

Our example has shown how rigid software-embedded rules (i.e. workflow status) and assumptions (i.e. definition of roles and authority to change) can obstruct informal actions and flexible behaviour. Specifically, we have observed how the strong emphasis on administrative process control introduced by software can reduce the scope for interaction among designers and the opportunity to obtain feedback from other functions. Inflexible software-stored parameters and procedures can also reduce the scope for exploration of alternative product configurations, causing an early configuration freeze.

Similarly to our first example, this has lead to the conclusion that the way knowledge is configured while being embedded in software (i.e. according to specific software-embedded assumptions) can, at different times, support conservative or promote innovative behaviour. Further rigidities can emerge as a consequence of the often unquestioned, repetitive behaviour that follows the conversion of routines as 'expressions' into computer-embedded 'representations' that are replicated throughout the organization.

These results have highlighted the need to add to the Evolutionary Economics' characterization of routines by exploring the *unstable elements* that challenge existing knowledge bases and alter the patterns of routines.[32] Our evidence has illustrated an example of a failure to re-establish the informal patterns of communication broken up by software implementation and emphasized the need to support the emergence of new patterns by pursuing a new equilibrium between standardized, common, and flexible, function- or activity-specific knowledge and routines. Studying the evolution of routines that follows software introduction has therefore provided important new insights into the mechanics of knowledge creation and reproduction at the level of the organization.

NOTES

1.   This chapter is also available as L. D'Adderio (2003), 'Configuring software, reconfiguring memories: the influence of integrated systems on the reproduction of knowledge and routines' *Industrial and Corporate Change*, special issue on the 'Theory of the firm, learning and organisation', 12(2), April. A short version also appeared in the Proceedings of the ACM/SAC Conference in Madrid, Spain 2002.
2.   The 'organizational memory' approach builds on the idea that organizations learn and that there is an incentive to store knowledge because of the path-dependent nature of learning (Cohen and Levinthal, 1990). This follows the realization that the knowledge and experience that resides within the organization needs to be somehow *preserved*, for

instance, as members of the organization retire or move on, and also *shared* among organizational members. The ability to acquire, retain and retrieve knowledge and experience can dramatically influence subsequent behaviour. For instance, while new knowledge is shaped by old knowledge, learning produces knowledge that must be memorized if it is to be of consequence in other situations. Thus 'memory is knowledge held away from its source of application, and its retrieval a type of learning' (Spender, 1995: 4). Retaining and sharing an organization's cognitive resources is essential both to *avoid duplication of efforts* in knowledge collection and maintenance, and in promoting *consistent decision-making*. Knowledge retention and sharing also allow for *organizational competencies to be continually re-constituted* (Holsapple, 1987, in Bannon and Kuutti, 1996: 2, emphasis added). In setting an emphasis on the *processes* of knowledge creation, retention and reuse, the notion of organizational memory can therefore provide a valid standpoint to explore organizational cognitive dynamics.

3.   See Chapter 2 for a theoretical discussion of the notion of routines 'as expressions' and 'as representations'.
4.   Cf. note 2, Chapter 1 for a definition.
5.   See also Chapter 4.
6.   Software producer's web page.
7.   In practice, this is achievable only in advanced and successful implementation circumstances.
8.   In the case of aircraft component failure, for example, an organization can trace the original configuration and modify it so that new aircraft models can incorporate the improved configuration: when a bolt fails, for instance, it is possible in principle to trace who designed it, who produced it, who tested it, who maintained it, when, and how often. This capability is especially important for artefacts that are built in batches (i.e. cars, aircrafts) (Interview/NG).
9.   The 'why' is the rationale behind a certain decision; the 'how' instead represents the way in which a particular design solution was achieved or executed (i.e. the sequence of steps by which a part or system is designed).
10. Cf. note 1, Chapter 1 for a definition of tacit knowledge.
11. I.e. the designer of the part may have left the firm; the part's supplier may be out of business; the organization may have lost the competences that sustained the design/production of that configuration.
12. In this case the evidence illustrates that the substitution of software for paper and CAD sketches creates a barrier to the interpretation of information for some functions.
13. Here the word 'routines' is intended in the narrowest of its definitions (cf. March and Simon, 1993).
14. Advanced software systems, for example, can incorporate 'knowledge-based' applications, which automate small design routines, thus producing an opportunity for substantial time saving, avoiding duplication of effort, and supporting economy of action by reducing the amount of repetitive work required. These technologies capture the technological workflow allowing the software to record the procedure used by engineers in the design of an artefact (Interview/RM).
15. On the dual role of software see also Orlikowski (1992).
16. While some literature, such as BPR, has implicitly examined the role of IT in storing process knowledge, this has failed to analyse the cognitive and motivational implications of delegating organizational procedural memory to software. Our approach aims to make up for BPR's lack of attention towards the *epistemic* content of routines; it also highlights the need to move beyond the abstractedness of those theoretical contributions that focus essentially on knowledge types thus neglecting the importance of their link to organizational practices (cf. Nonaka, 1994).
17. In order to fully characterize the role of software as a repository of organizational memory, therefore, we need to shift our attention from the individual decision-maker (engineer or manager) to also account for the role of organizational routines and practices in deploying knowledge (Coombs and Hull, 1997). This theoretically entails complementing the insights provided by the 'organizations as Interpretive Systems' approach (Bannon and Kuutti, 1996; Spender, 1995; Walsh and Ungson, 1991) with those in the field of Organizational Knowledge and Learning (Cohen, 1991; Cohen and Sproull, 1991; Dosi and Egidi, 1991; Dosi, Marengo and Fagiolo, 1996; Levitt and March, 1988; Nelson and Winter, 1982). While the majority of contributions in the latter have been centrally concerned with the *stability* of routine patterns (cf. Nelson and Winter, 1982), however, we intend to concentrate on the *dynamic* evolution of routines, in characterizing how routines evolve as a consequence of software implementation.

18. Software provides an ideal ground to study the interplay of the two levels of routines: routines as expressions and SOPs. According to Dosi, the *relation between the two levels*, however defined, is a promising area of investigation' (in Cohen et al., 1996: 18–19). The inscription of routines in software (cf. the workflow process later in this chapter) provides an excellent standpoint to observe such dynamics and therefore the 'reproduction of routines'.

19. While principally involving Engineering, Production and the Engineering Release Systems Departments, the issues discussed here involve several other functions including Industrial Design and Manufacturing.

20. Engineering is responsible for designing an artefact and releasing its configuration to Production. The production function uses the configuration to build (partial and full) prototypes for testing purposes. Once testing is completed and modifications are approved, Production releases the final configuration to Manufacturing for building.

21. PDM represents in fact only one (though a fundamental) piece of the greater integrated software infrastructure.

22. While the issue of the incentives and costs associated with knowledge codification is important, this does not constitute the focus of this work, which instead concentrates on the cognitive implications of software introduction for the organization.

23. Cf. also Chapter 4.

24. The persistence of department-specific specialized technologies, languages and methods is a likely scenario for many organizations. This is attributable to several reasons: (1) legacies can be 'best in class' applications that display superior performance to the generic integrated system module that should replace them; (2) local resistance to change; (3) legacies are modified over time to embed new layers of knowledge and functionality so that eventually it is very difficult to know what kind of functions a legacy exactly performs, which makes re-engineering infeasible; (4) legacy applications sometimes represent the most efficient means to convey tacit and local, function-specific knowledge.

    The persistence of clashes and inconsistencies is also attributable to the fact that often a new software implementation project begins (i.e. the implementation of a new package, or new version of same package) before an old one has been completed. This implies that at any one time, several overlapping and in some cases clashing technologies coexist in a firm. This is known in IT literature as 'the continuous building site' problem.

25. Several sets of rules and assumptions are embedded in software at different stages of its design and deployment life cycle. These include assumptions embedded by software designers about the industry and the sector where the software is to operate; rules and models to make the software work in a specific way (i.e. object-oriented programming philosophy); and it includes also management rules, which are imposed at the user level/adoption stage. All these assumptions and rules (software-embedded knowledge) interact with organization's knowledge and processes and influence the organization's cognitive dynamics as well as its behaviour. See also Chapter 4.

26. Relative differences exist also between different revisions of the same PDM system.

27. For work about how assumptions are embedded in technology see also Pickering (1995).

28. Even visible rules are often not worked around or questioned as practitioners tend to follow the 'path of least resistance'. For example, an engineer would have to modify the software to circumvent the rule. In practice, however, not many engineers have the skills required to reprogramme such a complex software tool, or indeed have the time or motivation to do so.

29. See Chapters 5, 6 and 7 for additional examples of how software can exert an important influence over an organization's flexibility, innovative and adaptive potential.

30. Literature that emphasizes organizational homogeneity includes transactional theories, which assume that organizational members largely share the same cognitive structures (Wegner, 1986).

31. This need for studies that characterize the nature and workings of such communities has been recently reflected in an upsurge of contributions in Sociology, Organization Science, Economics and Management Theory (cf. Cohendet and Meyer-Krahmer, 2001; Cowan, David and Foray, 1998; Knorr-Cetina, 1999; Lave and Wenger, 1991; Steinmueller, 1998). This work provides evidence that contributes to deepening this debate.

32. While providing invaluable insights into the nature and role of organizational routines and capabilities, Evolutionary Economics has so far essentially focused on elements that operate towards preserving stability, such as processes of knowledge accumulation and the persistence of continuity due to path dependency. So far relatively little attention has been paid to how routines change, at times break up, or even subside. These mechanisms lie at the basis of the formation of capabilities. The need to further our understanding of the dynamic aspects of organizational knowledge creation and reproduction and capabilities

formation is highlighted in several contributions including Dosi, Nelson and Winter (2000), and Cohen et al. (1996). For further discussion see Chapter 2.

6. Bridging Formal Tools with Informal Practices: How Organizations Balance Flexibility and Control

This chapter analyses the influence of 'flexible' software systems over the organization's ability to balance flexibility and control. While authors have traditionally focused on manufacturing, this chapter discusses flexibility at the design stage, particularly focusing on the tensions generated during the handover of a product configuration from Engineering Design to Manufacturing. In doing so, it focuses on the ability of software to select which knowledge sources and actions are allowed to or prevented from becoming an input into the product definition and development process. By concentrating on how two fundamental engineering processes (the BoM freeze and the WIP process) are reconfigured as a consequence of software implementation, the chapter draws implications for the organization's ability to flexibly adapt to change and innovate.

INTRODUCTION

The issue of flexibility has recently attracted the attention of both academics and practitioners. The notion is often invoked in response to the environmental and technological uncertainty that organizations are increasingly experiencing; in the experts' opinion, the answer to such uncertainty and environmental turbulence lies in flexible products, flexible processes, flexible tools and flexible organizations. While the advantages of flexibility have been discussed in the Innovation Studies and Economics literature, however, few contributions so far have examined flexibility in the specific context of Product Design and Development; even fewer have explored in-depth the efforts required to support flexible organizations, products, processes and tools.

Flexibility[1] can be characterized as the organization's ability to react to the threats and to effectively exploit the opportunities brought about by change; it is therefore directly and strategically linked to the organization's innovative and adaptive potential. By focusing on the Design and

Development Process, this chapter illustrates some of the mechanisms underlying organizational flexibility and therefore the adaptive and innovative potential of the firm. We argue that flexibility in Product Development is related to the organization's ability to adapt to change by modifying its products and processes so to maximize the opportunities brought by change while minimizing the disruption change often entails. In particular, we demonstrate that this capability is related to the organization's ability to maintain an appropriate balance between control and variation; this in turn entails the ability to balance the conflictual elements that characterize PD and related business processes: stable, ordered elements (i.e. routines, rules and heuristics) on the one hand and unstable, unordered elements (i.e. unstructured and informal processes) on the other. The chapter illustrates how the choice of design technology (in our case an integrated software system) can exert a fundamental influence on flexibility by affecting the organization's ability to incorporate late design changes and multidisciplinary design feedback into product definition. This in turn affects the organization's ability to adapt to change and innovate.

FLEXIBILITY IN THE LITERATURE

The notion of flexibility was first introduced to the economics literature in order to characterize the ability of firms to deal with fluctuations in demand for their output. For example, flexibility in the firm's operations was defined by Stigler (1939) as those attributes of production technology which accommodate greater output variation; similarly, Hart (1942, in Carlsson, 1989) related flexibility to the firm's ability to respond to uncertainty, understood in terms of fluctuation in market's demand and market imperfections. Since then, a considerable body of research has linked flexibility and firm competitiveness.[2] Efforts to advance our understanding of flexibility, however, have so far been characterized by some important limitations.

A first limitation in the literature is that the great majority of authors have focused on methods to measure and improve flexibility in Manufacturing (Adler, Goldoftas and Levine, 1999; Thomke, 1997). In his study of manufacturing operations, for example, Upton defines flexibility as 'the ability to change or react with little penalty in time, cost, or performance' (1994: 73). Only relatively recently have authors begun to address the issue of flexibility in the context of Product Design and Development (c.f. Cusumano, 1992; Iansiti, 1995; Ulrich, 1995). In defining flexibility as 'the incremental cost and time of modifying a design as a response to endogenous and exogenous change', Thomke (1997: 105) has shown how design flexibility can have a significant impact on the development process, particularly in environments of high uncertainty and instability. In his study of the management of Product Development in turbulent environments, he has found that a flexible approach, which embraces change, is preferable to traditional models, which are based on the assumption of a clear and stable product concept and specification. Such a flexible approach hinges on a number of factors: the ability to build system knowledge that describes the interactions between product architecture and design details, to make rapid decisions on critical changes, and the ability to run rapid, test-driven design iterations; flexibility therefore involves the structure of the design itself, attribute choices made by designers, and is related to the choice of a particular design technology (ibid.).

Authors have only recently begun to examine the *link between technology and flexibility* during Product Design and Development; while inexplicably underplayed, this is a critical issue, given that technology can play an important role both in supporting and hindering design flexibility. The recent emergence of computer-aided design and engineering tools, combined with rapid prototyping technologies provides an example. These are deemed to have reduced the cost and time of design changes significantly, thus procuring higher flexibility and product development performance (Sachs et al., 1992).

According to Thomke (1997), a firm's choice of design technology exerts an important influence on its design flexibility; moreover, because of differences in flexibility, firms will pursue different development strategies with respect to the management of design risk: the lower the design flexibility, the more likely a firm will invest in a reduction of risk that a design will change. As a result of low flexibility, for instance, design changes may be prevented, by 'freezing' specifications and solution approaches and by not allowing changes that are a result of information available after such a 'design freeze'; this would occur even though a design freeze would forego significant design improvements opportunities from using information that becomes available after a design had been frozen. In contrast, high flexibility can in principle allow firms to invest less time and fewer resources on activities aimed at minimizing risk while embracing exogenous and endogenous changes as an opportunity to continuously adapt and improve products.

While these initial contributions on the relationship between technology and flexibility are valuable, they can provide a misleading impression that the introduction of new technology (especially IT based) is necessarily and straightforwardly linked to an improvement in flexibility. Due to the complex interactions between technology and organization, this outcome is far from automatic, meaning that, in order to understand the influence of technology on flexibility, we require a more in-depth analysis of technology adoption in organizations. Such an in-depth investigation can reveal important issues that so far have been largely neglected by existing contributions.

Software and Flexibility

A first issue is the relationship between software and flexibility. Often in the management and technical literature, software is portrayed as a major enabler of a flexible strategy. To date, however, analysis has been mainly confined to assessing the 'impact' of software tools on flexibility (Sachs et al., 1992; Thomke, 1997). As argued earlier (Chapter 3), this view is underpinned by a somewhat rationalistic and deterministic characterization of technology behaviour within organizations. By concentrating on the impact of software on the organization, these contributions fail to address the fundamental issue of how organizational variables, in turn, shape software configurations and therefore fail to highlight how the overall flexibility outcome is the emergent result of such complex, two-way interactions.

Specifically, such a narrow characterization of software does not allow scholars to assess critically the implications of software introduction on product, process and organizational flexibility. For example, how does software influence the organization's flexibility and adaptive potential? And more precisely, what is the role of software-embedded rules and assumptions in altering the organizational balance between control, stability and variation, instability? What is the influence of software on opening and closing design and action spaces? Which are the implications of embedding process knowledge in software? Does it favour or reduce inter-personal and inter-functional communication and knowledge sharing? How do software-embedded rules and routines interact with other, more informal, organizational processes?

The 'Object' and the 'Process' World

A second important limitation of the existing literature, as anticipated in Chapter 3, concerns the overly rational representation of the design process. More recently, authors in the field of science and technology studies (STS) have emphasized that traditional models of engineering design are rationally constructed plans whose purpose is to impose *control* by expressing how the process *ought to* work rather than how it works in actual practice. While an important part of the design landscape, formal elements of rationalization and control represent only one side of the story: the actual development process is characterized by as much informality and dis-order as by formality and order (Bucciarelli, 1988).

Bucciarelli, for example, has argued that actual design is the outcome of the interaction between an 'object world' and a 'process world' (ibid.).[3] On the one hand, there are 'object-world' elements, which include various categories of tools, such as organizational charts, plant layout, project breakdown schemes, all of which serve as *reference maps* for the design activity. The tools support the introduction of *structure* into the process by dividing the action space into a sequence of clear separate 'states'; they provide a vision of permanence, certainty and order, contributing to introduce *control* and *discipline* into an otherwise extremely chaotic process (ibid.). The order introduced by object-world elements is necessary for the organization to position actors within a structure and hierarchy and to facilitate decision-making; order also contributes to the closure of a too complex system for a cognitively limited mind, helps create the appearance of certainty, and reduces cognitive dissonance (Thiétart and Forgues, 1995).

On the other hand, there are 'process-world' elements; these include those informal elements (i.e. informal contacts, missed deadlines, etc.) that constitute an integral, but often neglected, part of the design process (Bucciarelli, 1988). While introducing potential disruption and anarchy, elements of disorder do not necessarily hinder the success of design and development activities; to an extent, they are in fact required to ensure that sources of variation and creativity can enter the process. For example, process-world elements can become a channel for tacit processes and informal actions and therefore prevent inflexibility. A process that is solely based upon orderly elements can indeed become repetitive and rigid; an excessive emphasis on order can cause lock-in into established patterns, which can eventually lead to inability of the organization to adapt and innovate.

In failing to account for the disordered and unstable side of PD, much software and management literature has missed an opportunity, first, to account for the important role of normative elements in PD and, second, to capture the fundamental dynamics of the co-evolution of formal and informal elements in PD. The constant interaction of object- and process-world elements in PD introduces *tension and conflict*, on the one hand between ordered and ordering elements which bring stability, and on the other the unordered elements, which cause instability. The ways in which such tensions between *canonical and non-canonical practice* (Brown and Duguid, 1996), *espoused and actual practice* (Orr, 1987; 1990, in Brown and Duguid, 1996), *'modus operandi' and the 'opus operatum'* (Bourdieu, 1977) and between *'time objective' and 'time in-process'* (Bucciarelli, 1988) are accommodated represent an important factor in determining an organization's ability to adapt and innovate.[4]

By recognizing this dialectic, we can move beyond the dichotomy depicted in much of the existing literature to observe how the two categories of elements co-evolve and coexist side by side as an integral part of any development process. This chapter attempts to go one step further in arguing that the tensions between these two worlds influence dramatically the organization's flexibility potential. In doing so it will address some fundamental but as yet unexplored questions. For example, how do ordered and disordered elements co-evolve, and how are they related to the flexibility, adaptive and innovative potential of the organization? What is the role of software in influencing the balance between stable, ordered and unstable, disordered elements? The ability to manage these conflicts, we propose, lies at the very basis of the organization's adaptive and innovative potential.

Automatic Routines and Individual Behaviour

A third neglected issue in the literature is flexibility as the unpredictable outcome of the interactions between predictable automatic routines and individual behaviour. Evolutionary Economists have emphasized that the routinization of activity represents the most important form of storage of the organization's specific operational knowledge (Nelson and Winter, 1982); essential co-ordinating information is stored in routines, which, in providing a unique point of reference for processes and activities and in unifying diverging perceptions, represent a place where organizational conflict is absorbed. Routines correspond to the 'regular' elements of a firm's behaviour, which help to predict a firm's response to its changing environment; they represent essential elements of stability, embodying the principles of rules-driven behaviour (ibid.).

While these contributions are fundamental in shifting the focus of our attention from active decision-making to automatic behaviour, innovation scholars have more recently attempted to reverse such an emphasis, arguing that relying solely on routine mechanisms to explain a firm's response to change may result in a deterministic explanatory mode. In acknowledging the role of routines in influencing behaviour and organizational response to change and uncertainty, they have emphasized that human beings, who make and obey rules, are free to unpredictably change them (Fransman, 1994).

Precisely how and when are rules being challenged and how this may affect the organization's adaptation and flexibility potential has not been satisfactorily addressed in the Evolutionary literature. Although very valuable in emphasizing the importance of elements of stability, persistence, knowledge and experience accumulation, the evolutionary approach has often underestimated the role played by informal and unstable elements. These include the mechanisms by which routines are continuously being challenged and modified, or abandoned and substituted by other more informal or flexible processes. While some authors have highlighted the divergence between 'routines as representation' and 'routines as expressions', the interactions between the two have not been satisfactorily explored.[5]

We therefore need to examine the *dynamics of routines' evolution* in much greater depth. For example, how do automatic routines and deliberate processes interact? The outcome of these interactions is related to flexibility and therefore to the organization's innovative and adaptive potential. When are routines being uncritically followed and when are they instead being questioned? Which are the implications of embedding rules and routines in software? How does this influence the organization's response to change and therefore its flexibility?

The Interaction of Formal Tools and Informal Practices

A fourth and final point concerns therefore the need to understand the complex dynamics of interaction between formal tools and informal practices. For this purpose, we need to turn to more recent contributions in the fields of STS and Computer-Supported Co-operative Work (CSCW). Mambrey and Robinson (1995), for example, have studied the workflow of internal documents within the German Federal Ministry of Family Affairs. They have shown how, in such highly hierarchical and rational organization, existing rigid procedures are often bypassed and intricate, informal routines emerge (in Berg, 1998). Their evidence shows that, while the formal workflow model plays an important role in the work, it does not determine it.

Other work has examined the interactions between formal tools (in this case an electronic medical record system) and the informal practices performed by doctors and nurses at a Dutch hospital's intensive care unit (Berg, 1997a). The evidence here illustrates how formal tools are attributed central roles in organizing work within many workplaces. The tools operate on circumscribed inputs using rules that contain a model of the workplace in which they are supposed to function (ibid.).

According to Berg (1997a), the studies assessing the role of formal tools in organizations can be divided in two main schools: (1) the *naïve formalists*, who believe that formalization allows for the detachment of knowledge from its local context without losing its essence, allows comparability across sites and times, and manipulation into higher-order levels of abstractions while retaining direct relevance to that which is represented; and (2) the *empiricists* who argue for the fundamental poverty of the realm of the formal in comparison with the richness of the empirical world. On the one hand, the formalists have assumed the superiority of models and the purity of their logic; on the other, the empiricists have emphasized the interpretative skills or superior flexibility of human workers. While reaching opposite conclusions, however, both schools have built their analyses upon a presumed *dichotomy* between the formal and the informal. The formal is symbolic, clean, abstract and homogeneous; the empirical is messy, heterogeneous, concrete and not (to be) ordered within one single scheme.

Others have more recently expressed the need to move beyond this dichotomy. While formal tools can indeed transform workplaces in various ways, their generative power can be attributed neither to the tool nor to the human workers: 'Rather, the generative power of this configuration lies in the *interrelation* of the formal with the informal' (Berg, 1997a: 406). Through interaction, formal tools and informal practices are co-produced; the generic tool is re-configured to model the procedures, while the procedures are re-configured to fit the tool (ibid.).

The power of formal tools then lies in the *distance* between representation and represented, in the *tension* between the tool's model and what it models; since the formal tool embodies the impoverished version of what work is like, humans working with the tool need to re-add detail or to repair the tool's functioning whenever it is used in practice (Collins, 1990). The interactions between formal tools and informal practices can therefore be described as a fragile, unstable equilibrium, characterized by never-ending frictions, loose ends, and unforeseen consequences. While devices or routines may be created to 'fix' recurrent tensions, these will also tend to generate new problems. The existence of a gap between the tool and actual practices therefore produces a fruitful tension that can generate *new capabilities*. The capacities and characteristics that formalists and their opponents attribute to the formal tool or to a human agent appear in fact to be *highly distributed* (Berg, 1997a).

It is in the light of this discussion that the notion of flexibility assumes a new dimension. For example, does flexibility exist in relation to the tool's properties, or to the processes and actors that use the tool? Or, does it instead emerge as the outcome of their interactions? In analysing the co-evolution and co-production of software-embedded (formal) and informal practices, this chapter illustrates how fundamental engineering processes (the BoM and WIP process) are changed as they are embedded in software; our evidence also shows how software rules and philosophies are revised and reshaped according to the requirements that emerge during software implementation and use. We will demonstrate that the flexibility potential of the organization will ultimately result from the (temporary) resolution of the tensions and interactions between software-embedded and local practices.

FLEXIBILITY IN PRODUCT DEVELOPMENT AND PDM SOFTWARE

Characterizing Flexibility in Product Development

While the Product Development process is often portrayed in literature as a smooth sequence of ordered stages, its landscape is in fact characterized by overt conflict, whereby elements of order and disorder, stability and instability coexist side by side.[6] On the one hand, there are *stable elements* such as established organizational routines and procedures, ordering and scheduling tools and technologies; these support a relatively smooth flow of knowledge and activities across heterogeneous organizational functions while providing common reference points to the distributed development activities, thus supporting inter-functional and inter-organizational co-ordination. On the other hand, there are informal and unstructured processes, unexpected events, and unclassified inputs from the external or internal environment that can bring instability in the development process and can function as *continuity-breaking mechanisms.*

The task of achieving and maintaining flexibility is thus inevitably related to the organization's ability to strike, at any point in time, a balance between stable and unstable, ordered and disordered elements. If, on the one hand, this balance moves too much towards stability and control, processes become excessively rigid and repetitive, and therefore variation, innovation and adaptation can be hindered. Excessive control also often implies that rigid tools and procedures are worked around, as practitioners tend to regain flexibility by reverting to informal processes. If the balance moves too sharply towards the unstable end of the spectrum, on the other hand, processes become disordered and inefficient, creating redundancy and duplication of knowledge and efforts; continuity can be endangered as well as the organization's ability to exploit its own accumulated knowledge and experience. Flexibility and the organization's ability to change and adapt are eventually likely to emerge from the continuing efforts to resolve the tensions and the conflicts that arise form the co-presence of these contrasting but complementary categories of elements.

Software systems are being increasingly designed and adopted with the explicit objective to promote flexibility. Specifically, integrated systems are designed to support flexibility by bringing greater control to the product development process. This can be achieved: (1) by providing a single common data and process repository that enables centralized data and process management; and (2) by supporting the management of product and process configurations that enable consistency and concurrency of data and actions.

While these are the aims and assumptions embedded in software at the design and implementation stages, there is no evidence of how they perform in practice. Specifically, we need to explore how these assumptions effectively influence the balance between control and variation, stability and instability, and therefore an organization's potential for flexibility and adaptation. First, however, we shall begin by briefly describing the structure and content of Product Development activities as described by one of our interviewees at our main case organization.

Flexibility in the Early and Late Stages of Product Development

The proportion of uncertainty and risk that organizations face varies substantially during the different stages of Product Development: uncertainty (i.e. the number and width of fluctuations in a product configuration) tends to be higher at the beginning while decreasing as product definition progresses and irreversible choices are made; the risk of changes, instead, tends to augment as a product design progresses along the development chain; the systemic interdependencies among parts dictate that, during later design stages, any changes applied to a product part will inevitably trigger a cascade of changes in other inter-linked product systems and subsystems. Differential requirements for variation and control should therefore be in place to allow organizations to cope with such variable uncertainty and risk conditions at different stages of product development.

The *early stages* of PD are characterized by a very high level of change, as the product definition evolves very rapidly from product concept towards the final product configuration.[7] During these initial stages (cf. curve A, Figure 6.1), a substantial amount of data is generated from the various enterprise functions (within and beyond PD); these heterogeneous data and information sources flow into product definition in a disordered manner and the product configuration begins to take shape. At this point in time, product configuration fluctuations are numerous and extremely wide, while design cycles are relatively short and design iterations very frequent (Interview/NG). Critical design parameters are changing on a daily basis. The process of implementing changes to product definition at these early stages should be very informal: the engineer in charge of designing a specific part or assembly should hold sole responsibility for decisions to introduce and control changes; as parts and assemblies are being developed separately and a final total product configuration is not yet defined, there is no direct impact on other products as changes are implemented (ibid.).

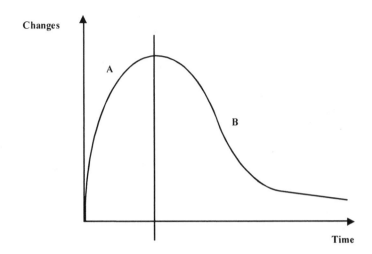

Source: Interview/NG

Figure 6.1 Incidence of change along product design life cycle

Compared with later development stages, the early stages are characterized by very high levels of configurational variation, due to the fact that the product is still highly undefined. Maintaining flexibility at this stage depends upon the ability to sustain a high level of change and experimentation; this can be achieved by providing a designer with sufficient time and scope to explore numerous alternative solutions and product configurations. A configuration freeze that is introduced too early can in fact become a source of rigidity; this is because it will not allow sufficient time and scope for numerous product variants to be generated and tested as well as because it will prevent later changes from being implemented (Interview/NG).

Further scope for rigidity at this stage can be created by not providing engineers with sufficient autonomy and 'privacy' to experiment with different alternative design solutions. It is in fact essential to allow an engineer to try ambitious solutions, which may fail, without his/her activity being exposed to people outside that specific segment of development (Interview/NG). There is therefore a rationale for keeping the design iterations generated at the initial stages of part/assembly development within a small circle of colleagues without sharing with the larger organization.[8] Control requirements at these early stages are minimal and therefore only very loose control mechanisms should be applied, as a high level of control could hinder creativity and experimentation. The design and implementation of software should ideally incorporate these early requirements for experimentation as trial and error (ibid.).

After a product configuration is *released* to Production the balance between the requirements for variation and control shifts towards the latter. At this stage, the basic product structure is defined and detail work begins, which will eventually deliver a feasible product that is ready for manufacture. Major product concept and structure fluctuations, from this point onwards, are rare and should very seldom involve changes in the key elements around which the product configuration and definition has been developed. Scope for changes at this stage is therefore minimal and essentially involves detail work (cf. curve B, Figure 6.1).

Once a configuration is released, or 'frozen', all relationships among parts, assemblies and systems that compose a product are established, and all relationships and interactions between different parts of the process and different people involved in the process are made explicit. As a consequence, an engineer's work becomes dependent upon the changes implemented by other colleagues. It follows that every change must be communicated, circulated, verified and approved before it can become operational: the process of incorporating changes therefore is formalized (ibid.). Formal control procedures are established, which are needed to preserve the integrity and efficiency of the development process as well as supporting a valid, consistent and concurrent product definition. In order to allow this, any changes must always be shared and communicated and must ideally be accessible to every interested party in the extended enterprise.

This task, however, is highly problematic due to the nature of the product configuration, which evolves constantly, as new parts are added and others modified. The dynamic nature of product configuration implies that various development functions will often be working at the same time on different versions of the same part. During these stages it is of utmost importance to determine for each product configuration the correct component parts, the right versions of each component, and the appropriate information required to complete individual manufacturing and maintenance tasks.[9] Variation and change at this stage should be reduced drastically; the need for variation is replaced by the need for control, aimed at supporting a precise product definition, which is required for optimizing production and manufacturing. Software should be designed and implemented to enable control and discipline at these later stages of product and process development.

Software and Flexibility: The Embedded Assumptions

Product Data Manager software is conceived with the aim to support flexibility by improving the organization's ability to respond and adapt to change; its philosophy supports a proactive approach towards change which consists in improving the organization's ability to introduce changes even when they are late or unexpected, as opposed to reducing the possibility for changes to occur. For example, PDM is designed to facilitate the early incorporation of multidisciplinary feedback into product definition while also allowing for the input of late design changes in response to new information coming from either the internal or the external environment.

To support these capabilities, PDM systems store and control the huge quantities of information generated by engineers during the PD process; this allows product administrators to control product life across multiple locations. More specifically, PDM is designed to manage the evolution of the product configuration after its first release (freeze); afterwards, as product definition matures, PDM is programmed to ensure that the correct design information is distributed to and accepted by the various enterprise organizations responsible for transforming the design into a finished product (i.e. Engineering, Production, Manufacturing, and Maintenance Centres) (software manufacturer's web page).

According to the software producer, these capabilities are technically enabled by the software's ability to store knowledge about the systemic structure of the product (i.e. product parts list) and of the processes and activities that are used to generate that product, including concurrent knowledge about the individuals' and functions' input into the design (i.e. design workflow). In particular, PDM embeds the following functionality: (1) *vaulting* capabilities, which control access to shared data by providing users with a single source of product information and offering access to the most current data, in principle, wherever that data resides; (2) *workflow* capabilities, to distribute data; PDM contains enterprise workflow and data controls which are designed to ensure that the product is stepped through a predefined series of states based on accepted industry 'best practice'; (3) *configured product structures* to relate data to product components across the entire product life cycle. By controlling the access, distribution, and management of structured product and process data, these capabilities facilitate the management of critical enterprise functions such as engineering change co-ordination, location of control, multiple manufacturing effectivities, advanced configuration, etc. (software manufacturer's web page).

These technical features, designed to underpin PDM's ability to support flexibility, are the result of specific assumptions embedded in the software package during its design, implementation and use.[10] First, PDM supports flexibility by imposing discipline and control to both processes and product data and structures. PDM is designed to perform essentially as an *ordering tool*, aimed at introducing *control*, structure and stability into the PD process.

According to the DMU[11] project manager at our organization: 'A flexible approach requires control – otherwise anarchy rules. PDM brings control – the key to managing flexible processes' (Internal Document/DMU). While PDM is conceived and implemented to introduce order into an otherwise unruly PD process, there is no evidence in the existing literature of precisely how its disciplining and controlling features work in practice. For example, what is the influence of software on the organization's flexibility potential? Does the software adequately take into account the differences in the requirements for control and flexibility across different stages of PD and the various organizational functions?

Second, PDM is designed to support flexibility by *selecting and directing knowledge and actions*; this may entail, for example, preventing the exploration of incompatible configurations and the implementation of infeasible changes. This can be conceptually characterized as an attempt to increase the 'fitness of design spaces' by promoting their selective contraction and, at the same time, expansion. The contraction of design spaces can be achieved, for example, by disallowing actions which are inconsistent with the actions of other individuals in the development process, or by invalidating designs which are incompatible with others being concurrently developed elsewhere in the organization; search spaces can be instead expanded by improving communication and knowledge-sharing across teams and functions and by allowing designers to attempt numerous alternative configuration solutions. While the software's selection capabilities exist in principle, we need to explore precisely how they perform in practice. For example, what is the influence of software on the designers' ability to explore alternative configurations and incorporate changes? Is the software-embedded expansion–contraction model efficient in practice as it is in theory? What is the overall influence of software's selection capabilities on the flexibility outcome of the development process?

Third, software is designed to support flexibility by acting as a *normative, standardizing element*.[12] Its implementation is followed by a push towards the articulation, codification and storage of existing organizational rules and routines, often involving their partial or total rewriting according to software-embedded assumptions and current best practice.[13] According to our manager, 'Lack of [standardized] procedures breeds low quality due to lack of data integrity, history and process repeatability – this is not sustainable. PDM can provide an environment to support flexible procedures' (Interview/DA). Software supports the introduction of prescriptive, normative elements within the design and development space, which characterize what the process *'ought to be'* rather than what it is in practice; the routines, rules and assumptions embedded in software provide a common reference point across the whole of the organization which is meant to synchronize and harmonize heterogeneous processes and actions. While software as a normative element performs an important function, its influence has not yet been explored. For example, what are the implications of the increased emphasis introduced by software on formal and codified knowledge and routines? How do codified, formal software routines interact with more flexible and informal working practices?

Fourth, PDM is designed to support flexibility by *increasing the visibility and transparency* of actions and product/process structures across PD and the extended organization. This can be achieved by loading a released design solution into a common PDM-managed database, which is, in principle, accessible by all the other functions. While this assumption can work in theory, its wider implications have not been yet investigated. For instance, which are the consequences of the increased transparency and visibility of design on the engineer's ability to explore alternative design configurations, to incorporate multidisciplinary feedback into product definition, and to implement late changes to a released product configuration?

In order to begin to answer these questions we need to abandon the predominant view of software as a stand-alone tool with fixed properties to explore the deeper interactions between software-embedded and organizational routines. This analysis will reveal how the theoretical assumptions embedded in software perform in practice. In other words, it will enable us to characterize how software and the organization are co-produced.

PDM and the Management of Product and Process Complexity

We begin our analysis by assessing how PDM manages product and process complexity. At the *product* level, complexity is determined by the multiple and inter-linked layers of product parts, assemblies, systems, features, etc., which are ordered in a hierarchical 'configured product structure'. Structural complexity derives from the difficulty of managing the evolving product configuration (the evolution of individual product parts, plus their relationships) and all its variants (i.e. three-door, hatchback, ABS, etc.). Managing such complex and interrelated structures is a daunting task. The vehicle programme ongoing at the time of this study, for example, included a standard vehicle configuration plus 32 different vehicle variant configurations. This meant that a very high number of parts and assemblies, and variant configurations had to be created, controlled, and maintained at any one time. A product configuration is usually managed through a variety of Documents and Processes, including the Engineering Parts List (EPL), the Bill of Materials (BoMs), and the Engineering Change and Deviation processes.

At the *process* level, complexity is related to the difficulty of co-ordinating the numerous heterogeneous and distributed activities that characterize the PD process. This involves the synchronization of development activities over time and across multiple organizational domains. Process complexity can be managed with a variety of tools including the Work in Progress (WIP) and the 'effectivity' process. The management of product and process complexity is achieved within PDM by controlling two fundamental documents and development milestones: the EPL and the BoM. The software in principle can also manage the links between the two processes, thus supporting the ability to automatically extract BoMs from the EPL. The presence of an effective EPL and BoM is fundamental to support the Digital Mock-Up (DMU) environment described in Chapter 4. The two documents are described below.

The Engineering Parts List and the Bill of Materials

The Engineering Parts List (EPL) is a means to manage structural complexity in Product Development. The List is the ensemble of all parts pertaining to a product and all its variants. A senior IT manager at our automotive organization compares the List to 'a large bucket containing all parts related to a specific Development Programme' (Interview/KT). Attached to each part in the EPL are two sets of data: (1) *base data*, concerning information about a part (i.e. part number, name, cost, weight, engineer responsible, drawing number, etc.); and (2) *usage data*, concerning configurational information (i.e. the relationships among parts, quantity, zone, functional applications, Assembly Indent, Usage Restriction Code, Source Code, etc.). The position of the parts in the EPL 'bucket', however, is not casual (Interview/KT). Far from performing as a random container of product parts, the List establishes the exact place that each part must occupy within the overall product structure.

The EPL is in fact a *hierarchically structured* description of all parts generated within the scope of an individual vehicle programme (i.e. a vehicle or vehicle family). In the List, the complex product structure is divided into several hierarchically organized levels, starting from the individual part/component at the bottom, and culminating with the entire vehicle configuration at the top of the hierarchy, and vice versa (Figure 6.2). Thus, starting from the top, each product represented in the List can be hierarchically decomposed into its constituent elements: *systems* (i.e. body or chassis), *sub-systems* (i.e. body side), *features* (i.e. door), *variants* (V-1, V-2, V-3, … Vn in Figure 6.3), *assemblies* and, finally, into the individual *parts* that compose an artefact.

The Engineering List is used to extract a vehicle's configuration, which is then verified through Prototype Build and Test. The List is created and maintained by the Engineering Release Systems (ERS) function, which is in charge of managing the production of a skeleton structure to which engineers can add information progressively, as this is being generated (Interview/MC). The List can be maintained manually, or it can be managed by PDM software, as it is the case for our organization.[14]

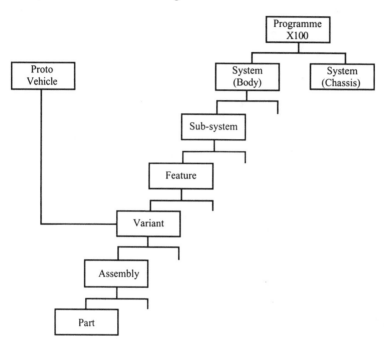

Source: Interview/KT

Figure 6.2 Schema of the EPL in Lotus Notes

While the List contains all parts that belong to an entire vehicle programme, a Bill of Materials (BoM) is an ordered list of the parts, sub-assemblies, assemblies and raw materials that characterize a *specific* product. Also created by the Engineering Release function, the BoM defines the type, number, quantity and relationship of parts and assemblies for each vehicle variant. A BoM is therefore a subset of the List. Figure 6.3 illustrates the differences between the EPL and the BoM. The EPL and BoM structures can be visualized in Product Data Manager in the '*Engineering View*' (E/View).

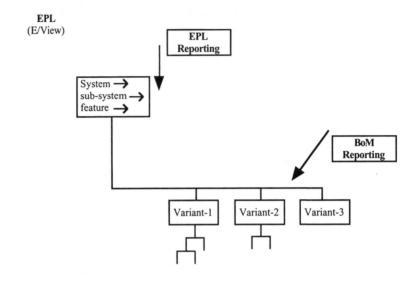

Source: Interview/MC

Figure 6.3 BoM and EPL reporting

PDM and the Management of Change

The EPL structure can be modified via two categories of change engines: Engineering Changes and Manufacturing Deviations. Product Data Manager introduces important changes in the ways these change processes are managed.

An Engineering Change Order (ECO) is any change applied to the List before BoM freeze (Figure 6.4). Its typical change cycle starts from Engineering, which raises an Order and sends it to the Engineering Release Systems (ERS) function; this implements the necessary changes to the List and the BoM, and sends the result back to Engineering (Interview/MC). Orders can be visualized in the *Engineering View* (E/View) in PDM. This is particularly convenient as the EPL structure exists only once in the E/View; because of this, any changes implemented to any parts or assemblies (for example, deleting or adding a part), need to be implemented only once to get automatically rebated in the List in all the vehicles containing the modified part affected by the change. Manufacturing Deviations instead include any changes that occur *after* BoM freeze; they can be visualized in PDM's *Manufacturing View* (M/View). The typical Deviation change cycle starts with the BoM freeze and the display of the released or 'frozen' configuration in the M/View; this original BoM can be visualized in Lotus Notes and is regularly updated with Orders and Deviations.[15]

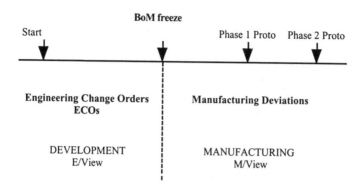

Source: Interview/MC

Figure 6.4 'Request to Change' documents

The process of implementing changes through Deviations is very complex as compared to Change Orders. In the E/View it is sufficient to implement the change once, for it to be propagated wherever the part is used; this is because in the E/View there is only one comprehensive structure from which all vehicle variants can be derived. All vehicles stored in the M/View, instead, are different as each one corresponds to a specific vehicle variant; every change introduced after BoM freeze must therefore be duplicated across all vehicle variant configurations, one at a time.

The specific process control mechanisms introduced by PDM have significantly altered the way the change process is managed. This bears important consequences for the organization's ability to achieve and maintain flexibility. Such implications are explored in the following case studies, which examine the introduction of PDM at a leading vehicle manufacturer organization.

FLEXIBILITY IN THE 'BOM FREEZE' AND 'WORK-IN-PROGRESS' PROCESSES: THE EVIDENCE

This section illustrates how flexibility and adaptation are achieved in practice in a major engineering process at a leading vehicle manufacturer.[16] The example shows how the 'Bill of Materials (BoM) freeze' process is being radically reshaped, following the introduction of an integrated information system and PDM software at the engineering end of Product Development. We argue that the changes introduced by PDM hold important implications for the ability of the organization to flexibly adapt to change and innovate. Additional evidence gathered through the observation of the changes affecting the Workflow process at the same organization is presented in the second case study.

The BoM Freeze Process

The following case study is based on a detailed account of the Prototype BoM process at the R&D end of a leading vehicle manufacturer as described by a senior engineering administrator. The emphasis is on the changes that occurred after the introduction of PDM and their implications for the organization's flexibility, innovative and adaptive potential.

BoM freeze: the ideal process
After highlighting the dichotomy between '*ideal*' and '*actual*' processes, our engineer begins to describe the idealized BoM process, which is embedded in software as standardized 'best practice' (Figure 6.5).

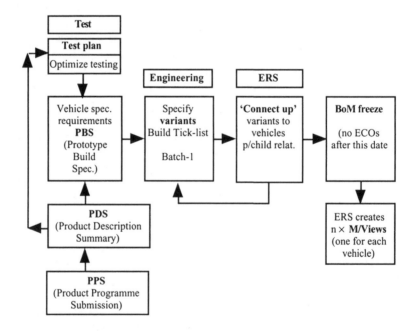

Figure 6.5 The prototype BoM process

The process starts with the definition of the vehicle specification (Interview/MC). The vehicle specification is driven by the *Test Plan* whereby testing requirements are optimized against the vehicle to be produced and its variants. The vehicle specification requirement document, named *Prototype Build Specification* (PBS) states the number of prototypes that will be required for that specific vehicle, or vehicle family.[17] Next, the prototype vehicles characteristics are specified according to the *Product Description Summary* (PDS) or marketing spec, which is a description of the standard vehicle to be produced and is driven by customer requirements, industry trends, bench-marking assessments; at other times, it can be driven by technology (i.e. testing) requirements. The PBS, or vehicle specification, is then passed on to the *Engineering Release Systems* (ERS) department, where engineering process administrators build a matrix-based tick-list in which vehicles and variants are identified and listed.

Next, the vehicle specification is passed on to *Engineering*, where it is divided into batches. Taking in consideration one vehicle batch at a time, Engineering fills in the tick-list matrix by identifying which variants are to be included in each vehicle specification. Subsequently, ERS will 'connect up' the variants to the vehicle. 'Connecting up' involves the creation of a parent–child (p/c) relationship between the variants and the vehicle. After that, when the volume of changes diminishes substantially, ERS calls the BoM freeze (date after which only small changes are permitted) and creates a number of configurations in PDM's Manufacturing View, one view for each vehicle variant configuration.

BoM freeze: the actual process

The initial stages of PD are characterized by a very high number of change cycles and design iterations, whereby parts and assemblies sustain substantial modification. Changes at this stage are implemented by raising an Engineering Change Order (ECO). These changes are normally either aimed at improving a part's design or performance, or they can arise as a consequence of other changes affecting related parts. The iteration cycles continue until the product structure and parts are completely defined and require only minor or no further alterations. The ideal process at this point dictates that Project Management should call the 'BoM freeze'. BoM freeze means that the product data and structure are sufficiently stable for the configuration to be released to production and manufacturing. Ideally, no more Change Orders should take place after the BoM freeze milestone, because these would entail unnecessary disruption for the downstream development functions.

According to our engineer, this is the point where the actual process begins to diverge from the ideal process. Theoretically, after BoM freeze, the

ERS function should create n × *Manufacturing Views* (M/Views), one for each vehicle variant (corresponding to V-1, V-2, V-n in Figure 6.3); the M/Views are created by loading specific product variant configurations into PDM software. From then onwards, the vehicle configurations must be maintained and modified individually, according to the manufacturing change requests (Deviations) as these come through. While this is what should happen in theory, the actual process is less straightforward, as the example of the X100 Vehicle Programme (ongoing at the time of fieldwork) illustrates.

The X100 is a complex vehicle programme, its complexity being partly due to the high number of vehicle variants that must be generated and the related level of data, assemblies and configurations that have to be created and maintained. By the time X100 has reached the BoM freeze milestone deadline, many parts have not yet being released, and a huge volume of change is still required before any prototypes can be manufactured: 'At this stage we are still being deluged with a substantial number of Change Orders' (Interview/MC). The process is still far away from the nominal conditions required to call a BoM freeze: the product structure is still highly unstable, the number of changes is high, and most of the changes required are still major changes. A project milestone date has been reached, whereby BoM should be frozen and whereby the product variants configurations should be moved from PDM's E/View to the M/View in order to facilitate the control of deviations. The development team however, is still lagging behind, striving to manage the enormous amount of data and assemblies.

In this instance, given the substantial amount of engineering change still required at the time of BoM freeze, the decision is taken not to create the Manufacturing Views as required by the idealized process embedded in PDM. The rationale behind this decision is that the migration from a single E/View to many M/Views would make it harder to implement serial changes, since every change must be individually propagated across each one of the variant configurations where the modified part is used. The production-oriented logic embedded in PDM is intentionally devised to control and inhibit the introduction of changes after BoM freeze. Its aim is to help control and stabilize a product configuration to the benefit of Production and Manufacturing. However, PDM works on the assumption that no major changes are required after freeze, a situation that does not often occur in practice.

In practice, many Change Orders of the type described above are still required to the first batch of vehicles (batch-1) after BoM freeze. The ad hoc solution adopted is therefore not to move the vehicle configuration from the E/View to the M/Views:

> Theoretically, engineers are not allowed to attribute a batch-1 effectivity status to an Engineering Change Order, they have to do it on a Deviation. However, most of the deviation requests we are receiving today are saying: 'please can you apply this Order into Batch-1'. Today we are beyond freeze date and yet most requests concern Orders with Batch-1 effectivity. It is clear that, if we can process that change into the E/View, as an ordinary Change Order, we need only to do it once. So that's the main reason why we kept in Engineering View. So that's what we are doing today, we are processing the Order into E/View with Batch-1 effectivity. [18] (Interview/MC)

Deluged by an excessive amount of change, the team has therefore decided to remain in the E/View. 'Today, although we are *after* the BoM freeze, we are keeping everything in the Engineering View. In the E/View you only need to make a change once, and it is automatically reflected everywhere the part affected by the change is used' (ibid.).

Given that the number of deviations incoming for specific vehicles are so few at the time of BoM freeze, while the number of Change Orders is still very high, the decision to bypass the software's rule and keep everything in the Engineering View facilitates the implementation of changes. Substantial effort would be in fact required to create and maintain the individual configurational databases in the M/View. The workaround is completed by attaching a Deviation document to the modified part. Because the change is implemented in the E/View, every time they load data from this into any Manufacturing Views, or every time they look at the data in the E/View, the Deviation document will always appear in association with the part. This way, the material specification Deviation associated with the part can always be visualized, even though the official manufacturing views have not been created.

The decision to work around the software-embedded procedure, however, holds important consequences. The software rule that requires the loading of the variant configurations in PDM's M/View is aimed at enforcing greater control over individual changes and on the way these affect each individual configuration. Manufacturing Views, for example, require an engineer to specify with precision from which view to which the change is to be propagated. For example, a rule embedded in PDM ensures that the software will create an error every time anyone tried to propagate a change where the part is non-existent. PDM, therefore, makes it necessary to be very specific as to where each part affected by the change is used, and which views a specific change is to be propagated to: 'This is due to the structure of PDM's logic, which is of an *incremental* nature, meaning that the software will allow only incremental changes and make any other type of changes very difficult to implement' (Interview/MC). The underlying philosophy of product manager and many engineering control systems is one of *sequential incremental change*:

In PDM you have to talk in terms of 'increment', you have to specify exactly what is it that you are going to change. In other words, you have a starting point today, and you can only change today's data. So you make an incremental change, which gives you a new starting point, then you can make a further incremental change, then a further incremental change etc. but they are all based on what has happened before. That gives you very clear control over the changes that you then send to production. (Ibid.)

Product Data Manager operates a selective action by allowing/disallowing specific actions to be performed and change-related data to enter/not enter the process. While PDM's logic is intended to provide better control and ease to implement changes, this can at times be perceived as a source of constraint and rigidity. In our case, to avoid such rigidity, the software routine is temporarily bypassed: the decision is taken to postpone the creation of the M/Views until the time when the number of Deviations that are required for a specific vehicle will effectively and substantially outweigh the volume of Engineering Orders.

Workarounds in computing and other technologies are well documented in the literature (Gasser, 1986). However, such literature has not sufficiently emphasized that, while it is always possible to bypass the software-embedded rules, this holds important systemic implications at the level of the organization. Working around a software routine may be feasible, but it always entails a degree of disruption. In our case, the decision to bypass the software rule by managing Deviations in the E/View inevitably generates confusion later in the process, when engineers try to propagate a change across different M/Views. Since the M/Views are modified independently, there would not be a common starting point for the incremental change; any further modifications would have to be done therefore on an ad hoc basis, which is often time-consuming, complicated and error prone. These were precisely the type of drawbacks that the software-embedded logic was designed to eliminate. Eluding the software's sequential logic implies duplication of work and a higher risk that later changes will be implemented incorrectly:

For example, a request arrived to ERS, asking to make a further change to an Order that had been made Batch-2 effective for the under-bodies; the problem was that that further change was requested to be made Batch-1 effective. Theoretically, this would be impossible, because the other change was Batch-2 effective and one cannot backdate effectivities, in theory. The reason that the first change had been made Batch-2 effective in the first place, was that there was a complex interrelationship of parts and effectivities; and it was decided that the easiest thing was to make the whole thing Batch-2 effective. But then all the effected items on the change where Batch-2 effective, and now they are prevented from making that change Batch-1 effective. (Interview/MC)

These problems are generated by the huge complexity of interrelationships between parts (structural complexity) and between effectivities of different kind (time or process complexity). 'You get a huge merry-go-round that you have to untangle' (ibid.). The control action exerted by software represents one way to handle such complexity: management rules and software routines act as stabilising factors within the unstable and disordered nature of product development. *Software-embedded rules* represent an attempt to discipline processes by imposing a sequential and ordered logic; they can help ensure that the work undertaken on one part is consistent and concurrent with work undertaken on related parts:

> A classic example of a rule is that you cannot release revision D of a part until after you have released revision C. One of the engineers gave us a Deviation saying: 'I want revision F of this part in the BoM'. But what is released today is just revision C. He hasn't released D, he hasn't released E, he hasn't released F, but he wants revision F in the BoM. He has already sent information to the supplier, and the supplier is going to produce the part according to revision F specifications. The problem is that that part is related to other parts, and the other parts have not been released to a revision that matches that parts revision, so you end up with a very long chain of interrelationships that you have to resolve. (Interview/MC)

Product Data Manager is designed to introduce *control* and to clarify structural and process–time relationships. Nevertheless, there are circumstances where the action exerted by PDM is perceived as constraining the flexibility of the process flow: 'PDM is introduced to control and discipline, but sometimes it gets in the way' (Interview/MC). A *production-oriented system*, PDM is designed to support data control and validation which is mandatory in the downstream Production and Manufacturing environments; this is supported by the software-embedded incremental change rule:

> That is a very good rule. But the problem is that we live in a very anarchic world, in development, there is very little time and there are very few resources. So it may be the case that even if the guy has not released his revision F of the part, he still wants to specify that he wants revision F in the vehicle. (Ibid.)

The influence of software on flexibility

In development's anarchic world the aim is therefore to strike an appropriate *balance* between control and variation, order and disorder. The ability to manage this balance is at the basis of an organization's flexibility potential. While some control is essential to co-ordinate action and keep up to schedules and deadlines, too much control can reduce the potential for variation and diminish the organization's ability to cope with unexpected or late changes.

The Prototype BoM process example has highlighted that constant *tensions* exist between elements of control that bring discipline, stability and *order* (i.e. software-embedded routines, Project Management rules) on the one hand, and unpredictable, unstable elements on the other, bringing *disorder* (i.e. product, process and organizational complexity, environmental uncertainty). The first set of tensions, corresponding to the tensions between 'time objective' versus 'time in-process' is illustrated in Table 6.1. The flexibility potential of the PD processes is therefore related to the organization's ability to adapt to and proactively exploit change, and to accommodate these tensions by striking an appropriate balance between these two conflicting and co-evolving categories of elements.[19]

This holds important implications for software design; in *designing a flexible system*, 'the first thing you have to do is to be very clear as to which operating philosophy you want'; for example, one can choose between a system that emphasizes discipline and a system that emphasizes variation; there are advantages and disadvantages involved with both these philosophies. An intrinsic risk is to emphasize too much one aspect while neglecting the other: 'You have a choice: you either design a system that allows you to have this total anarchy, or you make people work to the rules' (Interview/MC). The most appropriate approach to adopt varies substantially across sectors and organizations, and must take into account their differential structures (i.e. routines, hierarchies and incentives), regulatory and competitive environments, management attitudes, learning abilities etc.[20]

There are also implications for software adopter organizations. An information system must be ideally implemented in a way to avoid imposing too much control, which is a main cause of process rigidity and lock-in. The introduction of PDM at our organization corresponds to an attempt to impose greater control over the unstable and disordered variables in the development environment; its implementation has highlighted a second set of *tensions between informal processes and an ordering tool*, which embeds a set of rules that aim to discipline that process. The software's emphasis on order and control, however, is perceived as excessive and as a result has provided an incentive for the development team to work around process and software rules in order to preserve flexibility: 'We are a very schizophrenic company. On the one hand we want control, and control means there are rules.' When faced with the choice between reinforcing and relaxing the rules, our organization has two options.

The first is to enforce the rules: 'in other words you say to that engineer, you are not getting part revision F in the BoM because you have not released it'. The problem with too much discipline is that it can be constraining and may prevent adaptation: 'The problem is that we live in an anarchic world, he (the engineer) has already organized with the supplier that he is going to get revision F'. Even if a rigid system is put in place, this is likely to be partially bypassed in response to the requirements of the 'real' as opposed to the 'perceived' process: 'A good example is this freeze. There will be a freeze. This is a rule, but then, in practice, this becomes only an ideal date by which it would be nice if everything would be out for these guys [read: programme management].' If the rules act as a barrier, people will find a way to work around them. 'It is a schizophrenic world, everyone will tell you that there are rules, and that, of course, we must work according to the rules, but then they will immediately break those rules' (Interview/MC). Informal processes in these cases assist the process of organizational adaptation and stabilization in a conflictual situation characterized by tensions between stable, ordering and unstable elements.

Alternatively, another option would be 'to implement a system that can allow a very substantial amount of change and anarchy into the process'; this type of system would be especially beneficial upstream in development, where a greater scope for experimentation and change almost always leads to more efficient and innovative product designs. The downside of relaxing control and delaying the freezing of the vehicle configuration, however, would be inevitably felt downstream in Production.

> You could design a system that gave you total freedom, but then you come up with problems when you try to send data to Production. If you try to send production data to production suppliers it must be released and authorised for production, and the system must tell you what is the requirement. (Interview/MC)

This emphasizes a third type of *tension* and conflict, existing between *upstream* (Design, Engineering) and *downstream* (Production, Manufacturing) development functions. While, on the one hand, excessive control tends to introduce rigidity at the Engineering end, on the other, insufficient control can represent a liability at the Production end, whereby practitioners will have to cope with an excessive amount of change and with delayed and unreliable data. This is evident when we look beyond the boundaries of the Engineering and Design functions, over to Production and Manufacturing: 'We are not affected by this problem in our compartmentalized world [read: upstream functions in PD], but the volume of changes is causing huge problems to Manufacturing. They are unable to react to the volume of change.'

While in the Engineering environment variation is highly desirable, in a Production environment control is mandatory: 'For our prototype we want to be able to control the anarchy. In production you definitely want sequential incremental change.' Allowing too much variation could work against the

Table 6.1 Tensions: major issues

IDEAL PROCESSES (THEORY)	Co-evolution of ideal and actual processes: + PDM's logic and structure are based upon standardized industry 'best practice' + The number and complex relationships between product, process and organizational variables make the flexibility outcome always emergent	ACTUAL PROCESSES (PRACTICE)
ORDERING, NORMATIVE ELEMENTS	+ PDM is aimed at managing and ordering product, process and organizational data. PDM is also meant to control and discipline processes and actions + The complexity of the development process and the unpredictable nature of change introduce uncertainty and disorder into the process	DISORDERED ELEMENTS
FORMAL PROCESSES	Co-evolution of formal, software-embedded routines with informal, partially tacit processes.	INFORMAL PROCESSES
DESIGN AND ENGINEERING (UPSTREAM DEVELOPMENT FUNCTIONS)	+ PDM highlights tensions by forcing 'upstream' functions to take into account production and manufacturing needs early in the process + However, a rigid production-oriented environment can hinder innovation and flexibility upstream	PRODUCTION AND MANUFACTURING (DOWNSTREAM FUNCTIONS)

NEW KNOWLEDGE (EXPERIMENTATION, VARIATION)	+ Software can either allow or prevent the creation of new and the reuse of accumulated knowledge, depending on implementation circumstances. + In flexible implementation circumstances PDM can support experimentation as well as allowing experience and tacit knowledge to enter the process.	STORED KNOWLEDGE (ROUTINES, EXPERIENCE, INFORMAL NETWORKS)
CONTROL, DISCIPLINE	+ PDM and management tools exert control over process variables; while some control can facilitate data and process co-ordination, concurrency, validation, too much control can imply rigidity, and favour informal workarounds + Other elements, such as informal networks, experimentation and trial and error, ensure variation.	VARIATION
STABILITY	+ Elements of stability: routines, rules, procedures + Practice and other unstable elements challenge the established rules: evolution of routines	INSTABILITY
FORMAL TOOLS	Co-production of formal tools and informal practices	INFORMAL PRACTICES

very principle by which the software and other control processes are put in place: avoiding the duplication of efforts and facilitating the control and propagation of changes in order to provide stable and reliable releases to Production and Manufacturing.

By loosening up the system too much, there is the danger of pre-empting software of its function. This is not desirable, and also not entirely feasible, as 'There are controls in PM that you can't switch off, that force you for example to release the drawings in a sequential order'. One should:

> Come back to the basic question: what is the reason for the freeze? The reason for the freeze is that Manufacturing is incapable of coping with the huge volume of change; so we are going to freeze it, we say: this spec is what we are going to build it to. And there will be a minimal amount of change after that time. (Ibid.)

To achieve this requires controlling the BoM freeze: 'As far as the freeze is concerned, you have the choice between two operating philosophies: to delay BoM freeze or to freeze, but then accept that there will still be a substantial volume of change afterwards' (ibid.). If the freeze date feels unrealistic, the most obvious solution is to delay the freeze:

> Are we going to hit the freeze? Is there going to be sufficient data to manufacture the parts? Is the engineering at that level valid? Is it going to produce valid prototypes that we can manufacture, that we can test? Or are we not going to be able to get everything out in that date? If we decide the answer to that question is no, you have no choice but to move the freeze out, to delay the freeze. But if you delay the freeze, you delay the build. (Ibid.)

The other possibility is to keep the freeze milestone in place, but interpret it flexibly. 'Alternatively you can say: look, we are going to have a target date by which we would like all changes to be in, but we understand there will be a huge volume of change after that date' (ibid.). The changes are necessary as

> Everybody is scrambling at the last minute to get these changes in, and the majority of these changes are mandatory. For example, there may be parts that do not meet properly or cases in which, unless the change is implemented, the test would reveal invalid. There are all sorts of reasons for change. (Interview/MC)

This highlights the incompatibility between the *perceived* and *actual* *requirements*:

> If you are going to live in a freeze world, you have to create systems, processes, procedures and resources that enable you to live in that world. Today the systems, processes and procedures that we have assume that we are living in a freeze world. But the reality is that we are not living in a freeze world, because there still is a high volume of changes after the freeze ... there is a *mismatch* between the

perceived business process and the *real* business process. And all our procedures and processes and systems are based on the perceived business processes and not on the real business processes. (Ibid.)

This highlights a *fourth type of tension in PD*, between ideal and actual processes. Formal processes and rules are based upon industry best practice and management imperatives. The freeze itself, a fundamental development milestone, constitutes a normative element:

It [the principle behind the freeze concept] really comes out of the way we would like to operate. It's an ideal. In an ideal world we would be able to say: at this date we will freeze, and at that stage there will only be the tiniest need for change. In an ideal world. The problem is that we don't live in an ideal world. (Ibid.)

The 'ideal' freeze date 'is a very difficult target to achieve, because we need a huge department, we need a system that can react to a substantial amount of change' (ibid.). Meeting the freeze milestone would require either greater resources upstream in the release system, or downstream, in order to provide Manufacturing with the capability to respond and assimilate a high level of change: 'and of course we are talking about thousands of parts. And one vehicle every two weeks. You need a system to control that and you need people to operate that system. Alternatively, you muddle along, that's what we are doing' (ibid.).

This emphasizes a *fifth source of conflict* between the *resources available* and the *resources required* in order to support the 'ideal' processes:

I have a very clear vision of the requirements, but people [read: Programme Management] don't want to do it. The problem is that all the time people manage as if we were living in a freeze world. People do not face up to the fact that you actually need a quite sophisticated system [...], and quite high manning level to cope with that [...] and we don't have either. (Ibid.)

A possible solution would entail implementing a system that allows flexibility but also respects the control and stability required at the Production and Manufacturing end. According to our interviewee, therefore, a situation where 'You can impose your own rules, but are still able to slot things in, would be the ideal scenario' (ibid.). A flexible system should ideally facilitate the management of these contradictory requirements.

On the one hand we have seen that, by emphasizing control and discipline over variation, normative and formal tools over informal practices, stability versus instability, ideal versus actual processes, and the requirements of downstream rather then upstream development functions, the implementation of PDM at our organization has instead potentially reduced the ability to introduce late changes and feedback into product definition. On the other hand, however, we have also argued that the absence of control may hinder flexibility and cause rigidities downstream. In both cases the organization must strive to re-establish the balance between the underlying tensions generated. In this case, flexibility was restored by introducing informal workarounds which reduced the influence of software by allowing scope for slack and variation. We have argued that this has important implications in terms of data integrity and validity. Another method would have been to redesign and reconfigure software to accommodate higher flexibility requirements, as illustrated in the example below.

The Work-in-Progress (WIP) Example

Additional evidence shows that software-embedded control features can interfere with the early stages of product development. In particular, the example below illustrates how PDM's strong emphasis on administrative control early in the development of a product can reduce the scope for search and exploration and therefore adversely affect the innovation potential of the overall development process.

Product Data Manager systems embed rigid procedures aimed at tracking and controlling a development programme's progress throughout its various stages. After release, a product configuration is loaded on PDM and becomes subject to its disciplining action. The rationale for embedding a product configuration in PDM is to increase visibility and transparency of action by making the changes implemented available to every party involved in the process. While helping to improve data co-ordination and process concurrency, however, increased visibility can become a source of rigidity upstream, where engineers would prefer to experiment with configurations in their own private 'sandbox', rather than having to share their less then perfect attempts with the wider organization (IPDMUG). Here we can see at play some of the tensions previously highlighted between upstream and downstream functions, formal tools and informal processes, demand for control and need for variation.

Another example is the Work-in-Progress process in the memory chapter (5), which we can now interpret in relation to flexibility. There we have argued that a common problem with PDM systems is their inability to handle a mix of Engineering View and Development data. We have shown how this software characteristic turns into a liability when PDM's strict control features interfere with the early stages of product development. Product Data Manager's strong emphasis on administrative product control so early in the development of the product can reduce the scope for search and exploration and therefore decrease the potential for innovation of the overall development process.

Within PDM, the hand over of a design from an individual or group of individuals to another is made to represent a specific state in a procedure; according to these rules, a file record cannot move from one individual or group to the next without changing states. Every time an engineer working on a design wants to confer with a colleague, the system imposes that a change of state is triggered. Because the authority to change moves around with the file, the file must change 'owner' before it can be circulated to another individual or department. As a consequence, software can prevent informal communication and knowledge sharing among different individuals and functions in the development team; it can also prevent the designers from obtaining early feedback from other downstream development functions. Once again, we see tensions at play between normative and flexible routine elements, control and variation, formal tools and informal practices.[21]

The software, however, can be designed or configured to support greater flexibility rather than overly constraining the working environment. Alternative approaches to the design of PDM systems involve forcing the software to emulate paper-based processes. This is achieved by introducing 'user packets', which are intended to facilitate the sharing of documents among team members. In this case, while only one user can work on a 'master' design, other colleagues working on the same project can be notified that there is an updated master design and can obtain reference copies to store in their own packets. Packets are also designed to make it possible to move work around from department to department or from individual to individual, in logically organized 'bundles'. When an engineer requires the opinion of a colleague on a design, he/she can pass the entire job across to anyone else, as long as the master model and all the associated reference files are contained in and controlled by a packet. This operation will not trigger a change of state; besides, the formal workflow procedure is uncompromised by this informal re-routing because the authority to change the file's state does not move around with the packet, but remains with the designated individual.

This alternative solution, however, also holds implications. For instance, how far can informal teamwork and cross-fertilization carry on at the same time keeping overall management control of project costs and deadlines? As argued in the previous case study, excessive variation and a lack of control can also lead to lower overall flexibility. Product Data Manager systems can be designed and, to an extent, implemented in a way to support more or less control, or more or less slack and variation. How much control, and how many variations are needed varies substantially, depending on very specific implementation circumstances such as the user organization's own procedures and culture, the specific development programme, and the stage of development. The challenge for the organization is to strike an appropriate balance between allowing sufficient scope for variation while enforcing the much needed control. Within this fragile equilibrium between exploration of new and exploitation of old solutions (March, 1991), between expanding search spaces and delimiting the exploration territories (Levinthal, 2000), software represents a regulating factor.

Due to the complex interrelationships between software and organizational routines, characterizing software behaviour as simply 'enabling' or 'disabling' is unsatisfactory. Factors such as the rationale embedded in software, and the interaction of this logic with specific organizational features and variables (i.e. people, processes, materials and machines) fundamentally influence the organization's potential for innovation and adaptation.

CONCLUSIONS

This chapter has analysed the influence of software on the organization's ability to establish and maintain flexible products and processes. We have defined flexibility as the ability of an organization to react positively to change, by modifying its products and processes in a way to minimize the negative impact of unexpected changes while at the same time maximizing the opportunities these may procure. We have argued that this ability lies at the basis of an organization's potential to adapt and survive in increasingly competitive and turbulent industrial environments. Specifically, this work has related flexibility in Product Development to the ability of the organization to balance the tensions that constantly arise between conflictual elements, such as stable, ordered and formal elements, on the one hand (i.e. software-embedded routines, management rules, milestone documents) and unstable, unordered and informal elements on the other (i.e. unstructured, tacit, informal processes). Tensions have been also highlighted between ideal (or perceived) and actual processes; between the requirements of upstream and downstream development functions; and between new and accumulated knowledge.

We have shown how the organization's flexibility potential is the emergent outcome of the unravelling tensions between 'object-world' and 'process-world' elements. On the one hand there are constraints, which are constantly revised and reinforced by management rules, documents, procedures, routines and formal tools (such as PDM). Constraints are necessary because, by establishing boundaries they frame reality, fix specifications, and provide a reference point around which informal action can take place. On the other hand, constraints and rules are constantly challenged by the practice of design and development, which continually questions the rules of play.

Rules must be respected, but are also continuously challenged. If software-embedded constraints are perceived as being too rigid, the designers will revert to informal processes. As seen in the second example, changing the way software handles constraints can result in ensuring attendance to the rules. This is a very delicate equilibrium that must be continuously searched and maintained. Too much order and constraints, and the process can evolve into a sterile and repetitive mechanism; too few rules and constraints, and chaos could overtake the process. In the first example we have seen how, if administrators had not allowed engineers to bypass the process, the process would have come to a halt. On the other hand, we have seen that the major rules were not bypassed, as this would also have implied a breakdown in the system. We have therefore demonstrated that an organization's flexibility, innovative and adaptive potential depends thus upon its ability to strike at any point in time an appropriate balance between control and variation, order and disorder, stability and instability, formal and informal processes. The flexibility outcome is therefore continuously emergent and not given; and cannot be achieved simply by introducing normative, ordering and standardizing software systems, as the technology impact literature wants to suggest.

Conceptually, software influences the organization's flexibility by affecting its ability to strike an appropriate balance between variation on one side and control on the other. Often in the literature the influence (and expected benefits) of ICTs are explained in terms of increased control: software acts as a stabilizing and standardizing element which is often adopted to introduce order and control within a disordered and unstable organizational environment. A formal tool, software is designed to delimit the range of activities to the ones that are technologically and organizationally feasible. In other words, software operates a selection process sifting which actions and knowledge can or cannot be allowed to enter the development process.

The push towards control and codification brought about by software is intended to increase the transparency of actions and product/process structures. We have argued that the control mechanisms required to increase the visibility of an engineer's actions (i.e. the early release of a product configuration) can, in certain implementation circumstances, result in reduced autonomy and freedom for the designer to experiment and share knowledge across team and functional boundaries. The assumptions embedded in software alter the balance between tacit and codified knowledge, informal and formal practices, often privileging the latter at the expense of the former. Software adoption has provided an ideal ground from which to observe the co-evolution of formal, standardizing tools and informal, flexible working practices.

Most importantly, we have seen that while the disciplining action of software can be beneficial to certain, clearly structured, organizational functions and tasks whereby requirements for stability and control are high, it can represent a source of rigidity to other, more unstructured, functions and activities; we have shown how, in the latter case, an excessive emphasis on control may prevent the exploration of alternative technology configurations, as well as weakening the ability to incorporate heterogeneous knowledge inputs in the design (including inputs from customers and suppliers, and design feedback from other organizational functions and disciplines). This emphasizes how the requirements for flexibility and control vary across the heterogeneous functions and 'communities of practice' (cf. Brown and Duguid, 1996; Cohendet and Meyer-Krahmer, 2001) that make up an organization.

Finally, a number of implications can be drawn, which can be useful for both software developers and users. A challenge for *software developers* is how to ensure high system reliability at the same time allowing scope for rich, informal networks to develop; these are often a source of creativity and tacit knowledge. Product Data Manager systems should ideally be designed to enforce control while ensuring that informal communication and knowledge sharing are not pre-empted. The challenge for software systems manufacturers is therefore to design systems that: are flexible enough to discipline the process without totally inhibiting informal systems; and that enforce control but also allow for that vital scope for experimentation and variation that lies at the basis of a firm's flexibility and adaptive potential.

The challenge for Information Systems managers in user organizations is, analogously, to understand the differing requirements for variation/ exploration on one side and control/discipline on the other at the different stages of PD. Information Technology managers' responsibility is also to assess the actual behaviour of software systems during implementation and use in order to prevent the creation of process and cognitive rigidities. A pattern of implementation that facilitates the coexistence of formal and informal elements that characterize the process of product creation seems particularly fruitful whereby software allows for tacit elements and informal knowledge to enter the process side by side with the more 'prescriptive' elements. Managing the development process to maintain a balance between formal and informal elements would also help to ensure that the results of tacit knowledge processes and learning activities can enter the process, so as to avoid atrophy and lock-in into consolidated knowledge and procedures. It can also favour innovation by widening the search space for alternative solutions. Finally, it can also influence an organization's attitude towards risk and uncertainty, therefore ultimately affecting its adaptive potential.

NOTES

1. Something or someone that is flexible is able to change easily and adapt to different conditions and circumstances as they occur' (Collins, 1987: 550).
2. For a review of the literature, see Carlsson (1989) and Thomke (1997).
3. For a review see Chapter 3.
4. Analogously Thiétart (1995) has emphasized the existence of continuous processes of stability and instability, evolution and revolution in every organization. He compares organizations to chaotic systems where counter-acting forces are at play, some pushing the system towards stability and order (i.e. forces of planning, structuring and controlling), and others pushing the system towards instability and disorder (i.e. forces of innovation, initiative and experimentation). Organizations need to master the balance between order and disorder, change and stability if they want to survive 'at the edge of chaos'. According to Thiétart 'the science of chaos provides a new paradigm where two apparently irreconcilable visions of management – rational and quasi-mechanistic on the one hand, unexpected and disorderly on the other hand – can be reconciled' (1995: 43). The contribution of chaos theory is not further investigated in this book, as the strength of its explanatory potential against other bodies of literature remains as yet unproven.
5. For a discussion of the dialectic between 'routines as representation' and 'routines as expressions' see Chapter 3.
6. The latter view is implicitly present in Lindblom (1959), Parnas and Clements (1986) and Tyre and Von Hippel (1997).
7. Often several configurations are being created and maintained which correspond to different product variants.
8. Law and Callon (1995) have called this initial freedom a 'negotiation space'.
9. This activity is often referred to as Configuration Management.
10. See Chapter 4 for a wider discussion on software-embedded assumptions.
11. DMU stands for Digital Mock-Up (cf. Chapter 4).
12 On the role of software as a standardizing element see also Chapters 5 and 7.
13. See also Chapter 5.
14. In PDM, the links within and among levels are typically identified by parent–child type of relationships; this typology is common in advanced object-oriented databases and is aimed at facilitating the management of product system complexity (cf. Figure 6.2).
15. All Deviations are recorded in the 'Build Book' which is a list, or history of deviations and is managed by the ERS department.
16. Similar issues and trends were identified at our consumer electronics and an aerospace manufacturer.
17. This number is usually agreed between Project Management and Engineering and represents the outcome of a negotiation process whereby the technology requirements established by Engineering are verified against the costing and timing requirements assessed by Project Management.
18. Effectivities are a component of process complexity; they help determine at which stage of development each part is at any point in time (Interview/NG).
19. Beyond its theoretical relevance, this question is significant also for software producers, PD and IT managers. The former are engaged in the design of flexible software systems; the latter are concerned with how to preserve and support flexible product and processes.
20. Organizations differ substantially in terms of how much control and how much variation they require; the same approach applied in two different organizations can therefore lead to very different results. For instance, organizations characterized by unstable and inefficient routines and processes, and by low(er) accumulated learning may require a greater emphasis on control in order to counterbalance the prevailing effect of the unstable elements. In contrast, organizations characterized by higher hierarchical structures and well-defined and codified processes, may require greater scope for variation in order to prevent rigidities.
21. Software producers have recently acknowledged this limitation and are redesigning the future versions of the software in a way that minimizes its negative influence on informal knowledge-sharing.

7. Crafting the Virtual Prototype: How Firms Integrate Knowledge and Capabilities within and across Organizational Boundaries[1]

This chapter examines the influence of software on the creation of new and the integration of existing knowledge in the context of Experimentation and Prototyping activities. In particular, it explores the role of 'virtual prototyping' techniques, concepts and models in capturing design knowledge and in facilitating multifunctional processes' co-ordination and multidisciplinary knowledge integration. It argues that the role of software in supporting inter-functional co-operation and the co-ordination of knowledge and activities depends on the organization's ability to nurture integrating routines which support two-directional translation flows between 'local' (function-based) and 'global' (computer-embedded) knowledge and activity levels. These mechanisms also lie at the heart of dynamic capabilities' creation and maintenance.

INTRODUCTION

Experimentation as a form of problem-solving is fundamental to innovation (Rosenberg, 1982); it consists of 'trial and error, directed by a certain amount of insight as to the direction in which a solution might lie' (Barron, 1988, in Thomke, Von Hippel and Franke, 1998: 316). Studies in product and process development have shown that iterative trial and error is a significant feature of design (Wheelwright and Clark, 1992; Thomke, 1998), technology integration (Iansiti, 1997) and manufacturing (Adler, 1990b; Pisano, 1996). According to Leonard-Barton (1995), experimenting and prototyping generate new kinds of organizational capabilities: they help create 'requisite variety' in products and processes, as well as establishing a virtuous cycle of improvement; they also guard against core rigidities by introducing new sources of knowledge, new channels of information, and new methods for solving problems (ibid.).

While the importance of experimentation is widely acknowledged, few authors have so far attempted to characterize the technical and organizational mechanisms that sustain and enable experimental practices. These mechanisms often play a greater role in competitive success than simple mastery of new technologies (Pavitt, 1998). They underpin an organization's ability to achieve co-ordination and integration of knowledge, activities, skills and capabilities across organizational boundaries. In doing so, they lie at the basis of dynamic capabilities' formation and maintenance, as well as supporting the absorption of organizational tensions and conflicts.

By focusing on the area of product design and development,[2] this chapter examines the radical influence of advanced software-based prototyping technologies over the practice and the outcome of experimental and prototyping activities. An example of these advances is the Digital Product Model, also known as the Virtual Prototype.[3] As anticipated in Chapter 4, the Digital Model is, at the same time, a philosophy, a prototype, and a set of procedures: it is a philosophy, in that it outlines the technological and organizational path that organizations have to follow to integrate their development processes; it is a (virtual) prototype, because, as a digital entity backed by a relational database, it contains links to all data, information and codified knowledge required to design, engineer and manufacture an artefact; and finally, it contains a set of standard procedures, based on industry best practice.

Our main hypothesis is that the Digital Model technology radically reconfigures the mechanisms underlying the co-ordination and integration of experimental knowledge flows and activities, skills and capabilities across organizational boundaries. This hypothesis can be articulated into a number of fundamental but, as yet, unexplored questions: how do heterogeneous organizational functions or 'epistemic communities' (Knorr-Cetina, 1999; Steinmueller, 1998), and teams, or 'communities-of-practice' (Brown and Duguid, 1996), manage to co-operate during design and experimentation? What is the role of software-based technologies in supporting inter-functional co-ordination and the resolution of organizational tensions and conflicts? How do virtual prototypes influence the integration of heterogeneous knowledge sources (i.e. from various organizational domains) and types (i.e. tacit/codified, formal/informal, software-embedded/people-embodied knowledge) into product definition? Which are the technological and organizational mechanisms that sustain an organization's ability to integrate knowledge and activities across functional boundaries?

The chapter begins by analysing the ways in which integrated software-based technologies are reshaping firm-based experimentation and prototyping activities; an example of this is the influence of software on the relationship between digital and physical prototypes. The insights developed here are tested in the third section (case studies) where empirical evidence of the changes occurring at the interfaces between Industrial Design and Engineering as well as between Engineering and Analysis is presented. The chapter concludes with a discussion of implications and policy recommendations.

EXPERIMENTATION AND THE VIRTUALIZATION AND ACTUALIZATION OF INFORMATION

The Complementary Nature of Physical and Virtual Experimentation

The modes of experimentation in manufacturing organizations are radically affected by the introduction of software-based methods and technologies, such as computer simulations and Rapid Prototyping (Thomke, 1998). To date, the theoretical debate has been centred on a dichotomy between physical and virtual prototypes. Thomke, for example, focuses on learning by switching and choosing between different experimental modes (i.e. physical crash tests vs. computer simulations). He sees computer simulation as a 'substitute' for real experimentation in fields ranging from the design of drugs to the design of mechanical and electronic products (ibid.).

While there is a clear economic rationale in substituting physical prototypes with digital simulations, from a cognitive point of view there is an advantage in combining the learning that derives from both types of experimentation. All of the organizations interviewed as part of this study have emphasized that digital prototypes have not replaced but have been used to complement physical experimentation.[4] In other words, as this chapter sets out to show, the most interesting changes are taking place where old and new methods are being successfully combined. Indeed, it appears that the effective utilization of advanced software technologies is related to the extent of integration of the new with the existing methods, procedures and technologies (Thomke, 1997). In addition to the learning involved in creating a digital or a physical prototype, a second locus of learning involving learning by 'hybrid' (physical and virtual) and cross-functional experimental modes has emerged. Such hybrid modes are intended to facilitate the integration of existing and new technologies, skills, routines and capabilities by providing complementary problem-solving approaches. These methods, therefore, have important organizational implications: organizations that are more adept at adapting their routines and create new procedures which are capable of exploiting the potential designed into digital or software-based technologies are likely to generate competitive advantage. This realization holds important implications both for organizational learning and practice.

The 'Virtualization' and 'Actualization' of Information

How can we characterize the influence of digital technologies on experimental and prototyping activities? Drawing loosely from Levy's theoretical framework, we can describe an organization's experimenting and prototyping activities as involving a series of interactive cycles of 'virtualization' and 'actualization' of knowledge, materials and capabilities (Levy, 1997; 1999).[5] These cycles are supported by the introduction of integrated software technologies across most manufacturing sectors. Analysing the dialectic between the virtual and the actual can help us to understand and characterize the implications of 'virtual' technologies' introduction and use for product development.

Virtualization consists in the translation of the information related to a physical prototype into digital. An example of this is the technique by which a physical model (i.e. the clay model for a car body, or the epoxy model for a power drill) is 'scanned', or 'digitized' and translated into a digital 'cloud of points'. The inverse procedure, 'actualization', entails a translation from digital to physical. For example, a virtual 3D CAD model can be actualized into a number of different outputs: a Finite Elements stress plot, a two-dimensional (2D) drawing, a 3D rendering image, a CNC-machined physical model or a rapid prototype (also physical).

The technical ability to virtualize and to actualize a digital model into many different physical and virtual configurations is a form of 'digital flexibility' (Levy, 1997; 1999). The principle behind the creation of a Digital Model is that there is a single, updated source of product data that is available to all development functions and can be displayed according to each function's specific requirements.[6] Once generated by the Engineering function, for instance, the digital model can (and must) be used as a common reference point by all other organizational functions: the Toolmaker can use it as direct input to the tooling machines, Analysis can use it as input to finite elements or fluid–dynamic simulations, Marketing can use it to obtain customer or executive feedback, etc.

Virtualization and Actualization as Problematic Translation Processes

While the processes of virtualization and actualization that underpin digital flexibility are becoming a recurrent feature of the experimentation landscape in development organizations, they are far from straightforward. Below, it is shown how actualization and virtualization are not simply abstract or 'purely technical' but, because they are embedded in an organizational context, they inevitably involve the set up and maintenance of complex and highly problematic organizational routines.

First, experimentation and prototyping activities involve the interaction of various organizational functions, holding different culture, viewpoints, technological awareness, goals, incentives and capabilities. Hybrid prototyping techniques, as observed during our research, testify that experimentation, rather than belonging to a specific department or discipline field, or being confined to abstract calculation by lone inventors/engineers (as portrayed in much innovation literature) is instead a highly interactive activity which spans *discipline-specific* (i.e. Design, Analysis, Manufacturing, Testing, Marketing), '*internal*' (i.e. between Design and Production) and '*external*' (i.e. the toolmakers, the customers) organizational boundaries. The collective, cross-functional side of experimental activities represents one type of complexity.

Second, experimentation and prototyping activities involve the co-ordination of different knowledge types and levels, such as formal/informal, local/global, tacit/codified, personal/social and software-embedded/people-embodied. For instance, virtualization and actualization require both tacit and codified inputs for the translation to be effective. Both physical and digital prototypes, in fact, embody *the results* of tacit and codified processes: for example, tacit knowledge is required to interpret the results of computer simulations (corresponding to a first movement, from virtual to physical) (Petroski, 1996; Thomke, 1998). However, tacit knowledge is also required for the opposite purpose of translating the digital 'cloud of data' into a finished 3D model (corresponding to a second movement, from physical to virtual). The process of creating a 3D model from the digitization of a physical model, in fact, does not correspond to an automatic process of translation but involves substantial creative integrative efforts.

At this stage we can put forward two propositions: on the one hand, there is a constant tension, flux or 'state mutation' between physical and virtual prototypes, for example between 3D physical and 3D digital models. This suggests that there exists no actual dichotomy between physical and virtual prototypes, but rather a continuous flow created by the interactive multidirectional processes of translation between prevalently digital and prevalently physical 'states'. Feedback obtained from testing physical models can be used a posteriori to improve the 'virtual model'; vice versa, feedback from the digital model can be used to improve a priori the physical model. Whichever the sources or types of knowledge involved, what is clearly important is that hybrid prototyping techniques provide the richest standpoint to support the early integration of heterogeneous knowledge types and sources into product definition.

On the other, hybrid experimentation techniques tend to draw together the inputs from various organizational functions and disciplines, often causing the dissolution of traditional boundaries as well as forcing the organization to modify its routines in order to facilitate cross-boundary activities. It is therefore not simply an issue of assessing the relative importance of tacit vs. codified knowledge, but an issue of how to integrate different knowledge sources into product definition, and how to co-ordinate the activities of many different organizational functions around the design, testing and production of prototypes. The 'fitness' of the final artefact depends heavily on the effective co-ordination of the activities and knowledge inputs as well as the integration of many different iterative variation/selection processes that take place at several different organizational locations and levels. Once we look at experimentation activities not in abstract but in the context of actual practice, we realize the need to unveil the mechanisms that underpin 'the "artful integration" of local constraints, received standardized applications, and the re-representation of information' across organizational boundaries, levels and domains (Suchman and Trigg, 1993, in Bowker and Star, 1999: 44). The issues become particularly significant when analysing the influence of integrated information systems on development practices.

Supporting these propositions requires, therefore, an in-depth, contextually situated examination of experimentation processes; only a process-centred investigation can in fact uncover the evolution of the complex organizational and technological mechanisms which support an organization's experimentation and prototyping activities. This analysis reveals that the inverse processes of virtualization and actualization require processes of translation: virtualization requires a process of codification and simplification; actualization requires a process of reinstatement of subjectivity and local knowledge. Due to the technological and organizational complexity involved, the processes of virtualization and actualization are not at all straightforward, but involve establishing and maintaining routines that act as knowledge and activities co-ordination and integration devices. The case studies that follow document the processes of building and maintenance of translation routines at a consumer electronics manufacturer. Very similar patterns were observed at a vehicle manufacturer, our main case organization.

THE DIGITAL MODEL AS AN INTERFACING DEVICE AND THE EMERGENCE OF TRANSLATION ROUTINES

The R&D and Manufacturing unit of a leading consumer electronics organization is implementing the Digital Mock-Up strategy and technology, which is intended to provide the organization with the ability to digitally simulate the characteristics of the product and the production process as well as some features of the development organization. The DMU implementation involves radical changes in the technologies as well as in the methods and procedures for design, experimentation and prototyping. While radical changes occur at all interfaces between development functions, this chapter focuses on two cases, one involving changes occurring at the interface between Industrial Design and Engineering and a second at the interface between Engineering and Analysis.[7]

The Digital Model as Interfacing Device between Industrial Design and Engineering

The first case study analyses the changes occurring at the interface between Industrial Design (ID) and Engineering. As a result of the Digital Mock-Up implementation, new procedures are being introduced in both organizational functions; these are aimed at facilitating the translation and transfer of industrial designers' knowledge from solid clay models and paper- (or computer-) supported[8] sketches into a 3D Digital Model; the Model represents the major deliverable by the ID department, and is normally handed over from ID to Engineering after 'model sign-off'.

The new design and prototyping procedures, supported by a number of advanced software-based technologies, are especially devised to 'capture' and embed some of the industrial designers' and engineers' knowledge into the Digital Product Model during the early stages of PD. The managers, designers and engineers interviewed have emphasized the difficulty of transferring the designer's knowledge from a clay model, or a hand sketch, into a digital CAD model; they have also highlighted the difficulty of embedding the designer's intention into the Digital Model. This difficulty is essentially due to the visual and kinaesthetic nature of engineering knowledge (Ferguson, 1993a; 1993b; Henderson, 1991 and 1995; Vincenti, 1990).

Creating and modifying the 3D (SURFACE) CAD model

The principal output of the Industrial Design (ID) function is the 3D digital SURFACE model, which represents the outer part of the final product, commonly named 'skin' or 'shell'. Industrial Design creates the 3D model by combining mechanical functionality and Marketing requests and 'injecting them with the company style' (Interview/BK). The ID Surface Model is designed in E-CAD, a leading CAD software application;[9] when it is ready, it is signed-off to Engineering where the 'internals' are designed. Later in the process, the model returns to ID where, through various iterations, it is modified according to the changes introduced by downstream development activities (i.e. Engineering, Analysis, Production). The process of translating ID's sketches and clay models into a digital surface model is, in contrast to what is commonly suggested by much of the technical literature, highly problematic. Despite this, it is essential that efforts be made to ensure that as much as possible of the designer's knowledge and intent is incorporated into the digital product definition as early as possible in the development process. This in fact represents an important means to maximize the input of the ID function into product definition.

There are several methods available to create the Digital CAD Model. For example, the model can be created interactively in E-CAD starting from sketches made by hand or by using ALIAS, another widespread software application; alternatively, it can be obtained by scanning hand-refined clay models into the computer system.[10] The latter technique, involving the translation of a physical clay model into a Digital E-CAD Model, can be executed either manually, by measuring sections of a clay model and typing the data into the computer, or digitally, by 'scanning' the clay form. In both cases, 'the digital data obtained *has to be resurfaced in CAD by experienced CAD engineers* to become a quality surface model' (Interview/BK).

The scanning methodology, an example of 'reverse engineering', employs techniques which enable the machine to 'read' the surface of the clay model and translate it into digital data. The methodology used at the observed organization involves two steps: (1) scanning the model; (2) reconstructing the surfaces. The first step involves mechanical measurement, which produces an observational 'cloud of points' of digital data. The second step involves constructing lines and surfaces that closely approximate but, nonetheless, simplify or idealize the original clay model (Interview/BR).

This process is often compared to taking a snapshot of the clay model: theoretically, a simple and *automatic* process. Through deeper analysis, however, the procedure appears far from being automatic and seamless. Indeed, several designers and managers have described it as a highly problematic portion of the process:

> The second part of the methodology is to reconstruct the surfaces and that's where the problem stands at the moment ... *It isn't a press-button process*: for example, if you scan this clay prototype, you are picking up all the little problems, the draft angles go out of control ... So, whatever you scan, it cannot be the finished product.[11] (Interview/AS)

And also: 'what's important is that this representation isn't easily turned into the form of the model; so, the cloud of points is not necessarily the product' (Interview/BK). Some critical contributions on the use of Computer-Aided technologies in creative design have emphasized the lack of an interactive tool able to assist the transition phase from 2D sketching to an accurate CAD model:

In early phases of design, the progress of the design process is documented by sketches, package drawings and tape drawings. Increasingly, computer-aided systems are being introduced to replace and complement conventional design development steps. As a result of this development, numerous media gaps appear, characterized by multiple changes between various two- and three-dimensional representational media as well as physical and computer-internal models. In addition, the transition during the early phases of industrial design from the sketching design themes to the preparation of a CAID reference model *of spline quality* is not supported by computer-aided systems. (Boniz and Krzystek, 1996: 162–3, emphasis added)

At our consumer electronics organizations, the transition and translation of the design from a physical clay model into a Digital CAD Model is made problematic by what one engineer calls 'breaks in the process':

You get the *break in the process* which is where you are trying to go from the [physical] models to the E-CAD form, because E-CAD doesn't lend itself to complex free-formed surfacing. And then when you try to go back and make modifications again you get *another break in the system,* because the system does not allow you to make modifications. You really have to rework it. (Interview/AS)

Whichever technique is used for translating the surface data from both sketches and clay models into a CAD model, a careful reconstruction process is required. This process must ensure that the surfaces of the resulting digital model are high quality, because the quality and effectiveness of the work performed by downstream functions (i.e. engineering, tool-making, manufacturing) depends heavily on upstream surface quality:

The aim is to create *high quality* surfaces. If you create good quality surfaces you can then use them in making your 3D model. If you don't pay enough attention to surfaces you get a lot of problems downstream, you have difficulty to machine it, and in using SOLIDS. *It's just like laying the foundations.* (Interview/AS)

A quality SURFACE model is in fact mandatory to allow engineers to create a quality 3D SOLID[12] model; this is then circulated around the whole enterprise and becomes an intermediary among functions at all subsequent stages of development.

Visual and kinaesthetic knowledge

High quality design surfaces allow for smoother machining (and, therefore, actualization) of the 3D model into a physical shape at the Production stage. In order to obtain quality surfaces, the experience of the designer is mandatory:

In E-CAD terms this is where the skill is ... The problem with surfaces is that you do not only need to be able to use E-CAD, you need to be able to use forms, to understand forms, to understand what this [surface] is doing, to understand the term 'fair'. 'Continuity' is one thing, 'fair' is another: [a surface] can be totally continuous but not fair. *If you look down the surface you will see it.* (Interview/AS)

Surface quality is therefore a property that is difficult to capture geometrically and can only be assessed by building a physical prototype. The ability to 'look' and 'touch' a prototype is at the very basis of the processes of elicitation and capture of design knowledge. The continuing need for building physical versions of prototypes is related to the visual and kinaesthetic nature of engineering knowledge, as documented, for example, by Ferguson: 'the eyes and the fingers – the bare fingers – are the two principal *inlets to trustworthy knowledge* in all the materials and operations which the engineer has to deal with' (1993b: 50, emphasis added). Interestingly, the requirements for the use of visual and kinaesthetic knowledge by engineers are not eliminated by the introduction of recent digital technologies, but only transferred to more subtle design knowledge niches. The automatic scanning of the clay model leaves in fact *'pockets of ambiguity'* that only experienced and able engineers and designers are able to fill. This view is shared by the practitioners interviewed:

> Industrial designers are very skilled in creating this model by hand, and this is the most effective way of achieving the design shape ... *The problem with that* [computer representation] *is that every time you make a complex shape on the computer,* [in order] *to verify it, you need to have it cut.* Because of the ergonomic requirements of the shape, you want to make sure that it *feels right* in the hand. So you always have to have the shape cut ... with the guys working in foam, it means that you get instant feel if you are going in the right direction. *The problem then comes to get this complex [physical] shape into the digital model. That is difficult.* (Interview/AS)

Existing software-based technologies struggle to 'capture' the designer's subjective intent into the physical prototype:

> What you need is an easy method to create and then modify surfaces. When I say easy, it is still a skilled job. It is always going to be difficult to represent that [clay surface] in the computer, because *you can't take the computer to be subjective, or to understand that there is actually a change in curvature along here.* That needs to be defined by the eye, it is not possible for the computer to define the form on its own. You can have a start by scanning it and giving it its best fit, *but it won't be how the designer intended it to be.* (Interview/AS)

Working with a physical model, either hand-made or obtained by CAD-printing, is, therefore, a fundamental means to incorporate the designer's knowledge into the artefact:

The thing is *you can't judge a form on the screen.* You always need a clay, a cut piece. Now, whether you make it in a block using surfacing and give it to the machine tool to cut it, or whether you get a model maker to cut it, you need to handle it, to see it ... *At the end of the day you have to cut it.* (Interview/AS)

It is only by 'cutting', i.e. by using NC machining to generate a solid physical model out of the digital one, that some mistakes or imperfections can be detected and corrected: 'So you get this [computer] representation. Then you can cut. *Once you've cut, you can see immediately where the problem was: this* [model] *is not really what the designer wanted'.* (Interview/AS)

Building a physical prototype therefore helps capture the designers' intent into the digital model, as efficiently as possible; it also helps to ensure that several knowledge sources (from different organizational functions) can be conveyed into the product definition process early, i.e. by circulating the resulting physical prototype around the organization; finally, it can be used for validation and verification of the digital model, that is the trustworthiness and adequacy of the model from several viewpoints (i.e. executive management, customers, engineers, marketing, etc.).

Translating into the CAD language
At a deeper level of analysis, software-based technologies reveal limitations in capturing the designers' knowledge and intent. This problem partly stems from the fact that such technologies are designed by engineers, with engineers in mind:

It is basically *an engineering way to describe surfaces.* Suppose you have one section here, another here and another here, the [resulting digital] surface will go through those sections. That is the nearest you could go to deriving a surface from a hand sketch. *That's how E-CAD describes it and the way an engineer would describe it.* (Interview/BK)

The software demands a *translation* from the designer's language into the engineer's and CAD language, in order to ensure the best possible approximation of the designer's intent within the final model and, therefore, to maximize the industrial design input into product development. The engineering bias in E-CAD, however, creates significant problems for the designers.[15]

We could get these things [the surfaces] created in E-CAD, we knew we could do it. But, initially, we couldn't get the designers to do it. *Because of the engineering paradigm that is in E-CAD*, the industrial designers did not want to use E-CAD to create these things. It is a culture mismatch, and also a mismatch of skills and interest. That's not the way they [the designers] like to work. They don't actually mind computers, they like the Mac, for instance, because that does the things they want it to do. But *E-CAD gives engineering what engineering wants, it gives the*

> *toolmaker what the toolmaker wants*, but you don't actually want to do the
> surfacing in E-CAD. (Interview/BK)

The methodologies used by industrial designers to define, construct and
modify surfaces differ substantially from those of an engineer, and so does
the industrial designer's way to understand surfaces. In order to clarify this
difference, an industrial designer recalls the example of the construction of
spline[14] curves in aerospace:

> [For us] ... it is the same as in the aircraft and the shipbuilding industry. They
> have applied similar methodologies in their 'lofting departments', which is where
> for years and years guys have been trained to generate smooth forms. They were
> initially doing it full size, using spline curves, and then taking sections from the
> spline curves ... They draw the curve they want, then they lift the sections from
> there using two-dimensional geometry techniques. It used to be done with a very
> long piece of wood, which had a number of weights on. These weights would
> create a naturally smooth surface. Then they would create sections ... [or] ...
> 'frames', and then they would stick those to the side which will hold them
> together. If you try to build the sections first, [there is] no way you would get a
> smooth shape. (Interview/BK)

These observations mainly refer to the *making* of a CAD digital surface. A
similar problem, however, arises in relation to *modifying* those surfaces (i.e.
after receiving feedback from other functions):

> For example, E-CAD surfaces ... are made of constrained patches. The geometry
> is based on a number of control points. In the engineering paradigm you modify
> the surface by modifying those control features, which were used to define the
> surface. This is not the way a designer wants to work. It restricts your ability to
> modify it, which is a problem because changes are inevitable, there is nothing
> more certain than changes. (Interview/BK)

In this context,

> The way E-CAD works ... is still not satisfactory, because it doesn't allow [you]
> to modify surfaces the way a designer would. The other methods they [software
> developers] have introduced is to use 'canonic' forms, circles on it, *but the only
> people that use* [canonic] *circles and lines are engineers, the designers don't like
> it.* (Interview/AS)

The ID's way to modify surfaces differs substantially from the engineers'
approach:

> Once the surface is there in 3D, you can see the way the light falls on it, the way it
> interacts with surfaces ... you want to be able to make changes, that's what the
> software is not good at. Once a surface is modified, the surface doesn't allow to
> maintain the relationship with the surrounding surfaces. I can't say: I would like

to maintain continuity there, a curvature, or a specific style line (i.e. I want that always to be at a certain number of degrees). You can't describe that. (Interview/BK)

This problem is significant as errors in surface continuity will generate problems later on, in the process of making a SOLID model:

> The boundary conditions are very difficult to control. I.e. if you have a gap between two surfaces, you have a tangency condition that is not respected, then when you offset these surfaces along the normal, so that you make a solid out of it, then those conditions get much worse, and you go outside your tolerance for closing the volume, and that requires rework. So *if you get it right from the beginning then it gets easier downstream.* (Interview/AS)

The process of generating a Digital Model is, in synthesis, anything but straightforward. It involves two major kinds of difficulties: (1) *capturing and translating* prototypes and other *knowledge inputs into a digital form*; this is difficult because it requires that industrial designers adapt to an engineering way to define and design surfaces; (2) once a digital surface is obtained, the difficulty resides in *incorporating feedback and changes* to it; this entails a method of modifying and controlling surfaces and their parameters that is, again, typical of an engineering approach.

The 3D CAD model as a standardizing device

A legitimate question may arise at this point: if the translation of the designers' intent into a digital model were so problematic, would this not offset the advantages of using the CAD tools? Why bother with adopting the software tools when their use appears so controversial and counter-intuitive? A mechanical engineer provides an answer: 'The problem is we need E-CAD for *achieving the benefits downstream in engineering:* the higher quality the surfaces are, the easier it is downstream, the easier the engineering, the easier the data transfer' (Interview/AS).

The operation of translating physical prototypes and sketches into a digital model, involving a process of reduction of ambiguity and of codification of designers' knowledge, is useful in allowing for part of the *knowledge to be shared* and passed on to engineering and other downstream development functions. The operation of codification and reduction of ambiguity allows for a different type of experimentation and flexibility to be generated: *digital flexibility*. Digital flexibility, in our context, consists in the fact that, once the model is translated into digital data, this can be extracted (or actualized) under many different forms, as well as updated. CAD-printing is one example, but there are many other ways of reproducing a digital model. Such 'digital' flexibility, however, is achieved only by reducing ambiguity and subjectivity; this is obtained by translating the language of each function into the CAD language, which is biased towards the model of the engineering language. In order for them to become a constituent part of the process, inputs into product definition must be therefore translated into the CAD 'language', and then back into the 'local language' during successive iterations.

The 3D CAD Model (SURFACE) thus becomes a *'collector'* of codified design knowledge coming from different functions and prototyping activities. The process of codification implies a strong 'reduction of ambiguity'. While, in fact, a certain level of ambiguity can be beneficial at the upstream development stages (i.e. as a means to convey the designer's intent and as an inlet for tacit knowledge), ambiguity often creates serious problems downstream at the Production and Manufacturing end. The difficulties encountered in transferring surface models into a common sharable CAD model are therefore justified in view of the *'downstream benefits'*; these include the ability to create a 3D Model that can be later used as an interface between all development functions. The 3D digital surface model is used in fact by Engineering to create the 3D SOLID Model, the main engineering deliverable. Once the 3D SOLID model is created, this can be used by all development functions as a basis for successive iterations. The CAD SOLID Model becomes therefore an *intermediary* for all subsequent interactions between 'upstream' and 'downstream' development functions.

Conceptually, the 'released' CAD model behaves as a *standardizing device* (cf. Bowker and Star, 1999; Fujimura, 1992; Henderson, 1991; Star and Griesemer, 1989): in the name of increased flexibility, it demands the translation of all codifiable development inputs into a language that is mostly familiar with engineers, while not necessarily with other development functions. This flexibility, however, only works if the model is re-appropriated and reinterpreted by each development function. The evidence collected here suggests that *local re-appropriation practices* are required in order to facilitate *the elicitation and input of local and tacit knowledge into the codified product definition*. An example of local re-appropriation of the global CAD model is the CAD-printing technique, whereby the data that represents the 3D CAD model is sent to NC machining whereby it is 'printed' into a physical prototype. A similar result can be obtained via stereolithography or other 'fast prototyping' techniques. These technologies generate a physical prototype out of digital data; the prototype is then used by designers to verify that the shape visualized on screen is effectively what they had intended. Any changes are later re-incorporated into the single, common 'digital product definition'. This emphasizes that there is a continuous flow and constructive tension between physical and digital states, as well as between local and global knowledge and activity levels. Only the local re-appropriation of the CAD model will allow the results of local tacit knowledge processes to be embedded into the artefact definition *(local adoption of the global CAD model).*[15]

While the function of the local departments therefore remains fundamental, a translation process must be in place which supports continuous knowledge exchanges between the local and the global (CAD) level; this should ensure that as many different knowledge types and sources as possible are incorporated into product definition, as early as possible. This especially includes heterogeneous, 'non-articulable' and, therefore, uncodifiable knowledge sources which are not easily captured by software. *These translation processes are at the heart of co-ordination and communication among various development functions.* Inter-functional communication and co-ordination depend heavily upon the effectiveness of these translation and integrative procedures. To borrow a term from the Sociology of Technology, the released 3D CAD model can be described as an *'obligatory point of passage'* (Latour, 1987) between different development functions. Inter-functional exchanges and knowledge transfers take place via translation and re-appropriation routines that *connect local and global knowledge and activity levels as well as integrating heterogeneous (specialized) knowledge sources.* These routines help to accommodate the tensions arising from the dialectic between standardization and non-standardized practices and codes as well as between *local* and *global* levels. This 'permanent tension between the formal and the empirical, the local/situated and attempts to represent information across localities' has been so far under-explored and under-theorized (Bowker and Star, 1999: 44).

It appears clear that part of the challenge that the organization faces concerns the ability to strike a balance between the global and the local knowledge and activity levels; this balance should ensure that 'central' control and co-ordination through standardization is achieved, while allowing for the incorporation of rich, formal and informal, local knowledge into product definition; this is important especially at the early development stages where the product specification is not yet clearly identified. The *interactions between local and global levels* should support the early incorporation of heterogeneous knowledge types (i.e. tacit and codified, internal and external) and sources (i.e. specialized, discipline-specific) into product definition. These routines also support the integration between existing and new technologies, skills and capabilities.

The Digital Model as Interfacing Device between Engineering and Analysis

The first case study has illustrated how the CAD (SURFACE) Model becomes a principal intermediary between Industrial Design and

Engineering. The example that follows captures a similar trend occurring at the interface between Engineering Design and Analysis; the intermediary, in this case, is the CAD (SOLID) Model.

A single common model

The Digital Mock-Up implementation has introduced radical changes also at the interface between Engineering and Analysis; these include the introduction of integrated software modules that enable engineers to perform analyses directly on CAD geometry. The assumption behind this is, analogously, that, once a 3D Digital Model is produced, it can be used as an interface for all subsequent interactions between development functions. Prior to the introduction of integrated software,

> A volume model had to be built *specifically* for analysis; then we would construct from the volume model the surfaces, and all this was very time consuming. Previously, you had too many things to do before you got the answer, *and you had to do them in order to get the answer* ... in the new paradigm, *you build a Solid Model*. This has to be built anyway, it is not built especially for the analysis. *Then we can do the analysis directly on the solid model.* (Interview/BK)

The main idea is that, by adopting the 3D (SOLID) Model, analysts get to work on the same model as the engineers: 'So, where there were several models and duplication, there is now *a single common model* which every function has to refer to' (ibid.).

Once the Model is generated, the software allows engineers to apply 'loads' and 'boundary conditions' *directly on their design geometry*, to automatically mesh the model, run an analysis and post-process the results without exiting the integrated software environment. Following the introduction of integrated software technologies, first-order analysis work is shifted from the analysts to the designers, who can perform simple analysis iterations that help improve their design and identify the 'best part model'. After an 'optimal' model has been identified, the first-order analyses can be sent directly to an analyst, which can set up higher-order analyses, such as Finite Elements Analysis (FEA), using a specialized analysis tool, without having to rebuild the geometry. The analysts' FEA model can then be sent back to the designers, enabling them to visualize the CAD geometry and automatically update the master assembly model in the software database (Deitz, 1997).

The integration of Design and Analysis

The aim of integrated software systems is, therefore, to help practitioners *'close the design loop*, by providing bi-directional associativity so that CAD geometry flows directly *without translation* to the pre-processor, analysis engine, post-processor, and then back to the master assembly model in the CAD system's database' (Deitz, 1997: 95, emphasis added). The integrated software's philosophy is to create a *seamless two-way information flow* between Engineering Design and Analysis, thus completing the communication and information loop between the two functions. Authors have named this phenomenon as 'the convergence of Design and Analysis' (ibid.).

Such integration and 'seamless communication', however, is not automatically achieved as a consequence of software implementation. The convergence of Design and Analysis in fact involves the *a priori translation of the Analysis language into CAD language.* This translation enables the analysts to perform iterations directly on the 3D geometry model created by the Engineers. As with the previous case study, the adoption of the 3D CAD model by Analysts is enabled by the prior migration of the FEA language to be a way of representing the model data that is familiar to Engineering.

The language migration, in this case, is accomplished by linking the features found in parametric, feature-based CAD systems, familiar to engineers, with components of finite-elements models, familiar to Analysis. This corresponds to translating the language of Analysis, which is based on abstract finite elements, into the engineers' language of geometric entities. This language translation is meant to render analysis more intuitive for engineers; the software, for example, 'is capable of presenting the results of an analysis *in terms of geometry and shape, which a designer can understand more easily*, rather than, say, stress plots' (Palframan, 1999: 16, emphasis added). In order to integrate design and analysis, the latter is therefore made more intuitive, thus enabling engineers to pose problems and interpret the results in an engineering context.

The analyst's specialized expertise

The engineers are therefore developing some analysis skills: they are increasingly using automated analysis software as an aid to identifying the critical design parameters, evaluating their interactions, and eventually determining the best overall design approach. The analysts' skills, however, are not being made redundant. Even though advanced software systems may automate many routine tasks, 'they can't replace engineers with specialized expertise' (Deitz, 1997: 100). *Specialized expertise* is, in fact, required at all stages of analysis. During pre-processing, for example, the body of the design is divided into elements; deciding the most appropriate shape and size of these elements requires a sound understanding of the physical model and the Finite Elements procedure (Onwubiko, 1989). While the pre-processing stage requires knowledge about expected stress patterns, the post-processing stage requires experience to interpret the results (ibid.).

As a consequence of the introduction of integrated software technologies, practitioners have therefore divided Analysis-related activities in two types. The first type of activity is concerned with an increase in the automation of the finite elements solution process using *linear elastic static analysis* in which the engineer's input only involves the choice of the appropriate mathematical model for analysis. The second type, which includes the *non-linear or dynamic analysis* of structures and fluids, still requires a greater degree of involvement and expertise in finite elements methods by the engineer (Bathe, 1996). In our consumer electronic organization:

> We have just purchased a modeller from the CAD provider which does the analysis. We intend to use this in two ways: firstly, to do FEA of simple parts to be used by the engineers. The engineers now will be taught how to use the analysis: they will build a SOLID model, and then will use the analysis on the SOLID model. The engineers have got a reason to build the model for FEA, and that also gives them skill and the skill is used in preparing the right model for analysis; secondly, because now we have these things [the 3D SOLID models] so much earlier than a number of years ago, we are now in the position of being able to give that model to the Moulder who has got experience with plastics. We can say: this is what the form is, this is what we want, tell us if we are right or wrong. We still use the expertise outside, it is an extended enterprise. (Interview/BK)

The 3D CAD model is therefore sent as information input to the Moulders who hold specialized knowledge and can perform higher-order type of analysis:

> The moulders ... have this sort of system [Mould-Flow], they would do the analysis for you, but then they need the information. So now we intend to use E-CAD's data preparation capabilities to interface with Mould-Flow. *The analyses are done by specialists* because you need somebody who knows how to get the information from E-CAD, knows the package, knows how to do the analysis and how to interpret the analysis. (Interview/BK)

The 3D Model is therefore used to communicate the design intent and to collect specialized knowledge from other development functions such as Analysis and the Mould-makers; it also supports the integration of such specialized knowledge sources back into digital product definition (the common database, and therefore the single Model).[16] The nature of the exchanges between Engineers and Analysts is also evolving: Engineers are able now, in turn, to prepare their 3D model in a way that is most useful to analysts. This, again, improves co-ordination in the opposite direction and promotes an inverse translation flow, this time from Engineering to Analysis. Meanwhile Analysis, as a development function, retains its fundamental role by 'specializing' on higher order, complex analysis problems.

The CAD (SOLID) model becomes, therefore, an intermediary between Engineering and Analysis: created by engineers, it is passed on and used by analysts for their trials. Again, similarly to the previous case study, the analysts' input into product definition and development is mediated by the CAD model which, at the end of the analysis process, embodies some of the analyst's knowledge. The model becomes the intermediary for all subsequent exchanges between Engineering and Analysis. As seen above, the improvement in co-ordination and knowledge transfer depends upon the adoption of a common product model, which in turn requires the partial migration of the analysts' language towards the language of engineers, or the CAD language. As seen in the first example, co-operation in experimentation entails the construction of specific experimentation procedures that support the translation of knowledge flows between functions and levels. While, on the one hand, the Analysts' language is modified to become familiar to Engineers (*translation from local to global*), on the other hand, the engineers' 3D model is 'locally' modified in order to be adjusted to meet the requirements of the Analysts (*translation from global to local*).

The Emergence of Translation Routines

In conclusion, the above evidence has shed light on the techno-organizational processes of selection and variation. We have seen that an interesting feature of the 'virtualization of information' is that, once digitized, information can be processed in many different ways as well as represented in many different guises. The digitization of physical prototypes allows for their early translation into 3D digital data models; these then become intermediaries in the subsequent interactions among organizational functions, an obligatory point of passage for the knowledge that is to flow from local functions into global product definition and vice versa. From an organizational standpoint, the adoption of the 3D modelling technology corresponds to the creation of one of a series of important interfacing devices. Now each function draws directly from the 'released' computer Model, performs its prototyping iterations and simulations, and then inputs the results back into the Digital Model.

While the 3D Model as a standardizing device performs an important co-ordinating function, we have also highlighted that this would not be effective unless routinized mechanisms emerge which ensure that the globally collected knowledge, elaborated into the form of the Digital Model, is re-interpreted and re-appropriated at the local level by each development function. At the level of the individual function or department, the digital models are actualized in many different digital or physical prototypes; the process of actualization or local re-appropriation is achieved by re-embedding into the digital model the context-, person- and department-related knowledge and contingencies. During these processes, ambiguity is restored, codified knowledge re-interpreted, local meaning is reconstituted, as the 'local' community of practice 'appropriates' the Digital Model. We have therefore analysed the emergence of 'translation routines' that support these two-directional translation flows.

These translation procedures support inter-functional co-operation by allowing multiple translations between the CAD language (and the language of engineers) and the 'local' discipline- and function-specific languages. Co-ordination between heterogeneous development functions is promoted by the creation and maintenance of these two-directional translation processes that facilitate the process of embedding local knowledge into global product definition as well as supporting the appropriation of the global model by local development functions. The existence of translation routines is also attributable to the need to draw from local and informal knowledge sources and to integrate these as much as possible into the software-embedded global product definition. Indeed, if non-articulable knowledge was as uninteresting as supposed by those economists who focus principally on the margin between codifiable and codified knowledge (i.e. Cowan, David and Foray, 1998), there would be no need for organizations to set up and maintain these complex translation procedures.

CONCLUSIONS

This chapter has analysed the influence of integrated software-based technologies on design and experimentation activities conducted across inter-organizational and inter-functional boundaries. In particular, it has focused on the way such technologies reshape the mechanisms by which heterogeneous organizational knowledge sources (i.e. from various functions and domains) and types (i.e. tacit, articulable and codified) are transferred within and across organizational boundaries and the way these are integrated into virtual and physical artefacts. In observing the day-to-day co-evolution of technological and organizational practices, the chapter has also addressed the implications of software introduction on collective knowledge-building activities, focusing on the way software systems affect the patterns of collaboration and knowledge sharing among heterogeneous organizational 'epistemic communities' (Knorr-Cetina, 1999; Steinmueller, 1998), and 'communities-of-practice' (Brown and Duguid, 1996). In this context, we have observed the role of virtual and physical prototypes as 'points of obligatory passage', 'knowledge repositories' and 'intermediaries' among different communities and as loci where organizational conflicts are absorbed, and temporary truces can be reached.

We have argued that the introduction of integrated software tools radically reshapes these fundamental processes, for example by introducing the so-called 'virtual prototyping' techniques and concepts. While emphasizing that the *Digital*, software-embedded *Model*, shared among all functions involved in PD and beyond, can act as reference point for all organizational functions and therefore help co-ordinate their differing viewpoints, we have also highlighted its limitations. We have argued that, rather than being straightforwardly supported by the introduction of standardizing software tools and models, inter-functional co-operation in experimentation and design involves the local appropriation of the digital model by individual development functions, according to their specific requirements, knowledge and objectives. While the digital model can potentially act as a standardized interfacing device and facilitate the transfer of knowledge across functional boundaries, this works only to the extent that it is supported by the construction of local appropriation routines.

We have therefore demonstrated that effective co-ordination entails the formation of *translation routines*, that integrate formal and informal, tacit and codified, local and global, software-embedded and people-embodied, heterogeneous and standardized knowledge sources and levels. Such integrative routines support two types of knowledge flows: first, they facilitate the translation of local into global knowledge as well as facilitating the early embodiment of local multidisciplinary knowledge into global product definition; second, they support knowledge translation from a global back to a local level, facilitating the re-appropriation of the digital model by each development function, according to their specific requirements and viewpoints. This continuous process of routine building and maintenance is therefore absolutely crucial for the software-embedded philosophy to work in practice. Formal and informal co-ordination mechanisms embedded in routines represent the principal means to repair discontinuities and bridge the techno-organizational gaps between heterogeneous functions, knowledge types and sources, and old and new technologies.

The notion of translation routines provides a more satisfactory characterization of how software technologies are able to co-ordinate actions and knowledge across different communities-of-practice and epistemic communities; it also explains how heterogeneous inputs from specialized organizational functions are integrated and how these are able to collaborate while maintaining divergent knowledge, interests and viewpoints. The notion of translation routines helps to explain how organizational tensions and conflicts, due to the coexistence of heterogeneous, specialized functions, are absorbed.[17] Indeed we have demonstrated that such heterogeneity (a consequence of the increase in division of labour and specialization) can enrich the development process by providing specialized knowledge inputs. Among these inputs is that portion of knowledge that is impossible to articulate but which, nevertheless, is required to improve the product definition process. The emergence of translation routines testifies that, contrary to the codification debate's belief, this portion of knowledge is not simply relevant but essential to the development process.

Further, we have importantly emphasized that the emergence of integrative routines also underlies the organization's ability to create and maintain *dynamic capabilities* and therefore, ultimately, to sustain its innovative, adaptive and competitive potential. Uncovering these mechanisms represents an important theoretical and empirical step as the existence of dynamic capabilities has been assessed so far only *ex post*, as a measure of improved performance. This finding also provides empirical support to the suggestion that the concept of dynamic capabilities is far from 'an empty box', and that it can, and indeed must, be explored in order to improve our understanding of organizational behaviour and performance (Winter, 2000; Winter and Zollo, 1999).

The above results have been obtained by moving past an abstract conceptualization of the experimental activities performed by development organizations and by studying knowledge as situated, that is integral to and not separated from knowledge-production activities; the insights provided by our case studies could only be acquired by treating Vincenti's (1990) conceptual separation between 'what engineers *know*' and 'what engineers *do*' as an indistinguishable whole. We believe that our approach represents the way forward for organizational studies centred around knowledge issues: understanding organizations as knowledge-repository and knowledge-creating systems cannot, and should not, be viewed as separate from understanding how knowledge processes work in practice. In a similar way, we have opted for a characterization of the knowledge creation and transfer processes as highly interactive, in the belief that to study them as processes typically performed by individuals could imply at best overlooking important issues, and at worst acquiring findings which are irrelevant or altogether misleading.

A number of speculative policy implications can be drawn. A first important implication for the management of the innovation process in the firm is the need to support and nurture the routinized mechanisms of translation that are identified in this chapter. While the function of translation routines is important in relatively stable organizational environments, their role becomes even more crucial in the context of fast and radical change of the kind often instigated by the implementation of a new, corporate-wide Information System.

A related concern for software adopter firms is the need to account for the difficulties involved in appropriating standard, software-embedded procedures and models. On the one hand, software-embedded 'best practice' procedures and models can be relatively easy to acquire.[18] Acquisition can be facilitated, for example, by purchasing a software system 'solution' that embodies industry best practice and by exploiting the technology transfer expertise of software producers and consultants to implement it. On the other hand, our evidence demonstrates that such standardized, 'coded' procedures and models are of little use unless they are locally appropriated and effectively transformed into actual routines and prototypes. It is only by locally appropriating and adapting the software-embedded, standardized practices, models and methodologies to the new idiosyncratic organizational context that these can in fact acquire value.

In this respect, our investigation strongly indicates that a diffusion approach runs the risk of seriously mis-stating the organizational costs and productivity effects of software adoption processes. It emphasizes that, in evaluating the costs and benefits of Information Systems implementation, the 'invisible work of customization' that is required to translate (or 'actualize') software-embedded procedures (and models) into actual routines (and artefacts) must also be taken into consideration. The standardization of practices does not in fact unequivocally imply reduced costs of knowledge acquisition, as knowledge, models and practices have to be 're-created' at each new organizational location. These implications should also be taken into account when drafting public policies that are aimed at supporting the transfer of best practice across firms, sectors and countries.

The above inferences are also relevant from the viewpoint of software systems producer organizations. As integrated, enterprise-wide systems become more and more generic, following the producers' intent to devise software solutions that can be applied to an increasingly wider range of firms and sectors, these are also likely to require an increasing amount of customization by the user organization. As a consequence, software producers need to build greater flexibility and customization potential into their systems in order to facilitate the process of adaptation of generic systems to local, context-specific, circumstances and requirements. This involves designing systems that, while embodying standardized practices and models, are also flexible enough to allow for extensive local customization and adaptation.

NOTES

1. Previously published in *Research Policy*, 30(9) December 2001: 1409–24.
2. Engineering experimentation and prototyping play a fundamental role in the knowledge creation process at the firm level (Rosenberg, 1982). However, this remains an under-investigated area in innovation studies, where authors have principally concentrated on research-intensive industries as a paradigm for knowledge creation.
3. While Digital Mock-up, Digital Product Model, Virtual Product Model and Virtual Prototype correspond in theory to different levels of simulation capability supported by different stages of software implementation (from less to more advanced), in practice these concepts are often used interchangeably (cf. Chapter 4).
4. A complementary set of interviews, conducted in various sectors including Aerospace and Formula One, has confirmed this evidence.
5. The 'virtual' has been defined by French philosopher Levy as 'that which exists only *potentially* and not in *act*' (1997: XIII). In order to become 'actual', the virtual requires a process of transformation, or *actualization*, which does not simply entail *logic deduction* (i.e. the pure logic working of a software programme) but *creative invention* (i.e. the interaction between people and information systems) (ibid.: 7, my translation).
6. In practice, the extent of this capability depends heavily on specific implementation circumstances.
7. Additional evidence shows that similar radical changes occur at the interfaces with other functions, including 'external' enterprise organizations such as the Toolmaker.
8. I.e. ALIAS or Macintosh photo-realistic conceptual renderings.
9. E-CAD is our pseudonym for the leading software application in the automotive and aerospace CAD markets (see also Chapter 4).
10. Often a combination of the two methods is used.
11. The finished product or main deliverable for ID is the 3D surface model.
12. A 'SOLID' model is a 3D virtual prototype generated in E-CAD from a SURFACE model.
13. Similar biases have been reported in several other CAD applications.
14. 'A *spline* is a flexible strip that can be made to go through a set of points in such a way as to produce a smooth curve' (Onwubiko, 1989: 134).
15. Re-appropriation procedures represent, therefore, an important means to ensure the integration of 'sticky information' (Von Hippel, 1994), tacit knowledge, local idiosyncrasies, requirements and viewpoints into global (software-embedded) product definition.
16. While our example centred around the interfaces between Design and Engineering and Engineering and Analysis, the same type of pattern emerges at other critical interfaces, such as the one between Engineering and the Toolmaker and Mould-maker, whereby the solid model is used as information input to these 'external' organizations (Interview/BK); similar translations also occur at the interface between Design and Prototyping where the 3D solid data is used as input to the Stereolithography and Laser-sintering machines which produce 'fast' prototypes by printing CAD data (Interview/KT).
17. In this sense they perform a governance role similarly to Nelson and Winter's (1982) routines.
18. The ease of appropriation, however, will vary among firms, this being a function of the relative 'fit' between standardized practices and existing organizational processes and structures.

8. Conclusions

This book has explored the dynamics of Integrated Software Systems implementation and use in the organizational context of Product Development. By analysing the adoption of software at leading manufacturers in-depth and in the context of actual practice, it has drawn out implications for the organization's learning, adaptive and innovative potential.

Organizations worldwide are intensively and extensively adopting integrated software technologies with the aim to bridge the internal divisions and discrepancies created by an increasing functional and epistemological specialization. Within this context, integrated software is acquired with the objective of controlling and co-ordinating a firm's activities, including those which are learning- or change-related, and, therefore, critical for the organization. Notwithstanding the relevance and diffusion of integrated software systems, however, the implications of their adoption for the innovating organization had not so far been analysed in sufficient depth and detail.

Much of the academic debate, for instance, has greatly underestimated the fundamental influence of software on organizational knowledge and learning dynamics, being principally concerned with assessing the impact of software on quantitative performance variables. These contributions fall short of acknowledging that integrated software technologies are radically affecting not only organizational activities but also knowledge and learning processes; the latter include, for example, the processes by which specialized knowledge is acquired, created, stored, shared and integrated across heterogeneous organizational functional boundaries; and the processes by which organizations are able to use such knowledge to create and maintain their capabilities.

The innovative, adaptive and learning potential of the organization has been assessed in terms of its increased ability to: maintain adaptive processes that allow for the exploration of a wide range of techno-organizational configurations; incorporate heterogeneous local feedback and requirements into global product (and process) definition; modify routines to respond to differential requirements for radical and incremental change at different stages of the product development process; flexibly control the combined physical and virtual evolution of product and process definition; integrate, synchronize and validate data, information and knowledge flows across the extended enterprise and along the total product life cycle. Due to its radical influence on all of these critical processes, the implementation of an integrated software system has provided a unique opportunity to observe how organizations are able to learn and unlearn, react and adapt to change, build and renew their capabilities.

Specifically, such a privileged viewpoint has enabled us to shed light over the continuously unresolved attempts of the organization to strike an appropriate balance between continuity and discontinuity, flexibility and control, change and stability, heterogeneity and standardization; it has also uncovered the processes by which complementary knowledge sources (i.e. tacit/articulable/codified, formal/informal, local/global, people-embodied/ software-embedded) can be co-ordinated and subsequently integrated into a consistent unique artefact's definition. For example, it has helped us understand how heterogeneous organizational functions and domains are able to co-operate while maintaining conflicting interests and goals, and while speaking idiosyncratic, discipline-specific languages. Moreover, and most importantly, it has provided a unique standpoint to observe the evolution of routines (including the technological and organizational mechanisms that bring routines to change or subside) as well as providing a substantially new understanding of the sophisticated processes that underpin an organization's ability to create, maintain and renew its capabilities.

In addressing these complex issues, we have encountered the crucial question of how to characterize consistently and usefully the influence of (information) technology on organizational knowledge and practice. The theoretical characterization adopted throughout the book was chosen in the belief that it represents an important advance over more traditional technological- or socio-deterministic accounts. In order to capture the complex dynamics of co-evolution of software and organization, we have abandoned the narrow notion of 'software-as-a-tool' adopted by much Innovation, Economics, IT and Management literature. In essentially treating software as a 'black box' which impacts over the organization, such literature is in fact substantially unable to capture the deeper and perhaps most relevant features of the two-way interaction between software and the organization.

The device adopted in this book was, therefore, to open up both software's and the organization's black boxes to reveal how software and organization-embedded processes interact. Such an in-depth analysis was enabled by a characterization of software not as a simple tool, but as an ensemble of assumptions and procedures that continuously interact with organizational routines, radically shaping and in turn being shaped by these. Our process-centric approach was, therefore, able to reveal how software-embedded rules and assumptions influenced organizational cognitive processes and activities, and how, in turn, organizational processes influenced the configuration of software procedures and their performance.

From an empirical point of view, this involved an in-depth, qualitative research methodology that analysed the co-evolution of software-embedded and organizational processes (including knowledge and learning processes) in their complexity and in the context of actual practice. Theoretically, this entailed moving beyond a 'purely cognitive' and abstract characterization of knowledge, present in much organizational and innovation theory, to study organizational cognition as an ensemble of 'situated', collective and 'distributed' processes. The result we aimed for was a research effort that held strong empirical validity while providing also deeper theoretical insights.

Specifically, this methodology has allowed us to confirm the validity of the initial hypothesis: Integrated Software Systems radically reconfigure existing organizational routines, knowledge and learning processes, therefore exercising a fundamental influence over the organization's adaptive, innovative and learning potential. Even more importantly, our analysis has revealed that software adoption influences the very process of formation and maintenance of organizational capabilities. This result is highly significant and extends our findings beyond the prediction of the initial hypothesis.

By observing the co-evolution of integrated software systems with organizational routines and situated cognitive processes, we have therefore drawn significant implications for both the theory and the practice of the innovating firm. These implications have helped to fill some gaps in our theoretical understanding of organizations as knowledge users and producers which have so far been underplayed or entirely neglected by existing contributions.

THEORETICAL IMPLICATIONS

Our study has principally aimed to contribute to the theoretical debates in Innovation Studies, Organization Science, Evolutionary Economics and Engineering Epistemology. It has also added to the STS and CSCW debates, by extending their insights to the realm of organizations.

We have thus emphasized the need to move beyond the codification economists' principal concern with knowledge *accessibility* and *diffusion* by emphasizing the more important and complex processes by which organizations manage to *turn the knowledge acquired into distinctive competences and capabilities*. In this context, we have revealed how (software-embedded and organizational) routines and capabilities evolve, focusing on the *tensions* and *discontinuities* which cause them to change and subside, rather than on mechanisms of stability and continuity (main focus of the Evolutionary debate).

In contrast with Economics, Organization and Innovation theory, we have also highlighted the need to shift the focus of our attention from abstract decision-making to the study of how cognitive processes evolve in practice. This was achieved by rejecting the widespread, but unproductive, dichotomy between cognition and the context of knowledge usage and production to concentrate, instead, on the situated and context-dependent nature of knowledge (present in much of the Sociology of Technology debate).

Further, this book has contributed to the Organization Science and Innovation Economics' debates, in highlighting the need to abandon the simplified and unproductive view of organizational learning as a summation of learning by individuals. While this characterization appears in much cognitive science-inspired literature (including Organization and Management studies and Engineering Epistemology), it has become increasingly clear that there are fundamental shortcomings in extending the inferences acquired at the level of the individual to the level of the organization. We chose to adopt a more sophisticated and perhaps productive approach and studied knowledge not as simply embodied in individuals but as *distributed* across many forms of external memory (including artefacts, routines and locally-shared languages). In doing so, we have illustrated how *collective* and *distributed* knowledge-building activities operate in Product Development.

Intrinsic limitations were also identified in the organization and Innovation Theory's frequent mischaracterization of 'organizational culture' as a *homogeneous* entity. We have argued that this characterization fails to account for the 'internal' divisions created by both 'communities-of-practice' and 'epistemic communities' that produce noticeable local variations in the organization's landscape in terms of knowledge, language and culture. By acknowledging the *heterogeneous* nature of the organization's landscape, we have therefore shed some light over fundamental issues such as the processes by which heterogeneous organizational knowledge sources are integrated and by which diverging, conflicting interests are co-ordinated. We have also highlighted how heterogeneity often survives the introduction of more rigid, standardizing software technologies; indeed, it is preserved as a source of variation, flexibility and innovation.

As mentioned above, we proposed an alternative to the received characterization of software-as-a-tool impacting upon people and organizations. This characterization has so far prevented scholars from addressing some of the most interesting and promising issues in relation to the role of software. Even those engineering epistemology studies that contain outstanding micro-studies of technology, have often failed to address the complex interactions of technology and humans, which configure and in turn are configured by the process of technology design and use. By highlighting the complex interactions between software-embedded and organizational processes, we have demonstrated that the implications of software adoption are always emergent and cannot be deterministically predicted.

In addressing the most fundamental gaps in our understanding of organizational knowledge issues and the influence of IT, we have therefore been able to draw some relevant theoretical and empirical findings that are summarized in the sections below.

PRINCIPAL RESEARCH FINDINGS

In order to characterize the influence of software on the organization's innovative, adaptive and learning potential, we have initially identified three major themes. Each one of these themes principally addressed one of the evolutionary categories of knowledge *retention*, *selection* and *variation*. Following our findings, we also added the fourth category of knowledge *integration*. The resulting themes (and chapters) were: (1) knowledge *retention* and *reuse* (Chapter 5: Organizational Memory); (2) knowledge *selection* (Chapter 6: Control and Flexibility); and (3) knowledge *variation*, and the *integration* of knowledge and capabilities (Chapter 7: Experimentation and Prototyping).

Besides providing a contribution to the theory, each theme also highlighted one, or more, specific challenges facing the innovating organizations. These challenges pointed to the (continuously unresolved) attempt by the organization to achieve, at each moment in time, an appropriate balance between: *standardization* and *heterogeneity* (i.e. balancing standardized vs. idiosyncratic knowledge sources and types, organizational functions and levels, product and process structures, software applications); *control* and *flexibility* (i.e. supporting flexible vs. inflexible product and process configurations, formal and informal processes, management-enforced vs. computer-embedded rules); *specialization* and *integration* (i.e. integrating local, function-specific vs. global, computer-embedded knowledge sources and activity levels); *continuity* and *discontinuity* (i.e. combining new and existing knowledge and capabilities, supporting the emergence of new 'bridging' routines out of existing routinized patterns that have been broken as a result of software implementation). We have argued that managing the latter tension lies at the heart of the organization's ability to create and sustain their capabilities. The selected themes and the related implications of the above issues and challenges are summarized below.

Theme 1: Software as a Repository of Organizational Memory

The first theme has analysed the influence of software on the mechanisms by which organizational knowledge is structured, stored, retrieved and reused. It has been argued that, in the attempt to impose a new, common, 'language', software generates a push towards *greater standardization* and *reduction of* technological and organizational *heterogeneity* (i.e. local, idiosyncratic 'dialects'). We have shown how, while the newly introduced (standardizing) language and routines were aimed at reducing the duplication of efforts and at improving co-ordination by eliminating inconsistencies of data and actions across the organization, they clashed with existing organizational heterogeneities. These took the form of various 'epistemic communities' and 'communities-of-practice', each having their own knowledge base, culture, objectives, and discipline- or activity-specific languages.

We have argued that, while the introduction of integrated software is intended to eliminate the idiosyncrasies and support the creation of shared meanings, in early or unfavourable implementation circumstances it can generate even greater obstacles. It appears in fact that the very attempt to standardize across heterogeneous domains has paradoxically emphasized existing incompatibilities (of organizational, technological and epistemic nature) which were somehow previously latent, being accommodated by semi-formal communication patterns. Our example of the two (incompatible) product and database structures illustrated, therefore, a failure to establish a common, artificial language, due to the persistence of local 'dialects' (i.e. existing database structures, technologies and routines). Achieving shared meanings requires more than the mere co-ordination of information flows highlighted by some economists: it requires the integration of (often) incompatible meaning structures. The example also illustrated the failure of the software-embedded product and database structure to perform as a 'boundary object'; the new structure does not in fact possess the interpretive flexibility required to support inter-functional collaboration; rather, its behaviour is more similar to that of a standardizing device (similar to the Virtual Model in Chapter 7).

These results have emphasized the partial inadequacy of Organization and Innovation theory's frequent conceptualization of organizations as homogeneous entities that are characterized by coherent culture, knowledge and goals. Following the increasing division of labour and specialization, organizations are fragmented into functions that differ significantly in their relative ability to learn, interpret, know and memorize. These inconsistencies are often heightened by the introduction of software, which tends to disintegrate existing organizational patterns while challenging the stability of existing routines. Rather than being static and homogeneous, organizational knowledge and culture are *emergent* attributes that arise as a result of temporary equilibria and truces among conflicting elements. Organizational shared meanings, for this very reason, cannot be considered as given but require to be *continually reconstituted*. This observation leads to a fundamental paradox: the need for the organization to preserve heterogeneity (of knowledge and practices), therefore fully exploiting the advantages of specialization, while at the same time reaping the advantages of software-induced standardization. Resolving such a paradox entails preserving organizational heterogeneity, while at the same time ensuring co-ordination across domains and functions. This objective can be achieved, for instance, by supporting the emergence of new patterns which are capable of integrating standardized knowledge and procedures, on the one hand, with flexible, idiosyncratic knowledge and routines, on the other (as argued in Chapter 7).

Further, in discussing the implications of delegating *procedural* memory to software, we have argued that this performs as 'dual enabler', providing constraints that allow some actions while preventing others. This behaviour is even more relevant due to the tendency of software-embedded rules and routines to sink in and become invisible to the decision-maker. In these cases, the active interpretation emphasized by 'interpretive' literature is at times replaced by passive and automatic behaviour. While supporting the synchronization of efforts and economy of actions, software can therefore increase the risk of rigidity and lock-in. The example of the engineering workflow showed how strict software-embedded rules (i.e. workflow status) and assumptions (i.e. definition of roles and authority to change) might obstruct informal actions and flexible behaviour. While engineers can theoretically work around the software constraints, this is often prevented by the fact that software-embedded rules are often hidden from the user, and that, even when visible, they are not easy to customize or avoid. In contrast with the 'technology impact' literature, we have therefore emphasized that behaviour is not always the result of deliberate choices about technology use/misuse/disuse; hence, the need to adopt a learning view centred on routines behaviour, focusing on the organizational action that lies beneath explicit choices.

Theme 2: Influence of Software on Control and Flexibility

The second theme analysed the influence of software on the organization's flexibility and adaptive potential. We have argued that achieving and maintaining flexibility depends on the organization's ability to balance elements of control, stability with elements of variation and instability. This, for instance, involved managing the tensions that arise between formal and informal processes (i.e. software-embedded procedures and informal, tacit processes), standardized and non-standardized tools (i.e. software-based and paper-based tools), flexible and inflexible artefacts (i.e. released and work-in-progress documents).

Often the influence and benefits of ICTs are explained in the literature in terms of increased control: software acts as a stabilizing and standardizing element that brings order and control into the often disordered and unstable organizational environment. Integrated software tools help to achieve this by radically altering the balance between tacit and codified knowledge, informal and formal practices, often privileging the latter at the expense of the former. Software implementation provides, therefore, an ideal ground from which to observe the co-evolution of formal, standardizing tools and informal, flexible working practices.

What is not normally acknowledged in literature is that the software-induced push towards standardization, control and codification, which is meant to increase the transparency of actions and structures and, therefore, to support inter-functional co-ordination, can lead to organizational rigidity (i.e. reduced ability to share knowledge across functional or team boundaries). For instance, we have seen that, while increased control and visibility can benefit downstream functions where requirements for stability and control are high, it can become a source of inflexibility for those upstream functions whose tasks rely upon a high level of informality and creativity. Here, it can prevent the exploration of a wide range of alternative technology configurations, as well as decreasing the designer's ability to draw from heterogeneous design sources (i.e. knowledge from customers and suppliers, and design feedback from other functions).

The early integration of heterogeneous knowledge inputs into product definition performs the important function of delimiting search and design spaces to those territories, which are also compatible with other (internal and external) knowledge and requirements. As a consequence, software can also importantly influence the overall 'fitness' of the artefact. Further, by influencing an engineer's ability to be notified of and to incorporate changes to the design, software can also affect the organization's ability to flexibly react to the threats, and to effectively exploit the opportunities brought about by change. From all the above considerations, we concluded that integrated systems importantly influence the organization's innovative and adaptive potential.

Exploring the tensions between formal tools and informal practices has also emphasized that organizational stability and equilibrium are continuously emergent. By highlighting that instability and change, rather than stability and continuity, represent the prevailing conditions, this adds to our understanding of the dynamics of routine evolution. In highlighting that the consequences of software introduction depend upon the outcome of complex interactions between technological and organizational configurations, these results also hold important implications for the design and the implementation of software. We have seen, for example, that the same software package can produce completely opposite outcomes in terms of overall process and organizational flexibility in different implementation circumstances. This finding exposes the narrowness of the 'technology impact' view, which concentrates on the one-way influence of software on organizations thus failing to capture the fundamental influence of the organization's contingencies on software design and implementation.

Theme 3: Software and the Integration of Knowledge and Capabilities

The third theme has addressed the influence of software on the mechanisms by which heterogeneous organizational knowledge sources (i.e. from various functions and domains) and types (i.e. tacit/codified, formal/informal, computer-embedded/people embodied) are transferred across organizational boundaries and integrated into product definition. It also addressed the issue of the influence of software on collective knowledge-building activities, i.e. how software affects collaboration and knowledge sharing among heterogeneous organizational functions, or 'epistemic communities', and teams, or 'communities-of-practice'.

In this context, we have therefore observed the role of virtual and physical prototypes as 'boundary objects', 'points of obligatory passage', 'knowledge repositories' and 'intermediaries' among different communities and as loci where organizational conflicts are absorbed, and temporary truces can be reached. In characterizing the role of the digital, software-embedded, model as global knowledge repository and intermediary among different communities, we have also highlighted its limitations.

We have argued that, while the digital model can potentially act as a standardized interfacing device and facilitate the mutual flows of knowledge and activities across functional boundaries, this works only to the extent that it is appropriated and modified by each individual development function, according to its specific requirements, knowledge and objectives.

We have demonstrated that effective co-ordination in design and experimentation involves the formation of translation routines, which connect formal and informal, tacit and codified, local and global, heterogeneous and standardized knowledge sources and levels. These integrative routines support two types of knowledge flows: they facilitate the translation of local into global knowledge thus facilitating the early input of local multidisciplinary knowledge into global product definition; and they support knowledge translation from a global back to a local level, thus facilitating the re-appropriation of the digital model by each development function according to a format that is most familiar to that function.

The notion of translation routines explains more effectively how ICTs are able to co-ordinate actions and knowledge across different communities-of-practice and epistemic communities. It also explains how organizational functions are able to collaborate while maintaining divergent knowledge, interests and viewpoints. For example, it helps us understand how organizational tensions and conflicts, due to the coexistence of heterogeneous, specialized functions are absorbed; such heterogeneity (a consequence of the increase in division of labour and specialization) is in fact to be preserved as it can enrich the development process by providing specialized knowledge inputs. Among these inputs is that portion of knowledge which is impossible to articulate but which, contrary to the codification debate's belief, represents an essential input to the product definition process.

Finally, and most importantly, in capturing the emergence of such routines, we have shed light over those phenomena that lie at the very basis of the formation and maintenance of organizational capabilities, including the mechanisms by which organizations manage to integrate new and existing knowledge, technologies and capabilities. This represents an important theoretical and empirical step as the existence of dynamic capabilities had been assessed so far only *ex post*, as a measure of improved performance.

Cross-theme Patterns

While each theme occupied a specific chapter, all three recurred, in different measure, in each of the chapters. First, the *knowledge retention* theme (Chapter 5), which analysed the implication of delegating product and process memory to software, was also present in the flexibility chapter (6) where we discussed the interactions of software-embedded (formal) and people-embodied (informal) practices; the issue of knowledge storage and reuse was also present in the prototypes chapter (7) where we studied the implications of embedding local, specialized knowledge into global (computer-embedded) product and process definition. Second, the *knowledge selection* theme (Chapter 6), which examined the knowledge/action screening process operated by software-embedded rules was also addressed in Chapter 5 (memory), in relation to the processes of de-contextualization, articulation and codification that are required to embed local, tacit and function-specific knowledge into software. Third, the *knowledge variation and integration* theme, Chapter 7, which analysed the influence of software on the organization's ability to integrate new and existing knowledge sources and capabilities, was developed also in the memory chapter (5), where we addressed the integration of both generic and specialized knowledge sources and software applications; it was also present in the flexibility chapter (6), where we discussed the firm's ability to incorporate heterogeneous knowledge sources and types into the virtual product definition. The above results emphasize that, while the distinction between the processes of accumulation, selection and variation adopted in Evolutionary theory is valid theoretically, it tends to lose substance when confronted with the complex organizational reality.

The same observation applies to the *tensions* and *paradoxes* that emerged from the theme chapters. First, the tension between *standardization* and *heterogeneity* (Chapter 5), related to the need to exploit organizational function-based idiosyncrasies and retaining specialized software applications while ensuring inter-functional communication and collaboration was also emphasized in the flexibility chapter (6)'s discussion over the need to standardize processes while allowing scope for heterogeneous knowledge sources to enter the product-definition process. Second, the paradox between ensuring *control* and retaining *flexibility*, which emerged in Chapter 6 in relation to the implications of embedding control features into software, was also present in Chapter 5 (memory) where we discussed the implications of implementing an integrated, computer-managed product/database structure; the paradox was also highlighted in Chapter 7 (prototypes) in relation to the complementary nature of computer-controlled simulations (digital flexibility) and hand-made prototypes (interpretive flexibility). Third, the trade-off between *specialization* and *integration* was addressed in Chapter 7 (prototypes), in relation to maximizing the input of heterogeneous functions into product definition while maintaining co-ordination of knowledge and efforts. This was also introduced in Chapter 5 where the clash between functions having different knowledge, languages and cultures was highlighted; it also emerged in the discussion on the integration of local, specialized knowledge sources and activities into a global product definition (Chapter 6). Finally, the paradox between *continuity* and *discontinuity* (Chapter 7) analysed the emergence of organizational mechanisms able to integrate existing and new competences, routines and technologies; the paradox was also present in Chapter 5 in the dialectic between existing and new software applications and product/process structures, and in Chapter 6 in the tensions highlighted between perceived/actual processes, between control/variation and between formal tools and informal practices.

IMPLICATIONS FOR TECHNOLOGY MANAGEMENT POLICY AND PRACTICE

The results that emerged from the discussion centred around the above themes and challenges have therefore confirmed that the adoption of integrated systems holds fundamental implications for the innovating organization which go well beyond those commonly described in the literature. These implications are of primary concern both for those attempting to advance the theoretical understanding of the influence of (information) technology in organizations and for practitioners involved in the design and implementation of large-scale information systems. While we have so far explored the implications for theory, important inferences can also be drawn which are relevant to practitioners; these include IT, Operational and Change Management engineers and managers, and software developers.

A first important implication concerns the need for practitioners in software adopter organizations to carefully consider the consequences of embedding knowledge and assumptions into software; this was referred to as 'delegating memory to software'. Our argument has two types of implications. The first concerns the relationship between the structure (or language) of the existing technology and that of the software. We have argued that significant discrepancies can emerge as the software imposes a new standardizing language, which may be unfamiliar to some organizational functions. Intense inter-organizational conflicts can arise in this case, which can be due both to cognitive inertia (i.e. the unwillingness of certain functions to migrate towards the new language supported by the software), and to the partial inability of the new generic software technology to capture the specific knowledge of some functions or departments and convey this into product definition. Faced with this problem, the organization must choose between enforcing the new software and coping with emerging conflicts and reduced efficiency as experts learn to make the most of the new tool; or supporting the coexistence of new and old technology by creating interfaces between them. This problem is often reflected in the trade-off between enforcing an integrated generic system throughout the organization and allowing instead the new generic system to coexist side by side with existing legacy, and often specialized and best-in-class, applications. We have seen that, while an 'interfacing' strategy may be efficient from a data transfer viewpoint, this does not necessarily facilitate the transfer of knowledge across functions and therefore the formation of shared meanings. The second related point is that, due to the rationalizing effect of software over existing organizational structures, processes and communication flows, partial or ineffective implementation can result in further disintegration of existing (and frequently informal) organizational patterns of communication and knowledge transfer. This calls for a closer scrutiny of the way in which software-embedded assumptions materialize in practice.

Second, we have argued that organizational flexibility is not the straightforward outcome of software implementation, even if the software being implemented has been conceived to support a 'flexible', object-oriented, open architecture. Rather, flexibility is the overall outcome of the complex interactions between technology, people and organization. In our example, flexibility depends on the organization's ability at any point in time to strike a balance between more formal, standardizing and more informal, flexible routines. The task of maintaining this balance is rendered more difficult by the differential requirements for flexibility at different stages of PD (i.e. greater need for flexibility upstream, and for control downstream) or by different organizational functions (i.e. more creative, unstructured functions do not often cope well with high levels of control which is perceived as a source of rigidity). An important consequence of focusing on such interactions is that often software needs to be extensively customized in order to support overall organizational flexibility. This holds important implications for the adopting firm as well as for software producers. Specifically, information systems managers need to account for differing flexibility/control requirements across the organization and along the PD life cycle. It is also a responsibility for IT managers to ensure that software systems implementation facilitates the coexistence of formal and informal elements and to foresee and prevent the formation of process and cognitive rigidities. An important implication for software producers is that, although software might have been designed to support integration, flexibility and innovation, the opposite might occur if the deeper interactions of software processes and organizational processes are not adequately accounted for. This draws the attention to the fact that the flexibility built into software design may not be reflected in the overall flexibility of the technology-organization compound. It also suggests the level of depth and organizational knowledge that software producers must acquire in order to design products, which effectively support and do not hinder innovation in adopter organizations.

Third, this work has emphasized the importance for practitioners to support the emergence of translation routines, which ensure the integration of heterogeneous knowledge sources, types and levels from various organizational functions and distributed repositories. These routines also support the integration of existing and new knowledge, skills and capabilities. We have seen how, to support inter-functional integration and communication, practitioners must ensure that an appropriate balance is maintained between global and local knowledge and activity levels; this can be achieved by exploiting the co-ordinating role performed by standardized, virtual objects while, at the same time, supporting the emergence of more flexible boundary objects and infrastructures. A related concern is the need for software adopter firms to account for the difficulties involved in appropriating standard, software-embedded procedures and models. This is because, while software-embedded 'best practice' procedures and models can be relatively easy to acquire, they are of little use unless they are locally appropriated and effectively transformed into actual routines and prototypes. This led us to emphasize the inability of the diffusion approach to account for the organizational costs and productivity effects of software adoption processes. We have shown that the standardization of practices does not unequivocally imply reduced costs of knowledge acquisition, because knowledge, models and practices have to be 're-created' at each new organizational location. We have indicated that these implications are also relevant for drafting public policies that are aimed at supporting the transfer of best practice across firms, sectors and countries. From the viewpoint of software systems producer organizations, we have argued that, as integrated, enterprise-wide systems become more and more generic, they also require an increasing amount of customization by the user organization. Producers need to build greater flexibility and customization potential into their systems in order to facilitate the process of adaptation of generic systems to local, context-specific, circumstances and requirements. This involves designing systems that, while embodying standardized practices and models, are also flexible enough to allow for extensive local customization and adaptation.

Finally, we have argued that, while software is often described by practitioners as a straightforward 'tool' which can be used or disused, its influence is so pervasive to affect the very basis of the knowledge generation, adaptive and learning processes, at many levels. Because the influence of software is often automatic and not always visible, software-embedded routines cannot always be worked around by practitioners. This book has therefore pointed to the need for users to account for the tight interconnections between software and organizational routines, which render the outcome of processes and actions less clear and predictable then it might superficially appear.

Due to the level of empirical depth and detail in which our analysis has delved, many other inferences could be drawn which could be useful to practitioners and IT policy-makers. However, as the major ambition of this work was to advance theory, it is the author's decision to leave to practitioners the task of finding other important implications by comparing our evidence and analysis with their own experiences.

AVENUES FOR FUTURE RESEARCH

This research has highlighted significant areas within organizational knowledge studies and studies of IT and technical change that, because of their theoretical and empirical relevance, deserve further exploration. Further work is required in relation to a number of key issues.

First, we need to advance our understanding of the processes by which organizations create, accumulate and embed knowledge into artefacts. Specifically, we need to further explore the role played by epistemic communities and communities-of-practice in knowledge production. The collective mechanisms of knowledge codification, for instance, have just begun to be investigated empirically (and, to an extent, theoretically). Our contribution in this direction could be therefore taken further, for example by exploring the role of epistemic communities and communities-of-practice in the codification processes. This would include deepening our analysis of the role of communities in adopting and appropriating (and at times questioning, adapting and rejecting) the codified knowledge developed elsewhere in the organization or 'externally' acquired in the form of standardized models and standardizing technologies (i.e. integrated software). The related role of routines as governance mechanisms which absorb conflicts among such diverse communities also is of considerable interest and deserves further attention.

The mechanisms of memory reuse would also provide grounds for future investigation. We have analysed the processes of embedding knowledge in (software) technology and how these processes tend to reconfigure the knowledge stored according to technology-embedded structures, and we have discussed how at times this makes knowledge 're-activation' and reuse more problematic. It would be relevant to conduct research into the ways in which the 'frozen', codified or accumulated knowledge can be retrieved, re-articulated and subsequently brought to bear in decision-making. This could also help us understand the processes of rebuilding and retracing the complex socio-technical processes which generated the stored knowledge in the first place. For example, it could provide a deeper understanding of the circumstances in which technology fails, at the same time helping to trace and reconstruct responsibility in case of failure. This is especially important in relation to the issue of designing dependable computer-based systems.

While knowledge codification seems to have more recently become the focus of an increasing portion of research, the mechanisms of knowledge articulation also require further investigation. Rather than concentrating solely on articulation as a means to translate tacit into codified knowledge, it would be interesting to attempt to fully appreciate the relevance of what is lost during the process of articulation, including identifying a distinction between those relative portions of knowledge that can be effectively articulated and consequently made explicit, versus those which are likely to remain tacit. For example, which portion of knowledge comes from an implicitly recalled codebook, and which instead remains tacit because uncodifiable? Can software tools be designed which are able to convey uncodifiable knowledge in the process? Although these issues are dismissed by codification economists as uninteresting, they are instead of utmost importance as they can help identify and support those tacit and local knowledge pockets which fundamentally contribute to form the basis of an organization's innovative and competitive advantage.

Further investigation is also required into the organizational mechanisms that favour the intake of new knowledge while ensuring its compatibility and integration with existing knowledge. This includes investigating the long-term evolution of flexible integrative routines, including how these change as software implementation progresses and they become increasingly stable and 'institutionalized'. How can organizations ensure that these adaptive routines are supported and nurtured over time? What role can software play in this context? This task would entail a long-term fieldwork effort, as a historical analysis would in fact only highlight the codified, formal side of routine evolution, therefore failing to reveal the phenomena underlying the creation of capabilities.

A FINAL WORD

In conclusion, existing contributions on organizational knowledge have too often adopted an approach based on a narrow, abstract, static, context-independent and individualized notion of knowledge. In an attempt to move forwards, this research has emphasized the need to study knowledge neither as a commodity, nor as a static, abstract cognitive entity exclusively owned by individuals, but as a process which is context-dependent, collective, dynamic, contingent and often embedded with tensions and conflicts. It has pointed out that the specific role of organizations in knowledge creation, accumulation, transfer and integration has frequently not been accounted for. Even when taken into consideration, organizations have been often narrowly characterized as homogeneous, rather stable entities characterized by consistent objectives, incentives, culture and knowledge. Instead, we have emphasized that an organization's landscape is made of communities with idiosyncratic knowledge, culture, incentives and objectives. We have seen that, while these communities' aims and viewpoints are often incompatible, they often find a way to coexist by forming temporary truces, which are continuously being challenged and restored. We have also criticized the characterization of (information) technology as a narrow tool, which deterministically influences knowledge, people and organizations and indicated the need to embrace a more sophisticated analysis of the co-evolution of organizational, software-embedded processes.

We have demonstrated that important theoretical and empirical insights can be achieved by adopting a micro, in-depth and context-related approach that focuses on the complex, and always unresolved, tensions between technology and the organization. This work has shed light over the continuously unresolved attempts of an organization to strike an appropriate balance between elements of continuity and discontinuity, flexibility and control, change and stability, heterogeneity and standardization. Moreover, it has uncovered the processes by which complementary knowledge sources (i.e. tacit/articulable/codified, formal/informal, local/global, people-embodied/computer-embedded) can be co-ordinated and subsequently integrated into a single, consistent artefact definition. In doing so, it has helped to explain just how heterogeneous organizational functions and domains are able to co-operate while maintaining conflicting viewpoints, interests and goals, and while speaking idiosyncratic, discipline- and function-specific languages. Finally, and most importantly, it has provided a unique viewpoint to observe the evolution of organizational routines, including those mechanisms that can cause a routine to change or subside. It has thus provided us with a substantially new understanding of the sophisticated processes that allow organizations to create, maintain and renew their capabilities.

The study of the influence of integrated software systems over the organization's practices and cognitive dynamics has therefore enabled us to draw important theoretical and empirical implications for the firm as knowledge user and producer.

Appendix: Internal Company Documents

Digital Mock-up: Benefits to the X100 Programme (X100)

Digital Mock-up: Scope of Work (DMU)

An Integrated Product Development Strategy (IPDS)

Philosophical Approach to DMU Development (PHI)

The Workflow Process (WIP)

References

Adler, P.S. (1990a). 'Managing high tech processes: the challenge of CAD/CAM', in M.A. von Glinow and S.A. Mohrman, *Managing Complexity in High Technology Organisations*, New York: Oxford University Press.

Adler, P.S. (1990b). 'Shared learning', *Management Science*, 36: 938–57.

Adler, P.S., Goldoftas, B., Levine, D.I. (1999). 'Flexibility versus efficiency? A case study of model changeovers in the Toyota production system', *Organization Science*, 10(1): 43–68.

Akrich, M. (1992). 'The de-scription of technical objects', in W.E. Bijker and J. Law (eds), *Shaping Technology/Building Society – Studies in Sociotechnical Change*, Cambridge, MA: MIT Press.

Amann, K. (2002). 'PLM market outlook solid despite economic downturn', CIMdata, July.

Anderson, J.R. (1983). *The Architecture of Cognition*, Cambridge, MA: Harvard University Press.

Aoki, M. (1986). 'Horizontal vs. vertical information structure of the firm', *American Economic Review*, 76(5): 971–83.

Argyris, C. and Schon, D.A. (1978). *Organizational Learning*, Reading, MA: Addison-Wesley.

Arora, A. and Gambardella, A. (1994). 'The changing technology of technological change: general and abstract knowledge and the division of innovative labour', *Research Policy*, 23: 523–32.

Arrow, K.J. (1974). *The Limits of the Organization*, New York: Norton.

Arrow, K.J. (1979). 'The economics of information', in M.L. Dertouzos and J. Moses (eds), *The Computer Age: A Twenty-Year View*, Cambridge, MA: MIT Press, 306–17.

Arthur, W.B. (1994). 'Complexity in economic theory – inductive reasoning and bounded rationality', *American Economic Review*, 84(2): 406–11.

Bannon, L.J. and Kuutti, K. (1996). 'Shifting perspectives on organizational memory: from storage to active remembering', *Proceedings IEEE HICSS 96*, Hawaii.

Bathe, K.J. (1996). *Finite Elements Procedures*, New York: Prentice-Hall International.

Berg, M. (1997a). 'Of forms, containers, and the electronic medical record: some tools for a sociology of the formal', *Science, Technology and Human Values*, 22(4): 403–33.

Berg, M. (1997b). *Rationalising Medical Work: Decision-Support Techniques and Medical Practices*, Cambridge, MA: MIT Press.

Berg, M. (1998). 'The politics of technology: On bringing social theory into technological design', *Science, Technology and Human Values*, 23(4): 456–90.

Boland, R.J. and Hirschheim, R.A. (eds) (1987). *Critical Issues In Information Systems Research*, John Wiley Information Systems series, Chichester: Wiley.

Boniz, P. and Krzystek, P. (1996). 'Reverse engineering in combination with digital photogrammetry', in M.J. Pratt, R.D. Srinam and M.J. Wozny (eds), *Product Modelling for Computer Integrated Design and Manufacturing*, London: Chapman and Hall.

Boulding, K.E. (1966). 'The economics of knowledge and the knowledge of economics', *American Economic Review*, 56(2): 1–13.

Bourdieu, P. (1977). *Outline of a theory of practice*, Cambridge: Cambridge University Press.

Bowker, G.C. and Star, S.L. (1999). *Sorting Things Out: Classification and its Consequences*, Cambridge, MA: MIT Press.

Brady, T., Tierney, M. and Williams, R. (1992). 'The commodification of industry applications software', *Industrial and Corporate Change*, 1(3), 489–513.

Brown, J.S. and Duguid P. (1996). 'Organizational learning and communities-of-practice – Toward a unified view of working, learning and innovation', in M.D. Cohen and L. Sproull (eds), *Organizational Learning*, Thousand Oaks, CA: Sage Publications, pp. 58–82.

Brown, J.S. and Duguid, P. (2000). *The Social Life of Information*, Cambridge, MA: Harvard Business School Press.

Bucciarelli, L.L. (1988). 'Engineering design process', in F.A. Dubinskas (ed.), *Making Time: Ethnographies of High-Technology Organizations*, Philadelphia, PA: Temple University Press, Ch. 3: pp. 92–122.

Button, G. (1993). 'The curious case of the vanishing technology', in G. Button (ed.), *Technology in Working Order – Studies of Work, Interaction and Technology*, London: Routledge.

Callon, M. (1995). 'Four models of the dynamic science', in S. Jasanoff (ed.), *Handbook of Science and Technology Studies*, Thousand Oaks, CA: Sage Publications.

Carlsson, B. (1989). 'Flexibility and the theory of the firm', *International Journal of Industrial Organization*, 7: 179–203.

Chandler, A.D. (1962). *Strategy and Structure: Chapters in the History of the American Industrial Enterprise*, London: MIT Press.

Chandler, A.D. (1990). *Scale and Scope: The Dynamics of Industrial Capitalism*, Cambridge, MA: Belknap Press of Harvard University Press.

Coase, R. (1937). 'The Nature of the Firm', *Economica*, 4: 386–405.

Cohen, M.D. (1991). 'Individual learning and organizational routines: emerging connections', *Organization Science*, 2: 135–9.

Cohen, M.D., and Sproull, L. (1991). *Organizational Learning*, Thousand Oaks, CA: Sage Publications.

Cohen, M.D., Burkhart, R., Dosi, G., Egidi, M., Marengo, L., Warglien, M. and Winter, S. (1996). 'Routines and other recurring patterns of organizations: contemporary research issues', *IIASA Working Paper*, March.

Cohen, W.M. and Levinthal, D.A. (1990). 'Absorptive capacity: a new perspective on learning and innovation', *Administrative Science Quarterly*, 35: 128–52.

Cohendet, P. and Meyer-Krahmer, F. (2001). 'The theoretical and policy implications of knowledge codification', *Research Policy*, 30(9): 1563–91.

Collins (1987). English Language Dictionary, Glasgow: HarperCollins.

Collins, H.M. (1974). 'The TEA set: tacit knowledge in scientific networks', *Science Studies*, 4: 165–86.

Collins, H.M. (1990). *Artificial experts. Social knowledge and intelligent machines*, Cambridge (MA): MIT Press.

Cook, S.D.N. and Yanow, D. (1993). 'Culture and organisational learning', *Journal of Management Inquiry*, 2(4): 373–90.

Coombs, R. and Hull, R. (1997). 'Knowledge management practices and path-dependency in innovation', CRIC Discussion Paper, 2, University of Manchester.

Coriat, B. and Dosi, G. (1994). 'Learning how to govern and learning how to solve problems: on the co-evolution of competences, conflicts and organizational routines', prepared for the Prince Bertil Symposium, Stockholm School of Economics, June.

Cowan, R., and Foray, D. (1995). 'The changing economics of technological learning', IIASA Working Paper.

Cowan, R. and Foray, D. (1997). 'The economics of codification and the diffusion of knowledge', *Industrial and Corporate Change*, 6(3): 595–622.

Cowan, R., David, P.A. and Foray, D. (1998). 'The explicit economics of knowledge codification and tacitness', TSER/TIPIK Working Paper.

Crainer, X. and Obeng, Y. (1994). *Making Re-engineering Happen*, London: Pitman.

Cusumano, M. (1992). 'Shifting economies: from craft production to flexible systems and software factories', *Research Policy*, 21: 453–80.

D'Adderio, L. (1996). 'Data, information and knowledge in organisations', Project Report to the Economic and Social Research Council (ESRC), Brighton: SPRU, University of Sussex.

D'Adderio, L. (2000). 'The diffusion of integrated software solutions – Trends and challenges', prepared for the 3rd TSER/ESSY Meeting, Berlin, 3–7 April.

D'Adderio, L. (2001). 'Crafting the virtual prototype: how firms integrate knowledge and capabilities within and across organizational boundaries', *Research Policy*, 30(9) December: 1409–24.

D'Adderio, L. (2002). 'Configuring software, reconfiguring memories: the influence of integrated systems on knowledge storage, retrieval and reuse', Proceedings of the SAC Conference 2002, Madrid, Spain, ACM 1-58113-445-2/02/03.

D'Adderio, L. (2003). 'Configuring software, reconfiguring memories: the influence of integrated systems on the reproduction of knowledge and routines', *Industrial and Corporate Change*, special issue on the 'Theory of the firm, learning and organization', 12(2) April.

Daft, R.L. and Weick, K.E. (1984). 'Toward a model of organisation as interpretation systems', *Academy of Management Review*, 9: 284–95.

Dasgupta, P. and David, P.A. (1994). 'Toward a new economics of science', *Research Policy*, 23: 487–521.

Davenport, T.H. and Short, J.E. (1990). 'The new industrial engineering: information technology and business process redesign', *Sloan Management Review*, Summer: 11–27.

De Groot, A. (1965). 'Thought and choice in chess', *Psychological Studies*, 4, Paris: Mouton.

Deitz, D. (1997). 'The convergence of design and analysis', *Mechanical Engineering*, March: 93–100.

Dosi, G. and Egidi, M. (1991). 'Substantive and procedural uncertainty. An exploration of economic behaviours in complex and changing environments', *Journal of Evolutionary Economics*, 1: 145–68.

Dosi, G. and Marengo, L. (1994). 'Toward a theory of organizational competencies', in R.W. England (ed.), *Evolutionary Concepts in Contemporary Economics*, Ann Arbor, MI: University of Michigan Press.

Dosi, G., Marengo, L. and Fagiolo, G. (1996). 'Learning in evolutionary environments', IIASA Working Paper.

Dosi, G., Nelson, R.R. and Winter, S.G. (eds) (2000). *The Nature and Dynamics of Organizational Capabilities*, New York: Oxford University Press.

Downey, G.L. (1998). *The Machine in Me: An Anthropologist Sits among Computer Engineers*, New York: Routledge.

Eisenhardt, K.M. (1989). 'Building theories from case study research', *Academy of Management Review*, 14(4): 532–50.

Ergas, H. (1994). 'The 'new face' of technological change and some of its consequences', Working Paper, Harvard University, Centre for Science and International Affairs.

Ferguson, E.S. (1993a). 'How engineers lose touch', *Invention and Technology*, Winter: 16–24.

Ferguson, E.S. (1993b). *Engineering and the Mind's Eye*, Cambridge, MA: MIT Press.

Fleck, J. (1988). 'Innofusion or diffusation? The nature of technological development in robotics', Edinburgh PICT Working Paper 7, University of Edinburgh.

Foray, D. and Steinmueller, W.E. (2001). 'Replication of routine, the domestication of tacit knowledge and the economics of inscription technology', Conference in Honour of R.R. Nelson and S.G. Winter, Aalborg (DK), 12–15 June, 2001.

Fowler, D. (1998). 'Eurofighter's smoother take off', *The Engineer*, 22: 20–21.

Fransman, M. (1994). 'Information, knowledge, vision and theories of the firm', *Industrial and Corporate Change*, 3(3): 713–57.

Fujimura, J.H. (1992). 'Crafting science: standardized packages, boundary objects, and "translation"', in A. Pickering (ed.), *Science as Practice and Culture*, Chicago: University of Chicago Press, pp. 168–211.

Gasser, L. (1986). 'The integration of computing and routine work', *ACM Transactions on Office Information Systems*, 4: 205–25.

Glaser, B. and Strauss, A. (1967). *The Discovery of Grounded Theory: Strategies of Qualitative Research*, London: Wiedenfeld and Nicholson.

Grandstrand, O., Patel, P. and Pavitt, K. (1997). 'Multi-technology corporations: why they have 'distributed' rather than core competencies', *California Management Review*, 39(4): 8–25.

Hammersley, M. and Atkinson, P. (1995). *Ethnography: Principles in Practice*, 2nd edition, London: Tavistock.

Hayek, F.A. (1945). 'The use of knowledge in society', *American Economic Review* 35(4): 519–30.

Henderson, K. (1991). 'Flexible sketches and inflexible databases: visual communication, conscription devices, and boundary objects in design engineering', *Science, Technology and Human Values*, 16(4): 448–73.

Henderson, K. (1995). 'The visual culture of engineers', in S.L. Star (ed.), *The Culture of Computing*, Oxford: Blackwell, 196–218.

Henderson, R.M. (1992). 'Technological change and the management of architectural knowledge', in T.A. Kochan and M. Useem (eds.), *Transforming Organisations*, Oxford: Oxford University Press, pp. 118–132.

Henderson, R.M. (1994). 'The evolution of integrative capability: innovation in cardiovascular drug discovery', *Industrial and Corporate Change*, 3(3): 607–630.

Henderson, R.M. and Clark, K.B. (1990). 'Architectural innovation: the reconfiguration of existing product technologies and the failure of established firms', *Administrative Science Quarterly*, 35: 9–30.

Hirt, S.G. and Swanson, E.B. (1999). 'Adopting SAP at Siemens Power Corporation', *Journal of Information Technology*, 14: 243–51.

Holland, J.H. (1992). *Adaptation in Natural and Artificial Systems: An Introductory Analysis with Applications to Biology, Control, and Artificial Intelligence*, Cambridge, MA: MIT Press.

Hutchins, E. (1995). *Cognition in the Wild*, Cambridge, MA: MIT Press.

Hutchins, E. and Hazelhurst, B. (1995). 'Learning in the cultural process', in C.G. Langton, C. Taylor, J.D. Farmer, and S. Rasmussen (eds), *Artificial Life II: Studies in the Sciences of Complexity*, Reading, MA: Addison-Wesley.

Iansiti, M. (1995). 'Shooting the rapids: managing product development in turbulent environments', *California Management Review*, 38(1): 37–58.

Iansiti, M. (1997). *Technology Integration: Making Critical Choices in a Turbulent World*, Boston, MA: Harvard Business School Press.

Iansiti, M. and Clark, K.B. (1994). 'Integration and dynamic capability: evidence from product development in automobiles and mainframe computers', *Industrial and Corporate Change*, 3: 557–605.

James, W. (1950). *The Principles of Psychology*, New York: Dover Publications.

Jill, J. and Johnson, P. (1991). *Research Methods for Managers*, London: Paul Chapman.

Katz, R. and Allen, T. (1988). 'Organizational issues in the introduction of new technologies', in R. Katz (ed.), *Managing Professionals in Innovative Organizations*, Cambridge, MA: Ballinger.

Kay, N.M. (1994). *The Emergent Firm*, London: Macmillan Press.

Kling, R. (1991). 'Computerisation and social transformations', *Science, Technology and Human Values*, 17: 349–65.

Kling, R. and Scacchi, W. (1982). 'The web of computing: computer technology as social organisation', *Advances in Computers*, 21: 1–90.

Knight, F.H. (1921). *Risk, Uncertainty and Profit*, Boston, MA: Houghton Mifflin.

Knorr-Cetina, K. (1999). *Epistemic Cultures: How the Sciences Make Knowledge*, Cambridge, MA: Harvard University Press.

Koch, C. (1998). 'SAP/R3 – An IT plague or the answer to a tailor's dream?', Institute for Technology and Social Science, Technical University of Denmark, Lyngby.

Kogut, B. and Zander, U. (1992). 'Knowledge of the firm, combinative capabilities, and the replication of technology', *Organization Science*, 3(3): 383–97.

Latour, B. (1987). *Science in Action*, Cambridge, MA: Harvard University Press.

Lave, J. (1988). *Cognition in Practice: Mind, Mathematics, and Culture in Every-day Life*, Cambridge: Cambridge University Press.

Lave, J. and Wenger, E. (1991). *Situated Learning: Legitimate Peripheral Participation*, Cambridge, MA: Cambridge University Press.

Law, J. and Callon, M. (1995). 'Engineering and sociology in a military aircraft project: a network analysis of technological change', in S. Leigh Star (ed.), *Ecologies of Knowledge – Work and Politics in Science and Technology*, New York: State University of New York Press.

Leonard-Barton, D. (1992). 'Core capabilities and core rigidities: a paradox in managing new product development', *Strategic Management Journal* 13: 111–25.

Leonard-Barton, D. (1995). *Wellsprings of Knowledge – Building and Sustaining the Sources of Innovation*, Boston, MA: Harvard Business School Press.

Levinthal, D.A. (2000). 'Capabilities in complex worlds', in G. Dosi, R.R. Nelson and S.G. Winter (eds), *The Nature and Dynamics of Capabilities*, Oxford: Oxford University Press.

Levitt, B. and March, J.G. (1988). 'Organizational learning', *Annual Review of Sociology*, 14: 319–40.

Levy, P. (1997). *Il Virtuale*, Milano: Raffaello Cortina Editore.

Levy, P. (1999). *Cybercultura – Gli usi sociali delle nuove tecnologie*, Milano: Feltrinelli.

Lindblom, C.E. (1959). 'The science of "muddling through"', *Public Administration Review*, 19(2): 79–88.

Machlup, F. (1980). *Knowledge and Knowledge Production, Vol. 1 of Knowledge: Its Creation, Distribution, and Economic Significance*, Princeton, NJ: Princeton University Press.

Malerba, F. and Orsenigo, L. (1998). 'Knowledge, innovative activities and industry evolution', TSER/TIPIK Workshop, Paris, 4–5 December.

March, J.G. (1991). 'Exploration and exploitation in organizational learning', *Organization Science*, 2(1): 71–87.

March, J.G. and Simon, H. (1993). *Organizations*, 2nd edition, Oxford: Blackwell.

Marshak, J. (1974). *Economic Information, Decision and Prediction Selected Essays*, vol. 2, Boston: Reidel.

Miller, E. (1998). 'PDM moves to the mainstream', *Mechanical Engineering*, October.

Miller, E. (1999). 'Integrating PDM and ERP', CIMdata, March.

Moorman C. and Miner, A.S. (1998). 'Organizational improvisation and organisational memory', *Academy of Management Review*, 23(4): 698–723.

Nelson, R.R. and Winter, S.G. (1982). *An Evolutionary Theory of Economic Change*, Cambridge, MA: Belknap Press.

Newell, A. and Simon, H. (1972). *Human Problem-Solving*, New York: Prentice-Hall.

Nonaka, I. (1994). 'A dynamic theory of organizational knowledge creation', *Organization Science*, 5: 14–37.

Nooteboom, B. (1992). 'Towards a dynamic theory of transactions', *Journal of Evolutionary Economics*, 2: 281–99.

Onwubiko, C. (1989). *Foundations of 'Computer-Aided Design'*, New York: West Publishing.

Orlikowski, W.J. (1992). 'The duality of technology: rethinking the concept of technology in organizations', *Organization Science*, 3(3): 398–427.

Orlikowski, W.J. and Gash, D.C. (1994). 'Technological frames: making sense of information technology in organizations', *ACM Transactions on Information Systems*, 12(2): 174–207.

Palframan, D. (1999). 'Computer-aided engineering: the trick's in the training', *The Engineer*, 7: 15–16.

Parnas, D.L. and Clements, P.C. (1986). 'A rational design process: how and why to fake it', *IEEE Transactions on Software Engineering*, SE-12 (2): 251–7.

Pavitt, K. (1998). 'Technologies, products and organization in the innovating firm: what Adam Smith tells us and Joseph Schumpeter doesn't', *Industrial and Corporate Change*, 7(3): 433–51.

Penrose, E.T. (1959). *The Theory of the Growth of the Firm*, Oxford: Basil Blackwell.

Petroski, H. (1996). *Invention by Design – How Engineers Get from Thought to Thing*, Cambridge, MA: Cambridge University Press.

Pickering, A. (1995). *The Mangle of Practice: Time, Agency and Science*, Chicago: University of Chicago Press.

Pisano, G. (1996). *The Development Factory*, Cambridge, MA: Harvard Business School Press.

Polanyi, M. (1968). *Personal Knowledge: Towards a Post-critical Philosophy*, London: Routledge.

Prahalad, C.K. and Hamel, G. (1990). 'The core competence of the corporation', *Harvard Business Review*, 68(3): 79–91.

Richardson, G.B. (1960). *Information and Investment: A Study in the Working of the Competitive Economy*, Oxford: Oxford University Press.

Rosenberg, N. (1982). *Inside the Black Box*, Cambridge: Cambridge University Press.

Rothwell, R. (1993). 'Systems integration and networking: the fifth generation innovation process', paper prepared for the Chaire Hydro-Quebec Conference en Gestion de la Technologie, Montreal, 28 May.

Sachs E., Cima, M., Bredt, J., Curodeau, A., Fan, T. and Brancazio, D. (1992). 'CAD-casting: direct fabrication of ceramic shells and cores by three-dimensional printing', *Manufacturing Review*, 5(2): 117–26.

Sanchez, R. and Mahoney, J. (1996). 'Modularity, flexibility, and knowledge management in product and organizational design', *Strategic Management Journal*, 17: 63–76.

Simon, H.A. and Egidi, M. (ed.), Marris, R. (ed.), (1992). *Economics, Bounded Rationality, and Cognitive Revolution*, Brookfield, VT: Edward Elgar.

Software Producer's Manual (1998).

Spender, J.C. (1995). 'Organizational knowledge, learning, and memory: three concepts in search of a theory', Working Paper, Newark: Rutgers University.

Star, S.L. (1992). 'The Trojan door: organizations, work, and the 'open black box', *Systems Practice*, 5(4): 395–410.

Star, S.L. and Griesemer, J.R. (1989). 'Institutional ecology, "translations" and boundary objects: amateurs and professionals in Berkeley's Museum of Vertebrate Zoology, 1907–39', *Social Studies of Science*, 19: 387–420.

Steinmueller, W.E. (1998). 'Does information and communication technology facilitate 'codification' of knowledge?', TSER/TIPIK, Brighton: SPRU, University of Sussex.

Stigler, G. (1939). 'Production and distribution in the short run', *Journal of Political Economy*, 47(3): 305–27.

Stigler, G. (1961). 'The economics of information', *Journal of Political Economy*, 69(3): 213–25.

Stiglitz, J.E. (1977). 'Symposium on economics of information: introduction', *Review of Economic Studies*, 44: 389–91.

Suchman, L. (1987). *Plans and Situated Action: The Problem of Human–Machine Communication*, Cambridge, MA: Cambridge University Press.

Teece, D.J., Pisano, G. and Shuen, A. (1990). 'Firm capabilities, resources and the concept of strategy', Consortium on Competitiveness and Co-operation Working Paper 90–9, Berkeley, CA: University of California at Berkeley, Center for Research in Management.

Thiétart, R.A. (1995). ['Evolution of the strategy function'] 'L'évolution de la "fonction" stratégie', *Entreprises et histoire*, 10: 91–5.

Thiétart, R.A. and Forgues, B. (1995). 'Chaos theory and organisation', *Organization Science*, 6(1): 19–31.

Thomke, S.H. (1997). 'The role of flexibility in the development of new products: an empirical study', *Research Policy*, 26: 105–19.

Thomke, S.H. (1998). 'Managing experimentation in the design of new products', *Management Science*, 44(6): 743–62.

Thomke, S.H., Von Hippel, E. and Franke, R. (1998). 'Modes of experimentation: an innovation process – and competitive – variable', *Research Policy*, 27: 315–32.

Tyre, M.J. and Von Hippel, E. (1997). 'The situated nature of adapting learning in organizations', *Organization Science*, 8(1): 71–81.

Ullman, E. (1997). *Close to the Machine: Technofilia and Its Discontents*, San Francisco. CA: City Lights.

Ulrich, K. (1995). 'The role of product architecture in the manufacturing firm', *Research Policy*, 24: 419–40.

Upton, D.M. (1994). 'The management of manufacturing flexibility', *California Management Review*, Winter: 72–89.

Vincenti, W.G. (1990). *What Engineers Know and How They Know It – Analytical Studies from Aeronautical History*, Baltimore, MD: Johns Hopkins University Press.

Von Hippel E. (1994). '"Sticky information" and the locus of problem-solving', *Management Science*, 40(4): 429–39.

Walsh, J.P. (1995). 'Managerial and organizational cognition: notes from a trip down memory lane', *Organization Science*, 6(3): 280–321.

Walsh, J.P. and Ungson, G.R. (1991). 'Organizational memory', *Academy of Management Review*, 16(1): 57–91.

Wegner, D.M. (1986). 'Transactive memory: a contemporary analysis of the group mind', in B. Mullen and G.R. Goethals (eds), *Theories of Group Behaviour*, New York: Springer-Verlag, 1986, pp. 185–208.

Weick, K. (1979). *The Social Psychology of Organizing*, 2nd edition, Reading, MA: Addison-Wesley.

Wernerfelt, B. (1984). 'A resource-based view of the firm', *Strategic Management Journal*, 5: 171–80.

Wheelwright, S.C. and Clark, K.B. (1992). *Revolutionising Product Development*, New York: The Free Press.

Wildawsky, A. (1983). 'Information as an organizational problem', *Journal of Management Studies*, 20(1): 29–40.

Winter S.G. (1987). 'Knowledge and competence as strategic assets', in D.J. Teece (ed.), *The Competitive Challenge: Strategies for Industrial Innovation and Renewal*, New York: Harper and Row.

Winter, S.G. (1988). 'On Coase, competence and the corporation', *Journal of Law, Economics and Organization*, 4(1): 163–80.

Winter, S.G. (2000). Comments to the Dynamic Capabilities Session at the CCC Conference, Chicago, IL, 7–9 April.

Winter, S.G. and Zollo, M. (1999). 'From organizational routines to dynamic capabilities', TSER/TIPIK Working Paper.

Ziman, J. (ed.) (2000). *Technological Innovation as an Evolutionary Process*, Cambridge: Cambridge University Press.

Zuboff, S. (1988). *In the Age of the Smart Machine: The Future of Work and Power*, New York: Basic Books.

Index

absorptive capacity 23
actualization 14, 176, 191–2
  as problematic translation process
    176–8
adaptive potential, firm's 8, 135–6, 138,
    139–41, 143, 160–61, 169, 170,
    194, 197, 199, 203, 204
Adler, P.S. 79, 136, 173
aerospace industry 63, 72, 75, 184
agency 55
Akrich, M. 90
ALIAS 103, 180
Allen, T. 20
Amann, K. 102
ambiguity 45
  pockets of 182
  reduction of 17, 95, 121, 185, 186
Analysis function, Digital Model as
    interfacing between Engineering
    and 187–91
analysts, specialized expertise of
    189–91
Anderson, J.R. 107
Aoki, M. 121
architectural knowledge 32, 58
architecture, object-oriented 73, 86, 92,
    108–9, 209
Argyris, C. 23
Arora, A. 19
Arrow, K.J. 39
Arthur, W.B. 23, 28
articulation 47, 53, 56, 211–12
artificial intelligence 43
assembly drawings 93–4, 108
Atkinson, P. 65
authority, see control
AutoCAD 60
automatic routine behaviour 25–7, 38,
    112–13, 128, 129, 131, 140–41,
    203
automotive industry 62–3, 72

Bannon, L.J. 110, 112, 132
base data 150
Bathe, K.J. 190
beliefs formation 113
Berg, M. 32, 44, 46–7, 48, 51, 52, 53,
    54, 55, 56, 57, 58, 69, 141–2
bespoke software 74–6
best practice 30, 49, 112, 147, 154, 165,
    174, 195, 208, 210
Bill of Materials (BoM) 149
  access to 84
  definition of 151
  freeze 152–3
    PDM and flexibility in 64, 135,
      153–66
  learning about 61
  structure of 108
Boeing 19
Boland, R.J. 21
BoM, see Bill of Materials (BoM)
Boniz, P. 181
Boolean logic statements 115–16, 118,
    119
Boulding, K.E. 39
boundary objects 130, 202, 205, 210
Bourdieu, P. 46, 139
Bowker, G.C. 5, 17, 43, 44, 56, 121,
    122, 130, 178, 186, 187
BPR, see Business Process Re-
    engineering (BPR)
Brady, T. 76, 102
breaks in the process 181
Brown, J.S. 6, 17, 46, 47, 48, 49–50,
    52–3, 130, 139, 170, 174, 192
Bucciarelli, L.L. 44, 45, 138–9
Business Process Re-engineering (BPR)
    4, 30, 49–50, 73–4, 81, 112
Button, G. 52

CAD Data Manager (CDM) software 3,
    84, 88

management of workflow process delegated to 124–7

CAD software, *see* Computer-Aided Design (CAD) software

CAID model, *see* Computer Aided Industrial Design (CAID) model

Callon, M. 39, 171

capability and competition 22

capability maintenance process 33

Carlsson, B. 136, 171

case studies
data analysis 66–7
developing theory from grounded research 68
researcher's involvement in 65–6
selection of 64–5

CDM software, *see* CAD Data Manager (CDM) software

Chandler, A.D. 22, 33, 41

change
distinction between stability and 33
PDM and the management of 152–3
as prevailing condition 204–5

Check in Progress (CIP) 125

CIP, *see* Check in Progress (CIP)

Clark, K.B. 4, 5, 22, 33, 34, 35–6, 41, 45, 173

clay models, scanning of 58, 176, 179–83

Clements, P.C. 171

CNC models, *see* Computer Numerical Control (CNC) models

Coase, R. 39

codified knowledge 7, 8, 11, 31
boundaries between tacit knowledge and 12–13
in routines 30, 36, 37
see also knowledge codification debate

cognitive psychology 15–16, 25, 27, 32, 43

Cohen, M.D. 25, 26, 27, 29, 30, 41, 45–6, 61, 107, 112, 113, 123, 132, 133, 134

Cohen, W.M. 23, 111, 131

Cohendet, P. 10, 41, 133, 170

collective vs. individual knowledge building processes 21, 31–2, 47–8, 200

Collins, H.M. 39, 142, 171

combinative capabilities 23

Commercial Off-the-Shelf (COTS) software systems, *see* integrated Commercial Off-the-Shelf (COTS) software systems

common intentionality 20, 22

Common Object Request Broker Architecture (CORBA) 86

communities of interpretation 49

communities-of-practice 6, 17, 20, 21, 48–50, 106, 129, 130, 170, 174, 192, 193, 200, 202, 205, 211

competition 22, 136

component drawings 108

Computer-Aided Design (CAD) software 3, 19, 54, 61, 84, 88, 116, 137
changes in model status and ownership 125–7
failure of 57
SOLID model 181, 185, 186
analyst's special expertise 189–91
integration of design and analysis 188–9
single common model 188
SURFACE model
creating and modifying 179–81
as a standardizing device 185–7
translating into CAD language 183–5
visual and kinaesthetic knowledge required for 181–3

Computer Aided Industrial Design (CAID) model 181

Computer Numerical Control (CNC) models 84

computer simulations 175, 177

Computer-Supported Co-operative Work (CSCW) 8–9, 43, 51, 141, 199

concurrent design processes 93–5

confidentiality 62, 65

configured product structures 89

conflict absorption, inter-organizational 96, 208
flexibility potential of PD processes related to 136, 139–40, 142, 143, 160–66, 168
organizational routines as loci of 27–9
VPM technology and 65, 97–8, 174, 192–3, 205, 206

consultants 77

consumer electronics industry 63, 190
contextual aspect of routines 27–9, 200
contingent history 56
continuity-breaking mechanisms 143
control
  routines as mechanisms for 27–9
  software-embedded rules for 58, 89,
    124–9
    and flexibility 64, 94–5, 100, 111,
      124, 126–7, 130–31, Ch. 6, 201,
      203–5, 207, 209
    see also flexibility, balance
      between control and
convergence of Design and Analysis
  189
Cook, S.D.N. 15
Coombs, R. 132
CORBA, *see* Common Object Request
  Broker Architecture (CORBA)
core capabilities 23, 29
core competencies 23
core modules 76
core rigidities 29, 111
Coriat, B. 24, 27, 28, 29, 34
cost–benefit analysis 16, 195
COTS software systems, *see* integrated
  Commercial Off-the-Shelf (COTS)
  software systems
Cowan, R. 5, 12, 13, 14, 16, 17, 18, 20,
  40, 122, 130, 133, 192
Crainer, X. 33
creative invention 14
CSCW, *see* Computer-Supported
  Co-operative Work (CSCW)
customization 109, 195, 209, 210
Cusumano, M. 136

D'Adderio, L. 39, 41, 71, 72, 73, 121,
  131
Daft, R.L. 49
Dasgupta, P. 13, 40
data analysis 66–7
data communication entity 80–81
data conversion, reduction of 95
data core 80–81, 92
data ordering, sifting and control 96–7
data re-interpretation, reduction of 95
data vaults 88, 94, 105, 108, 147
database, persistent 78
Davenport, T.H. 85

David, P.A. 5, 12, 13, 14, 17, 18, 20, 40,
  133, 192
De Groot, A. 23
declarative memory, organizational 25
  definition of 107–8
  influence of PDM software on
    106–10, 129–30
    coexistence of incompatible
      structures 114–18
    emergence of shared meanings and
      organizational coherence 121–3
    PDM and the integration of
      heterogeneous technology and
      data structures 114
    role of PDM in influencing
      meaning formation 118–21
Deitz, D. 188–9
design as critique 58
design freezes 126–7, 137, 145, 146
  BoM freeze, *see* Bill of Materials
    (BoM)
design landscapes 57
design process
  individual vs. collective knowledge-
    building processes in 47–8
  rational characterization of 44–7
design spaces 148
digital flexibility 176, 185–6
Digital Mock-Up (DMU) 81–5, 150,
  196
Digital Model (DM), creation of, *see*
  Virtual Product Model (VPM)
  technology
Digital Model (DM) stage 83, 84
Digital Pre-Assembly stage 83, 84
Digital Product Model (DPM) stage 83,
  84, 196
distinctive competences 22–3, 24
distributed knowledge 32, 48, 59, 199,
  200
division of labour, *see* functional
  specialization
DMU, *see* Digital Mock-Up (DMU)
Dosi, G. 24, 26, 27, 28, 29, 31, 33, 34,
  132, 134
Downey, G.L. 62
dual enabler, software as 111, 128, 130,
  203
Duguid, P. 6, 17, 46, 47, 48, 49–50,
  52–3, 130, 139, 170, 174, 192

dynamic capabilities approach 22–3, 33–8
dynamic capability, definition of 34
dynamic routines 25, 32–8, 131, 141

E-CAD 179–85 *passim*
ECO, *see* Engineering Change Order (ECO)
effectivity process 150
Egidi, M. 23, 29, 39, 132
Eisenhardt, K.M. 66, 68
electronics industry 63, 72, 190
empiricists 141–2
Engineering Change and Deviation process 149
Engineering Change Order (ECO) 153, 155–8
engineering design process, *see* design process
Engineering Epistemology 8, 50, 199–201
Engineering function
  Digital Model as interfacing device between Analysis and 187–91
  Digital Model as interfacing device between Industrial Design and 179–87
Engineering Management Control systems 84
Engineering Parts List (EPL) 149, 150
  definition and use 150–51
  introduction of software to manage 64, 129–30
    coexistence of incompatible structures 114–18
    emergence of shared meanings and organizational coherence 121–3
    PDM and the integration of heterogeneous technology and data structures 114
    role of PDM in influencing meaning formation 118–21
  learning about 60–61
Engineering Release Systems (ERS) 115, 124, 125, 151, 152, 155, 156, 158
Engineering View 151, 152, 153, 156–8, 166
Enterprise Resource Planning (ERP) software 2, 72

epistemic communities 6, 15, 17, 18, 19, 20, 106, 129, 130, 174, 192, 193, 200, 202, 205, 211
EPL, *see* Engineering Parts List (EPL)
Ergas, H. 13, 19, 40
ERP software, *see* Enterprise Resource Planning (ERP) software
ERS, *see* Engineering Release Systems (ERS)
ethnographic research 46, 49, 61, 65–7
Excel spreadsheets 116
experimentation
  importance of 173–4
  and the virtualization and actualization of information
    complementary nature of physical and virtual experimentation 175–6
    virtualization and actualization as problematic translation processes 176–8
    virtualization and actualization of information 176
explicit knowledge 31; *see also* codified knowledge
external memory 6, 32, 48, 200

Fagiolo, G. 132
FEA software, *see* Finite Elements Analysis (FEA) software
feedback 94, 109, 126, 127, 131, 147, 167, 185, 197
Ferguson, E.S. 10, 50, 179, 182
field notes 66
Finite Elements Analysis (FEA) software 61, 77, 84, 103, 126, 176, 188, 189, 190
flat file structure 115–16
Fleck, J. 41
flexibility, balance between control and 64, 94–5, 100, 111, 124, 126–7, 130–31, Ch. 6, 201, 203–5, 207, 209
  definitions of flexibility 135, 136–7
  flexibility in product development and PDM software
    BoM freeze 64, 135, 153–66
    characterization of flexibility in product development 143–4
    conclusions 168–70

Engineering Part List and Bill of
  Materials 150–51
flexibility in the early and late
  stages of product development
  144–6
PDM and the management of
  change 152–3
PDM and the management of
  product and process complexity
  149–50
software and flexibility: embedded
  assumptions 146–9
workflow process 64, 126–7,
  130–31, 135, 166–8
flexibility in the literature 136–8
automatic routines and individual
  behaviour 140–41
interaction of formal tools and
  informal practices 141–2
'object' and 'process' world
  138–40
software and flexibility 138, 204
Foray, D. 12, 13, 14, 16, 17, 18, 20, 40,
  105, 122, 130, 133, 192
Forgues, B. 139
formal knowledge 8, 64
formal tools, interaction between
  practices and 54–9, 141–2, 160–61,
  166, 204–5
formalists 141–2
Fowler, D. 98
Franke, R. 173
Fransman, M. 40, 140
Fujimura, J.H. 56, 186
functional specialization 2, 194
influence of software on 3, 18–20,
  197, 201, 202–3, 206, 207
functions, communication and
  co-operation between 19–20, 79,
  85, 92, 95–6, 97–8, 106–7, 117,
  120–23, 126–31, 138, 143, 148,
  167, 169, 198, 203, 204, 207, 209
in experimentation activities 65, 173,
  174, 177–8, 187, 192–4, 205–6
further research, avenues for 211–2

Gambardella, A. 19
Gash, D.C. 41
Gasser, L. 52, 128, 158
generic systems 72, 208

genetic re-engineering 112
genotype 29, 38
Glaser, B. 68
Goldoftas, B. 136
Grandstrand, O. 23
Griesemer, J.R. 53, 186
grounded research, developing theory
  from 68

Hamel, G. 23, 33, 34
Hammersley, M. 65
Hayek, F.A. 39
Hazelhurst, B. 30
Henderson, K. 57, 179, 186
Henderson, R.M. 19, 20, 32, 41
hierarchical data structures 108, 115,
  120, 125, 126, 149, 150, 155
Hirschheim, R.A. 21
Hirt, S.G. 73, 77, 82
Holland, J.H. 123
Hull, R. 132
human work, logic of 52–4
Hutchins, E. 6, 7, 30, 31, 47, 48
hybrid knowledge 31, 53
hybrid prototyping 65, 175, 177–8

Iansiti, M. 5, 16, 22, 33, 34, 35–6, 40,
  136, 173
implicit knowledge 31; *see also* tacit
  knowledge
incompatible structures, coexistence of
  114–18
incremental change, software-embedded
  157–9
individual vs. collective knowledge
  building processes 21, 31–2, 47–8,
  200
Industrial Design function, Digital
  Model as interfacing device
  between Engineering and 179–87
inertia 28, 74, 128, 208
informal knowledge 8, 64
Information Systems managers 170
innovation potential, firm's 8, 111,
  126–7, 129, 131, 135–6, 139–41,
  143, 166, 169, 170, 194, 197, 199,
  204
inscription technologies 105
integrated Commercial Off-the-Shelf
  (COTS) software systems 71–2

Index

adoption of 78
  Digital Mock-Up (DMU) or the
    phased implementation of an
    integrated PD environment 81–5
  implementation of an integrated
    software environment 85–8
  integrated product development
    strategy 78–81
  integrated software applications
    88–90
alternative paths towards integration
  76–8, 119–20
assumptions embedded in design of
  90–91
  centralized data core and single
    product definition 92–3
  co-ordination of functions, intent
    and viewpoints 95–6
  data ordering, sifting and control
    96–7
  and flexibility 143–4, 146–9
  from 'serial' to 'concurrent'
    processes: synchronization of
    data and activities 93–5
  integration of software systems and
    organization 91–2
  issues and questions arising from
    98–101
  standardization and the reduction of
    data re-interpretation and
    ambiguity 95
  virtual and physical product 97–8
as enablers of BPR strategy 73–4, 112
increasing generic character of 72–3
influence on organizational memory,
  see declarative memory,
  organizational; organizational
  memory, influence of integrated
  systems on; procedural memory,
  organizational; Product Data
  Manager (PDM) software
perceived benefits over bespoke
  software 74–6
see also Product Data Manager
  (PDM) software
Integrated Product Data Manager User
  Group (IPDMUG) 67, 166
Integrated Product Development (IPD)
  Strategy 7–8, 78–81
integrated IT strategy supporting 85–8

integrated software applications 88–90
integrated software environment,
  implementation of 85–8
integrated software systems, *see*
  integrated Commercial Off-the-
  Shelf (COTS) software systems
interfacing 76–8, 119–20, 208
  Digital Model as interfacing device
    between Engineering and
    Analysis 187–91
  Digital Model as interfacing device
    between Industrial Design and
    Engineering 179–87
  temporary 81–2
internal documents, workflow of 141
Internet 62, 66, 67
interviews 66, 67
intranet systems 107
IPDMUG, *see* Integrated Product Data
  Manager User Group (IPDMUG)

James, W. 31
Jill, J. 65, 66, 67
Johnson, P. 65, 66, 67

Katz, R. 20
Kay, N.M. 40
kinaesthetic knowledge 182
Kling, R. 51–2
Knight, F.H. 39
Knorr-Cetina, K. 10, 17, 41, 133, 174,
  192
know-how 55, 111
knowledge appropriation 15, 30, 191–2,
  193, 195, 206
knowledge articulation 47, 53, 56,
  211–12
knowledge base, organizational 34–6
knowledge codification debate 11
  beyond the knowledge codification
    debate 21–2
  boundaries between codification and
    tacitness 12–13
  increase in knowledge codification
    and diffusion 13–16
  influence of information and
    communication technologies
    18–21
  process of codification as language
    creation 16–18

knowledge diffusion 11, 13, 22, 30, 36–7, 199, 210
knowledge integration 22
  alternative paths towards 76–8, 119–20
  influence of software on 7, 8, 37–8, 114, 209–10
    Virtual Product Model (VPM) 4, 9–10, 65, 97–8, 100–101, Ch. 7, 201, 205–7
  organization's capacity for 35–7
knowledge reproduction 13–15, 24, 30
knowledge retention and reuse, *see* organizational memory, influence of integrated systems on
knowledge selection 7, 8, 9, 100, Ch. 6, 201, 203–5, 206; *see also* control; flexibility
knowledge take up, *see* knowledge appropriation
knowledge variation, influence of software on 7, 8, 9, 100–101, 106–7, 122, 129–30, Ch. 7, 201, 205–7; *see also* knowledge integration
Koch, C. 73, 128
Kogut, B. 23, 110, 112
Krzystek, P. 181
Kuutti, K. 110, 112, 132

language creation, process of codification as 16–18, 30, 32, 122, 129–30, 208
Latour, B. 187
Lave, J. 10, 17, 31, 41, 48, 49, 133
Law, J. 171
learning as legitimate peripheral participation (LLP) 48
learning organization 23
learning/search routines 25
legacy systems 77, 87, 121, 208
Leonard-Barton, D. 22, 23, 29, 34, 41, 111, 112–13, 173
Levine, D.I. 136
Levinthal, D.A. 23, 131, 168
Levitt, B. 132
Levy, P. 14, 176, 196
Lindblom, C.E. 45, 171
local knowledge 55, 122, 200, 202, 212

flows between global knowledge and 57, 173, 186–7, 191–3, 195, 205–6, 207, 209–10
see also communities-of-practice; epistemic communities
locally contingent planning 44
logic deduction 14
Lotus Notes 103, 115, 151, 153

Machlup, F. 39
Mahoney, J. 121
Malerba, F. 5, 36, 41
manufacturing deviations 152–3, 156–9
Manufacturing View 152, 153, 155, 156–8
March, J.G. 7, 16, 23, 25, 27, 28, 33, 39, 41, 132, 168
Marengo, L. 33, 34, 132
Marris, R. 23, 39
Marshak, J. 39
meaning formation, role of PDM in influencing 118–21
meaning, reconstruction of 109–10
medical record system, electronic 141
meta-structures 37
Meyer-Krahmer, F. 10, 41, 133, 170
Miller, E. 72, 73, 85
Miner, A.S. 108, 112
Moorman, C. 108, 112
motivational/relational aspect of routines 27–9

NEC 35
Nelson, R.R. 6, 12, 23, 25, 27, 28, 30, 32, 39, 40, 41, 48, 132, 134, 140, 196
neoclassical economics 12, 50
Newell, A. 5, 31, 45
Nissan 35, 103
Nonaka, I. 39, 132
Nooteboom, B. 23

Obeng, Y. 33
Object Linking and Embedding (OLE) 86
object-oriented architecture 73, 86, 92, 108–9, 209
object-world elements 139, 168
observer-as-participant 65

OLE, *see* Object Linking and
Embedding (OLE)
Onwubiko, C. 189
operational routines 25
Organization Theory 5–6, 8, 49–50, 111,
130, 199–200, 202
organizational culture 6, 50, 76, 79, 82,
123, 130, 167, 200, 202–3
organizational knowledge
individual knowledge vs. 21, 31–2,
47–8, 200
see also organizational memory,
influence of integrated systems
on
organizational learning curve 79
organizational memory, influence of
integrated systems on 6, 7, 8, 9,
100, Ch. 5, 201, 202–3, 206, 211;
see also declarative memory,
organizational; procedural memory,
organizational; Product Data
Manager (PDM) software
organizational routines 23–5, 198–200,
210
automatic routine behaviour 25–7, 38,
112–13, 128, 129, 131, 140–41,
203
contextual aspects of 27–9, 200
dynamic aspects of 25, 32–8, 131,
141
individual vs. collective behaviour
31–2
motivational/relational aspect of 27–9
as representations and expressions
15–16, 29–31, 45–6, 113, 131,
141
uncovering roots of routines and
capabilities 38–9
virtualization and actualization
involving set up and maintenance
of 176–8
see also procedural memory,
organizational
Orlikowski, W.J. 41, 52, 132
Orsenigo, L. 5, 23, 36, 41

packets 127, 167
Palframan, D. 189
Parnas, D.L. 171
participant observation 65, 66–7

partnerships 80, 86
parts procurement and control systems
84
Patel, P. 23
path dependent processes 28
Pavitt, K. 2, 23, 40, 121, 174
PBS, *see* Prototype Build Specification
(PBS)
PDM software, *see* Product Data
Manager (PDM) software
PDMII 89
PDS, *see* Product Description Summary
(PDS)
PED, *see* Product Engineering Designer
(PED)
Penrose, E.T. 33
people-embodied knowledge 8
perfect rationality 23
applied to design process 44–7
peripheral applications 76
Petroski, H. 10, 19, 50, 177
phenotype 29
physical aspect of routines 27
physical prototypes 65, 97–8, 175, 177,
186, 192
scanning of 58, 176, 179–83
Pickering, A. 53, 133
Pisano, G. 5, 23, 24, 25, 33, 34, 173
plans, situated 44
PLM technologies, *see* Product Lifecycle
Management (PLM) technologies
Polanyi, M. 31, 39
power of default 128
practice
espoused and actual 46–7
interaction between tools and 54–9,
141–2, 160–61, 166, 204–5
precepts and 46; *see also*
communities-of-practice
Prahalad, C.K. 23, 33, 34
pre-integrated systems 76–7
problem-solving activity 25–7, 34, 35–6
procedural memory, organizational
25–6
automatic character of 26, 112–13
definition of 111
influence of PDM software on 107,
111–13, 130–31, 203
observations about procedural
memory and software 127–9

PDM and the management of the engineering workflow process 123

product engineering workflow 124–7

workflow process definition and control 123–4

process complexity, management of 150

process redefinition 79

process-world elements 139, 168

product complexity, management of 149, 150

product customization 109, 195

Product Data Manager (PDM) software 2, 72, 80–81, 84

aims and functions 87, 88–9, 108–9, 146–7

as enabler of BPR strategy 73–4

and flexibility

in BoM freeze 64, 135, 153–66

conclusions 168–70

embedded assumptions 146–9

Engineering Parts List and Bill of Materials 150–51

management of change 152–3

management of product and process complexity 149–50

in workflow process 64, 126–7, 130–31, 135, 166–8

growth of market for 72

model inspired by aerospace organization 75

as a repository of organizational declarative memory 106–10, 129–30

coexistence of incompatible structures 114–18

emergence of shared meaning and organizational coherence 121–3

PDM and the integration of heterogeneous technology and data structures 114

role of PDM in influencing meaning formation 118–21

as a repository of organizational procedural memory 107, 111–13, 130–31, 203

observations about procedural memory and software 127–9

PDM and the management of the engineering workflow process 123

product engineering workflow 124–7

workflow process definition and control 123–4

second generation (PDMII) 89

training courses in 60

product definition

consistency of 88–9, 91–3, 118, 146

evolution of 144–6, 147, 180, 183, 190–91

Product Description Summary (PDS) 155

Product Engineering Designer (PED) 125

product information, distribution of 88, 89

Product Lifecycle Management (PLM) technologies 101–2

product structure tree 125–6

Prototype Build Specification (PBS) 155

prototype verification 115

qualitative methodologies, advantages of 59–60

R & D organization 19

rapid prototyping 6, 99, 137, 175, 176, 186

re-interpretation of stored information 110, 112–13

release process 94–5, 115, 124, 125, 126

learning about 61

responsibility 109

reverse engineering 180

Richardson, G.B. 39

risk 137, 144

Rosenberg, N. 6, 33, 50, 173, 196

Rothwell, R. 19

routines, *see* organizational routines

routings devices, software-embedded 124

rules and constraints, software-embedded, *see* control

rules of thumb 23

Sachs, E. 137, 138

Sanchez, R. 121

satisficing behaviour 23
Scacchi, W. 52
scanning of clay models 58, 176, 179–83
Schon, D.A. 23
Science and Technology Studies (STS)
    8–9, 43, 51, 138, 141, 199
scripts 90, 99, 106
search spaces 148
SED, *see* Surface Engineering Designer
    (SED)
sequential incremental change, software-
    embedded 157–9
serial development processes 93–4
service technician training 46
shared meanings, organizational 107,
    114, 120, 121–3, 130, 202, 203,
    208
shared vision 20
Short, J.E. 85
Shuen, A. 5, 23, 24, 25, 33, 34
Simon, H.A. 5, 7, 16, 23, 25, 27, 28, 33,
    39, 41, 45, 132
situated knowledge 31, 43–4, 59, 194,
    199, 200
skills, integration of 79, 80
social structures and practices 107
Sociology of Technology debate 200
software application solutions, *see*
    integrated Commercial Off-the-
    Shelf (COTS) software systems
software-as-a-tool 6, 54, 99, 138, 149,
    198, 200–201, 203, 205, 210
software-embedded knowledge 8, 64
    and flexibility, *see* flexibility, balance
        between control and
    and organizational memory, *see*
        declarative memory,
        organizational; organizational
        memory, influence of
        integrated systems on;
        procedural memory,
        organizational
software life cycle 81, 82
software philosophy 9, 91, 117, 142,
    147, 160, 164, 174, 189
Software Producer's Manual 73, 108,
    125
software producers
    assistance with case studies 62
    challenges for 170, 209, 210

integrated product development
    environment supported by 86
integration of 80
training provided by 60
software selection, for case studies 61–2
software solutions, *see* integrated
    Commercial Off-the-Shelf (COTS)
    software systems
software user organizations, selection for
    case studies 62–3
SOLID CAD model 181, 185, 186
    analyst's specialized expertise 189–91
    integration of design and analysis
        188–9
    single common model 188
SOPs, *see* Standard Operating
    Procedures (SOPs)
specialist publications 62
Spender, J.C. 31, 112, 132
spline curves 184
Sproull, L. 112, 123, 132
SSTs, *see* Stable Systemic Traits (SSTs)
stable environment 16–17, 137, 204–5
Stable Systemic Traits (SSTs) 26
Standard for Exchange of Product Data
    (STEP) 86
Standard Operating Procedures (SOPs)
    29–30, 31
standardization 73, 86, 92, 95, 100, 106,
    110, 117, 121–2, 123, 129–30,
    148–9, 195, 201, 202, 203, 204,
    207, 210
    3D CAD model and 185–7
Star, S.L. 5, 17, 43, 44, 46–7, 48, 53, 56,
    121, 122, 130, 178, 186, 187
'states' in procedures 124, 139, 167
Steinmueller, W.E. 14, 15, 17, 18, 19,
    39, 40, 105, 133, 174, 192
STEP, *see* Standard for Exchange of
    Product Data (STEP)
Stigler, G. 39, 136
Stiglitz, J.E. 39
Strauss, A. 46, 68
STS, *see* Science and Technology
    Studies (STS)
Suchman, L. 5, 7, 31, 44, 48, 58, 178
SURFACE CAD model
    creation and modification of 179–81
    as a standardizing device 185–7
    translating into CAD language 183–5

visual and kinaesthetic knowledge required for 181–3
Surface Engineering Designer (SED) 125
Swanson, E.B. 73, 77, 82

tacit knowledge 5, 7, 8, 11, 31
    articulation and 47, 211–12
    boundaries between codified knowledge and 12–13
    formal tools and 55, 58
    and knowledge reproduction 13–15, 24
    process world elements as channel for 139
    reconstruction process requiring 109–10
    in routines 24, 25–6, 36, 37, 38, 111, 113, 177
    and shared meanings 121
    see also knowledge codification debate
technological links 83
technology implementation path 83–5
technology management policy and practice, implications for 208–10
Teece, D.J. 5, 23, 24, 25, 33, 34, 41
tensions 57, 139–40, 143, 166, 167, 168, 200, 207
    formal tools vs. informal processes 142, 160–61, 204–5
    ideal vs. actual processes 164–5
    physical vs. virtual prototypes 177, 186
    resources available vs. resources required 165
    time objective vs. time-in-process 160
    upstream vs. downstream development functions 161–4, 204
Test Plan 155
Thiétart, R.A. 139, 171
Thomke, S.H. 19, 136–7, 138, 171, 173, 175, 177
Tierney, M. 76, 102
TMS, *see* Total Modular Statement (TMS)
tools, formal, interaction between practices and 54–9, 141–2, 160–61, 166, 204–5

Total Modular Statement (TMS) 103
    coexisting with PDM 114–18, 119–20
translation routines 10, 36, 187, 191–4, 205–6, 209–10
transparency of actions 149, 166, 169, 204
triggers, software-embedded 124
Tyre, M.J. 7, 44, 171

Ullman, E. 40
Ulrich, K. 41, 136
unarticulated knowledge 12–13, 187, 212
uncertainty 23, 45, 135, 136, 137, 144
Ungson, G.R. 107, 132
unstable environment 16
Upton, D.M. 136
usage data 150
user discussion lists 67
user organizations, selection for case studies 62–3
user packets, *see* packets

vaulting capabilities 88, 94, 105, 108, 147
vehicle specification 155
Vincenti, W.G. 10, 50, 179, 194
Virtual Product Data Manager (VPDM) 88, 89
Virtual Product Model (VPM)
    technology 7–8, 83, 84–5
    and knowledge integration 4, 9–10, 65, 97–8, 100–101, Ch. 7, 201, 205–7
    conclusions 192–5
    Digital Model (SOLID CAD model) as interfacing device between Engineering and Analysis 188
        analyst's special expertise 189–91
        integration of design and analysis 188–9
        single common model 188
    Digital Model (SURFACE CAD model) as interfacing device between Industrial Design and Engineering 179

creating and modifying the 3D
SURFACE CAD model
179–81
SURFACE model as a
standardizing device 185–7
translating into CAD language
183–5
visual and kinaesthetic
knowledge 181–3
emergence of translation routines
191–2
experimentation and the
virtualization and actualization of
information
complementary nature of
physical and virtual
experimentation 175–6
virtualization and actualization as
problematic translation
processes 176–8
virtualization and actualization of
information 176
virtual prototyping, *see* Virtual Product
Model (VPM) technology
virtualization 176, 191
as problematic translation process
176–8
visibility of actions 149, 166, 169, 204
visual knowledge 182
Von Hippel, E. 7, 14, 44, 122, 171, 173,
196
VPDM, *see* Virtual Product Data
Manager (VPDM)
VPM technology, *see* Virtual Product
Model (VPM) technology

Walsh, J.P. 107, 132
web of computing 51
Wegner, D.M. 133

Weick, K.E. 6, 31, 32, 48, 49, 110
Wenger, E. 10, 17, 41, 48, 49, 133
Wernerfelt, B. 33
Wheelwright, S.C. 4, 45, 173
Wildawsky, A. 96, 112
Williams, R. 76, 102
Winter, S.G. 6, 12, 23, 24, 25, 26, 27,
28, 30, 32, 39, 41, 48, 111, 132,
134, 140, 194, 196
WIP process, *see* workflow process
work-in-progress process, *see* workflow
process
workarounds 46, 57, 128, 143, 157–9,
160, 166, 169
workflow charts 30, 46, 124–5
workflow process 150
introduction of software to manage
64, 130–31
balance of flexibility and control
64, 126–7, 130–31, 135, 166–8
observations about procedural
memory and software 127–9
PDM and the management of the
engineering workflow process
123
product engineering workflow
124–7
workflow process definition and
control 123–4
learning about 61

X100 Vehicle Programme 156

Yanow, D. 15

Zander, U. 23, 110, 112
Ziman, J. 7
Zollo, M. 194
Zuboff, S. 20